The Two Faces of Judicial Power

"Engst has written a game changer. Theoretically, this book pushes back on the idea that courts depend on outsiders to shape their power and instead argues that through their decisions, judges can exert direct and indirect influence on political actors. Empirically, the book is a breath of fresh air. In place of the usual measures of judicial choice is an innovative content analysis of judicial decisions—one that could be adapted to many different contexts."

—Lee Epstein, *Ethan A.H. Shepley Distinguished Professor, Washington University in St. Louis, USA*

"This book provides something I had not thought was possible—robust evidence that legislators limit themselves when they face the threat of constitutional review. It is brilliant work that furthers our understanding not just of the German Federal Constitutional Court, but all constitutional courts engaged in the abstract constitutional review of legislation."

—Chris Hanretty, *Professor of Politics, Royal Holloway University of London, UK*

"Recent decades have seen a rise in the power of courts, followed by political tensions around judicial decisions. Scholars have invested a great deal of effort trying to understand the interactions between constitutional courts and legislatures, but few are able to match the theoretical rigor, empirical novelty, and methodological sophistication of Benjamin Engst's *Two Faces of Judicial Power*. The book constitutes a major advance in the field of judicial politics in Europe and beyond."

—Daniel Naurin, *Professor of Political Science, University of Oslo, Norway*

"This compelling study of constitutional review in Germany is a welcome addition to the literature. Engst reminds us that the influence courts have over public policy lies not only in their power to strike down laws but in the way that this power influences the shape of pending legislation. He offers a careful theoretical account as well as an innovative approach to revealing the second face of judicial power."

—Jeffrey K. Staton, *Professor of Political Science, Emory University, USA*

Benjamin G. Engst

The Two Faces of Judicial Power

Dynamics of Judicial–Political Bargaining

palgrave
macmillan

Benjamin G. Engst
University of Mannheim
Mannheim, Germany

ISBN 978-3-030-46015-0 ISBN 978-3-030-46016-7 (eBook)
https://doi.org/10.1007/978-3-030-46016-7

This Palgrave Macmillan imprint is published by the registered company Springer Nature Switzerland AG
The registered company address is: Gewerbestrasse 11, 6330 Cham, Switzerland

Acknowledgments

Over the course of the past years, I have had wonderful friends, wise colleagues, and beloved family members by my side, who encouraged me to write the book at hand. I wish to express my admiration to them and hope the herein words can honor the level of gratitude I feel.

The book is based on my Ph.D. research and I would like to express my sincere gratitude to my advisers Thomas Gschwend, Christoph Hönnige, Jeffrey K. Staton, and Tom S. Clark for their invaluable guidance, their patience, countless advice, and support that allowed me to develop my research agenda. Christoph Hönnige and Thomas Gschwend made me part of a fascinating project funded by the German Research Foundation in the context of which this study took place. I was fortunate to work with Caroline E. Wittig as part of the project, who became a great friend and a reliable source of support and advice.

Moreover, I had the opportunity to move this project forward at four different institutions. In this regard, I thank the Graduate School of Economic and Social Sciences at the University of Mannheim for supporting me. I am deeply grateful to former and current members of the School of Social Sciences in Mannheim, above all to Christian Arnold, David M. Grundmanns, Marcel Neunhoeffer, Sebastian Sternberg, Lukas Stötzer, Tilko Swalve, and Steffen Zittlau. The passion of these scholars and friends to share their methodological knowledge and skills often helped me to adopt a new perspective on my research. I also wish to acknowledge Jan W. van Deth; his mentorship during my undergraduate and graduate years was crucial in my decision to pursue the path to this book. Additionally, I am grateful to the Lorenz-von-Stein-Society at the Mannheim Centre for European Social Research which has awarded my thesis the Lorenz-von-Stein Prize considering it an outstanding dissertation in political science at the University of Mannheim. I feel privileged and honored having received this special recognition for my work.

I am indebted to Tom S. Clark and Jeffrey K. Staton who invited me for an academic year at Emory University. This year was possible thanks to the generous funding from the German Academic Exchange Service. My gratitude goes to the faculty of Emory's Department of Political Science, who taught me a modern perspective on judicial politics. I wish to thank Adam Glynn for providing me with insights on causal inference that inspired my work on autolimitation. I am also grateful for the great friendship and valuable remarks on my work provided by Leeann W. Bass, Ashley Moraguez, and Steven W. Webster.

My research would not have been possible without the support of former colleagues and good friends at the Departments of Political Science at Georg-August-University of Göttingen and Leibniz University Hannover. In particular, Petya Alexandrova, Julia Hagen, Fabian Jakubowitz, Sarah Sinram, and Frederik Springer were open to listen to ideas and at the same time took part in spontaneous thought-provoking discussions about my work. I thank Christoph Garwe, Philipp Köker, Yvonne Lüdecke, Philipp Meyer, and Eva Ruffing, who not only provided their unique criticism on some of my ideas but also guided my thought process with fruitful suggestions to solve problems I encountered during my writing process. Their perspectives helped me polish my herein presented work. Furthermore, I would like to acknowledge the assistance I received from Felicia Riethmüller and Jonas Tafel in collecting the data to assess judicial power. I also thank my fellow graduate students and in particular Verena Fetscher, Moritz Heß, and Adam Scharpf for being the good friends I needed to get that breath of fresh air when a break was much needed.

Finally, I consider myself blessed to have lifetime friends like Julia F. Dutkowski, Daniela Hohmann, Marius Knierim, Melanie Kowalski, Sarah Lange, Farhad Omid, and Alexandra Schulz. They have been particularly supportive in clearing my mind when I was caught in unproductive thoughts while helping me keep my feet on the ground. Moreover, I owe a lot to my family for encouraging me at every stage of my personal and academic life, especially my beloved mother Christa-Maria Engst and my thoughtful, always caring father Michael Engst. No existen palabras que puedan expresar lo agradecido que estoy con la persona más importante en mi mundo, quien siempre me motiva a alcanzar mis metas. Gracias por tu apoyo incondicional Maria Geraldine Zúñiga Manrique.

Contents

List of Figures

List of Tables

CHAPTER 1

The Two Faces of Judicial Power

Highest courts with the power to review and invalidate political acts are an integral part of the system of checks and balances in any modern democracy. Following the waves of democratization after World War II and the Cold War (Huntington 1991), many democracies adopted codified constitutions and established courts empowered to protect constitutional rights Stone Sweet (Stone Sweet 2000, Ch. 2). Nevertheless, courts face a dilemma: they are not isolated players but they need to enter into a dialogue with the political branches. As they cannot enforce decisions themselves, the implementation of judicial decisions is dependent on the legislative and the executive branches. This is the reason why the judiciary is traditionally seen as "beyond comparison the weakest of the three departments of power" (Hamilton 1788, Federalist No. 78). In particular, courts have "no influence over either the sword or the purse" (Hamilton 1788, Federalist No. 78) and lack those institutional features necessary to demand compliance with their decisions.

Nevertheless, courts have become powerful institutions. The developments around prominent decisions by highest courts illustrate that the judiciary shapes societal and political processes. The landmark decision by the United States Supreme Court in *Brown v. Board of Education* (347 U.S. 483 [1954]) contributed to the process of ending segregation. Germany's abortion laws bear the hallmarks of the German Federal Constitutional Court (e.g., BVerfGE 88, 203) and the British Supreme Court has strengthened the rights of the British Parliament vis-à-vis the government in the negotiations over the United Kingdom's exit from the European

B. G. Engst, *The Two Faces of Judicial Power*,
https://doi.org/10.1007/978-3-030-46016-7_1

Union ([2017] UKSC 5). Moreover, decisions by the Austrian Constitutional Court (G258/2017), the United States Supreme Court (576 U.S. 644 [2015]), and the German Federal Constitutional Court (BVerfGE 105, 313) have significantly strengthened the rights of the LGBTQ communities in their respective countries. These are just a few examples of a general trend characterized by "the global expansion of judicial power" (Tate and Vallinder 1995).

Political problems are increasingly redefined as judicial problems, which has led to a process that scholars call judicialization (Stone Sweet 2000; Shapiro and Stone Sweet 2002; Hirschl 2008; Hönnige 2011) or even the transition to *juristocracy* (Hirschl 2004). There are different views on the development of judicialization. Stone Sweet (1998, 2000) argues that the process constantly increases, while others suggest that there are limitations to the process, which allow for variation (Vanberg 1998a, b, 2015; Santoni and Zucchini 2004; Brouard 2009; Hönnige 2009; Hönnige and Gschwend 2010). Nevertheless, both perspectives highlight the importance of the judiciary in politics and society. Constitutional courts and supreme courts are highly respected institutions receiving substantial public support beyond the levels of support for the political branches in many countries (Gibson et al. 1998).

Various factors are discussed to explain why highest courts are able to have an impact on political processes. On the one hand, public opinion in favor of the court is used as an exogenous explanation for political compliance. On the other hand, the strategic use of courts by political actors—who are unwilling to pass unpopular policies or assume that courts also constrain the political adversary once majorities shift—are endogenous explanations for the empowerment of courts (Vanberg 2015).

The assumption underlying arguments based on public opinion is that highest courts have become powerful actors due to the legitimacy that they receive from public support, which they can use to seek political compliance. Vanberg (2001, 2005) argues that courts are able to manipulate the transparency around their decisions. Decisions taken in a transparent environment raise public awareness and this leads political actors to comply with judicial decisions. He assesses his argument in the context of the German Federal Constitutional Court and Carrubba and Zorn (2010) bring evidence of his approach in the setting of the United States Supreme Court. Staton (2010) extends the research on public opinion in judicial decision-making and argues that courts are able to manipulate the mixture between the legitimacy for the judiciary and the transparency of decisions to encourage compliance. Accordingly, judges manipulate the transparency of the environment through strategic media communication. In addition, Sternberg et al. (2015) found that judges pay attention to public opinion on an issue under consideration when justifying referrals by opposition parties.

Endogenous explanations for political compliance are based on two perspectives (Vanberg 2015, 171–176). First, it is argued that political actors use (friendly) courts strategically when the political branches are unable or unwilling to correct or pass policies (Whittington 2005). This also allows the political branches to shift the blame over controversial issues or the uncertainty over the implications of policies to the judiciary (Salzberger 1993, 358–369). Second, a government in a sufficiently competitive political system may accept moderate judicial constraints at a given point in time, assuming that the court also constrains opposing parties once majorities shift (Stephenson 2003). This approach is based on electoral concerns and known as insurance theory (Ramseyer 1994). The theory is also used to explain more generally why political actors have empowered courts in the first place to review legislation (Ginsburg 2003; Ginsburg and Versteeg 2014). In line with these perspectives, highest courts have become powerful actors for the strategic purposes of political actors.

In sum, courts have become powerful institutions mainly due to public support in the institution and the willingness of political actors to (strategically) accept the judiciary. However, while existing approaches are suitable to explain the general compliance with judicial decisions, the findings do not explain the substantive influence of the judiciary. The strong focus on compliance leads to a bias, connecting judicial power only to the implementation of decisions. However, compliance is to a certain extent only the "base" (Dahl 1957, 203) or the precondition of judicial power. The outlined perspectives detach judicial power from the "means" (Dahl 1957, 203) that courts use to exercise power, namely judicial decisions. The next sections outline the need to more strongly account for the actual "choices justices make" (Epstein and Knight 1998) to fully understand the direct and indirect power of highest courts.

1.1 (Non-)Decisions as a Means of Judicial Power

An established definition of power is that "A has power over B to the extent that he can get B to do something that B would not otherwise do" (Dahl 1957, 202–203; similar Simon 1953; Bueno de Mesquita 2006, Ch.

7). This definition implies that power is a relational concept and it can only exist in the interaction between actors (Dahl 1957). The interaction of interest here is where the court exercises power over the governing majority. An essential part of a power relation is the instrument used to exert power (Dahl 1957, 203). Courts need a tool to obtain a certain response from the government, namely the judicial decision. In publishing judicial decisions, courts outline behavior that they accept or behavior that they do not accept. Moreover, courts have also come to outline behavior that they expect—an important observation further discussed in the next section. In sum, publishing decisions enables courts to exert direct power. In presenting decisions, courts show what is called the *first face of judicial power* (Isaac 1987, 7–10).

Bachrach and Baratz (1962, 948) criticize the traditional view on power as shortcoming and argue that:

> [P]ower is also exercised when A devotes his energies to creating or reinforcing social and political values and institutional practices that limit the scope of the political process to public consideration of only those issues which are comparatively innocuous to A. To the extent that A succeeds in doing this, B is prevented, for all practical purposes, from bringing to the fore any issues that might in their resolution be seriously detrimental to A's set of preferences.

From this perspective, judges also establish a general position through their decisions. Hence, they do not need to make decisions regarding every political issue; instead, the power of the judiciary is the influence of established positions on the government's agenda. Courts are powerful if the government already drafts new policies that match the court's interests instead of her own interests. In other words, the court is not explicitly involved but exercises power. The government presents policies different from those that it would present if the court did not exist. If the court's positions influence the government's agenda before an explicit judicial involvement, then the court shows what is called the *second face of judicial power* (Bachrach and Baratz 1962; Isaac 1987, 10–12).[1]

The perspective adopted in this study defines judicial power as the direct and indirect effect of judicial decisions on political and societal actors. Judges are able to constrain the political branches by making (or threatening to make) decisions. The government and the legislature alter their behavior based on the possibility that courts can review their actions. This perspective on power is in line with the literature on judicialization (see Hönnige 2011, 348–350).

It should be noted that there is an additional perspective linking judicial power to judicial independence (Cameron 2002; Staton 2010, 8–9). While the precise definition of judicial independence is contested (see Linzer and Staton 2015, 225), a common separation is drawn between *de jure* and *de facto* judicial independence (Feld and Voigt 2003; Melton and Ginsburg 2014; Rios-Figueroa and Staton 2014; Linzer and Staton 2015; Voigt et al. 2015): the former refers to formalized rules that grant the judiciary autonomy and insulate judges from any form of pressure (Staton 2010, 8–9; Rios-Figueroa and Staton 2014, 106–107), while the latter is linked to the compliance with judicial decisions. Hence, independence embodies the idea that judges can expect that their decisions are accepted and that they do not need to fear negative consequences in response to their decisions (Feld and Voigt 2003, 498; Voigt et al. 2015, 198). Thus, judicial independence is a matter of compliance, which I regard as a base of judicial power.

In sum, public support for the judiciary, judicial independence, and (political) compliance with decisions are important preconditions of judicial power. However, the means of courts to exercise power are judicial decisions. The aim of this study is to understand under what conditions judges make particular judicial choices and formulate requests directed at the political branches, showing the first face of judicial power. Moreover, this study seeks to identify the extent to which political actors anticipate judicial decisions, which allows courts to show the second face of judicial power. In the following sections, I establish the language used throughout this study and I further outline the two perspectives on judicial power, also raising two questions that are addressed in this book.

1.1.1 Judicial Choices and Their Implications

Judicial power—whether direct or indirect—originates from a court's ability to make decisions. In particular, the (fear of the) implications of judicial choices describe a court's ability to influence politics and society. Hence, in order to assess the faces of judicial power it is necessary to first define judicial choices.

Scholarship on the United States Supreme Court often groups judicial choices on a liberal to conservative dimension (e.g., Segal and Cover 1989, 561; Martin and Quinn 2002; Clark and Lauderdale 2010). This is useful in the context of the United States where scholars can rely on individual judicial votes to estimate ideal points of judges on the same dimension. Nevertheless, the publication of individual judicial votes is not common in cross-country comparison (e.g., Kelemen 2013). Therefore, defining judicial choices as conservative or liberal is not always compelling. Moreover, choices defined as conservative or liberal imply a focus on political proceedings and plaintiffs. However, the empirical chapters of this book account for all decisions made by a constitutional court. Hence, politically laden language seems inappropriate here.

Scholarship focusing on courts outside the United States often defines judicial choices as collective outcomes of a court. The research mostly accounts for a court's ability to overturn laws. Hence, scholars define choices using a dichotomous measure of constitutionality; i.e., a law violates the constitution or it does not violate the constitution (e.g., Vanberg 2001, 2005; Krehbiel 2016, 997). Similarly, courts may choose to veto policies or not to veto policies (e.g., Brouard and Hönnige 2017). Moreover, in many studies judicial choices are defined with regard to the actor addressed in a decision; for example, Helmke (2002, 295) defines judicial choices as "whether the justice voted in favor of or against the government" (similar Krehbiel 2016, 995). Carrubba and Zorn (2010, 818) use a similar measure in the context of the United States arguing that a decision on the merits is either in support of a government's position or not. There are also studies that regard judicial choices as directed towards the political opposition. Hence, a judicial choice either favors the opposition when a law is not constitutional or it does not favor the opposition when a law is constitutional (e.g., Hönnige 2008, 974–975; Sternberg et al. 2015).

The established language falls short when a plaintiff's prime aim is not for a court to overturn policy. Plaintiffs often refer to constitutional courts with aims to seek a reversal of a decision by a lower court or a repeal of an administrative act. The annulment of a law is only an implicit aim under such circumstances. This is why I argue that it is more reasonable to define judicial choices universally with regard to a plaintiff's referral. In other words, a judicial decision summarizes the judicial choice with regard to an act referred by a plaintiff. The outcome of a decision is a verdict on a referral. Thus, throughout this book judicial choices are defined as follows: A judicial choice is defined as *justified* once a plaintiff's referral is (at least partially) granted on the merits. A judicial choice is defined as *not justified* once a plaintiff's referral is not granted on the merits.

This language is appropriate for three reasons: First, the judicial choice is no longer defined with regard to one particular type of act. Instead, I account for all acts of constitutional courts review. Second, in constitutional decision-making, plaintiffs and legal questions vary, while the addressee of decisions is almost always the state. This latter aspect is inherent in the design of constitutional law, which was established to protect citizens from the abuse of power by the state (Stone Sweet 2000, 37–38). Hence, I use a definition of judicial choices that applies equally to whoever turns to the court. At the same time, it is reasonable to assume that justified referrals are not in the interest of a governing majority. These referrals would imply a misuse of political power, while referrals not justified do not hold a governing majority accountable. Therefore, the definition of judicial choices used embodies clear political implications. Third, the adopted language is not uncommon; for example, the German Federal Constitutional Court—as a representative, albeit powerful constitutional court (see Chapter 3)—uses the decision on the merits to assess whether a plaintiff's referral is (not) justified (Schlaich and Korioth 2015, Ch. 5).

In sum, a court either justifies or does not justify a referral and this defines the collective judicial choice made in a decision. The choice embodies explicit implications for the political branches and society. In the next section, I further elaborate on the outcome of decisions to conceptualize the first face of judicial power.

1.1.2 The First Face of Judicial Power

Most studies cited at the beginning of this chapter conceptualize judicial choices as binary choices between the options to strike an act down or not (Vanberg 2001, 2005; Hönnige 2009; Carrubba and Zorn 2010; Staton 2010; Sternberg et al. 2015; similar Helmke 2002). The previous section established more general language. However, empirically courts also declare acts as void and suggest implications for future political actions (Staton and Vanberg 2008; see "corrective revision" in Stone 1992, 241–244; see also discussion in Clark and Lauderdale 2010, 873–874). Hence, judges provide what I call *directives*, which are *statements by the judges included in a court's decision directed at political actors to request their action in response to a constitutional issue.*[2]

Directives are different from the judicial choice to invite an override of a statutory interpretation. Courts like the United States Supreme Court can interpret statue to uphold a law, which allows for settling a case. However, Hausegger and Baum (1999) found that the Supreme Court sometimes invites Congress to override a statutory interpretation. In other words, the judges settle a constitutional issue but ask Congress to revise the interpretation. While some scholars address this interesting behavior (Spiller and Tiller 1996; Hausegger and Baum 1999; Christiansen and Eskridge Jr. 2014, 1410–1411), this is not what is considered a directive here. Directives do not occur once the court has settled a constitutional issue; instead, directives ask political actors to respond to a constitutional issue.

"Restrictive interpretations" (Stone 1992; Davis 1986, 57; Brouard 2016) as used by the French Constitutional Council are also not considered directives here. The nature of restrictive interpretations is that the court defines how a law has to be applied to stay within the boundaries of the constitution (Brouard 2016, 223). In these decisions the court essentially does not justify a referral but one may argue that the court issues a directive. An action by political actors to implement the decisions is not necessary as the court settles the constitutional issue. The constitutional issue directed at political actors would exist only once a referral is justified. This is why restrictive interpretations do not meet the definition applied here and are not included on theoretical grounds. However, I acknowledge that the literature has found restrictive interpretations to be an increasingly common judicial choice in France (Brouard 2016, 230–231). Nevertheless, an assessment included in the empirical sections of this book shows that referrals that are not justified but include directives occur in low numbers for the case analyzed here. Therefore, it is reasonable to leave this judicial choice aside on empirical grounds too, albeit not without emphasizing the relevance for future research.

Landmark decisions often include directives. For example, decisions by the German Federal Constitutional Court were essential to design Germany's abortion laws (BVerfGE 39, 1; BVerfGE 88, 203). The decisions were so explicit that even judges raised concerns in separate opinions that the court was presenting solutions that were actually the responsibility of legislators (Landfried 1992, 54–55). However, when the German legislature passed new abortion laws, major provisions presented by the court became part of the new laws (see Landfried 1992, 53–56; Vanberg 2005, 126–128 on the abortion decisions).

The first column in Table 1.1 summarizes information on the possibility of directives among all 19 constitutional courts in the European Union.[3] There is evidence that courts in 13 countries can use directives and only three countries do not use directives, while for an additional three countries no information is available. The second column of the table summarizes the possibility of courts to present deadlines. Deadlines define the date until which the legislature should resolve a constitutional issue. Assuming

Table 1.1 Judicial directives and deadlines among constitutional courts in the EU

Country	*Directive possible*	*Deadline possible*
Austria	✓	✓
Belgium	✓	✓
Bulgaria	✗	✗
Croatia		✓
Czech Republic	✓	✓
France	✓	✓
Germany	✓	✓
Hungary	✓	✓
Italy	✓	✓
Latvia	✓	✓
Lithuania	✗	✗
Luxembourg	✗	✗
Malta		✓
Poland	✓	✓
Portugal	✓	✗
Romania	✓	✓
Slovakia		✓
Slovenia	✓	✓
Spain	✓	✓

✓= Measure exists; ✗= Measure does not exist

Note: Information obtained mainly regarding review procedures directed at laws. Based mostly on country reports by Starck and Weber (eds. 2007), Luchterhandt et al. (eds. 2007), Hufen and Nörr Stiefenhofer Lutz (eds. 2008), and Ludewig (2012). Information on European countries with supreme courts and detailed sources are summarized in Appendix A

that a judicial decision includes the opinion of the court, then deadlines hint at directives, at least to the extent that they request an action by the political branches within a certain timeframe in response to a constitutional issue. The possibility of using deadlines mirrors the use of directives among European countries, with Portugal being the only exception (Hufen and Nörr Stiefenhofer Lutz eds. 2008, 73).

The types of decisions that courts can make sometimes encourage directives. The Italian Constitutional Court can present so-called *sentenze monito* which declare a constitutional violation without directly invalidating the act referred to the court. Instead, the legislature is asked to address the constitutional violation presenting new legislation (Hufen and Nörr Stiefenhofer Lutz eds. 2008, 45–46). The court sometimes uses this approach to present specific guidelines that the legislature should follow (see decision No. 826 [1988]; No. 420 [1994]; cited in Hufen and Nörr Stiefenhofer Lutz eds.

2008, 46). For example, the court has done so in decisions strengthening the pluralism of broadcasting, which is an area of long-standing conflict in Italy (Eusepi 1995; Hibberd 2007). The Austrian Constitutional Court uses a comparable measure presenting *pro futuro* decisions. The court declares an act void at a point in the future, which gives the government time to respond to an act with new legislation (Ludewig 2012, 31–32). In decisions that declare a law incompatible with the constitution, the court often outlines the framework to which political actors should pay attention when drafting new legislation (Hufen and Nörr Stiefenhofer Lutz eds. 2008, 63). The Portuguese and the Romanian Constitutional Court possess special powers to direct a statement at political actors. Portuguese judges are required to notify respective legislative bodies once they observe a constitutional violation due to a legislative omission (Art. 283 II Portuguese Constitution). In a similar vein, the Romanian Parliament "shall be bound" to align a legislative act with a decision by the Romanian Constitutional Court if a law is declared unconstitutional before its proclamation (Art. 18 III Act on the Romanian Constitutional Court).

To sum up, highest courts not only declare acts constitutional or void, but courts also have means available to outline possible responses. The three choices that judges at highest courts can make are: (1) the choice to *not justify* a referral, which implies that an act referred to the court is in accordance with constitutional provisions and a plaintiff's claim is rejected; (2) the choice to *justify* a referral, which implies that an act referred to the court violates constitutional provisions and a plaintiff's claim is granted; and (3) the choice to justify a referral and present a *directive*, which implies that an act violates constitutional provisions and the court includes a statement directed at political actors to request their action to address a constitutional issue. The different outcomes have different implications for the implementation of decisions. First, no implementation is necessary when the court does not justify referrals. Second, an implementation of justified referrals is necessary. The governing majority is only constrained to the extent that the court does not allow certain behavior. Third, an implementation of directives is necessary. Moreover, the court constrains the government by stating requests. Assuming that the court wants the governing majority to comply with decisions, the question is: *When do judges choose one judicial outcome over the other?*

In order to answer this question, I use a separation of powers model to outline the bargaining over policy positions between the governing majority and the court. The model includes the possibility that the court can make the three outlined judicial choices. Based on the model, I argue that the court's judicial choice depends on the costs that the court fears from the evasion of a decision and the costs of the government to legislate again in response to a judicial decision.

Differentiating between more than two choices accounts for findings from the literature on the clarity of judicial decisions (Staton and Vanberg 2008, 505). Compliance with decisions is also a function of the clarity of decisions (Baum 1976; Spriggs 1996, 1127–1128; Staton and Vanberg 2008; Corley and Wedeking 2014). Staton and Vanberg (2008) argue that judges are able to manage trade-offs that they face by manipulating the clarity of their decisions. On the one hand, vague decisions allow judges to deal with policy uncertainty and the possibility to cover political noncompliance. On the other hand, specific decisions allow judges to increase the general awareness of decisions and pressure political actors to comply. This study extends the implications of Staton and Vanberg's (2008) model. The authors argue that if judges are able to cover possible noncompliance through vague decisions, they may not always choose to uphold laws; instead, striking laws down in vague decisions can serve strategic purposes. Hence, in order to design accurate separation of powers models, we need to compare choices that allow judges to manipulate the opinion clarity to the choice to uphold laws (Staton and Vanberg 2008, 516). The study at hand designs such a model. The two judicial choices that require an implementation—to only justify a referral or present a directive—reflect different levels of clarity. Referrals that are only justified leave behavior consistent with the decision ambiguous, while directives are specific to the expected behavior. Both judicial choices are included separately in the model presented here. In addition, the choice not to justify a referral but to uphold an act is included. Therefore, putting implications of the model designed here to the test should generate empirical findings that also hold relevance to the literature on opinion clarity.

The judicial choices considered here are derived from the content of published decisions. It is not necessary to know individual judicial votes for this approach. This is an advantage to the extent that publishing individual judicial votes is not the norm in cross-country comparison (Raffaelli 2012, 30; Kelemen 2013, 1345). Published votes only allow differentiating majority opinions from separate opinions. The actual outcome that has legal and political implications is reflected in the content of the majority opinion. This content can be classified according to the three choices outlined above. Hence, in order to understand judicial behavior, I focus on the content-specific outcome of published judicial decisions. These features exist in any legal system. They allow opening parts of the black box of judicial decision-making independently of individual judicial votes.

In making an explicit judicial choice, courts show their first face of judicial power. In the next section, I turn to the second face of judicial power.

1.1.3 The Second Face of Judicial Power

The assumption of the second face of judicial power is that judicial power is not only visible in the implementation of a particular decision; instead, judicial power also occurs once interests of the court influence the political and societal agenda, without the explicit involvement of courts. In short, political actors anticipate the possibility of a judicial involvement and change their behavior accordingly.

This idea itself is not new to judicial politics. Scholars convincingly argue that the threat of a possible judicial decision already fuels the process of judicialization (Stone 1992; Landfried 1992; Kommers 1994; Stone Sweet 1998, 2000; Vanberg 1998a, b, 2001, 2005; Langer and Brace 2005). Policymakers do not wish to receive the negative implications of a court decision, e.g., policy-seekers do not wish to lose major reforms to the judiciary and vote- and office-seeking actors try to avoid a public backlash when losing to popular courts. This is why these actors constrain themselves and alter their agenda in advance. The idea that "the legislature censors its own behavior preemptively in anticipation of judicial review" (Vanberg 2001, 352; similar Stone 1992, 122; Stone Sweet 2000, 75) is also known as *autolimitation*.

Early studies on autolimitation use case studies to outline how political actors discuss judicial decisions to foreshadow a possible judicial reaction. Stone (1992, 122–129) discusses in length the procedures established by the French government to consider legal issues. He argues that the legislature often postpones legislation to prevent a decision by the French Constitutional Council. In addition, (2000, 79–83) presents detailed case studies on Germany's development of industrial codetermination and the French legislation on media pluralism. He shows how past decisions of the constitutional courts in both countries influenced legislative debates and legislation. Landfried (1985, 528–531) also assesses the codetermination law and the German legislation on abortion (Landfried 1992, 55–56), outlining how the legislature considers possible judicial interventions when drafting legislation. The case studies make it plausible to argue that past judicial decisions can serve as legal signals to the legislature. However, the case studies involve highly salient and controversial topics, which are shaped by multiple referrals to courts and multiple legislative proceedings. Hence, one should be careful when generalizing from those studies. Moreover, the studies overlook the need for comparison. In order to understand whether considering past judicial decisions leads to different legislative behavior than not considering decisions, it is necessary to include legislative proceedings where judicial decisions were not considered. In other words, identifying autolimitation requires proceedings that can serve as counterfactuals. Changes to bills considered under the influence of past judicial decisions need to be compared with those changes to bills not considered under the influence of past decisions.

Langer and Brace (2005) present a large-N study to assess what they call the "preemptive influence" of state supreme courts in the United States on state legislatures. They find that the implementation of restrictive legislation addressing the death penalty or abortion takes longer once courts or the public hold liberal positions relative to policymakers. These findings suggest that state legislatures limit themselves in anticipation of a judicial review. The caveats of the study are that the focus is again on two controversial issues, while the dependent variable only allows the authors to assess the timing of the enactment of a law. This does not reveal the extent to which a court's views influence the government's agenda substantially. The government may take a policy off the agenda for a while but presents the policy that it wants to pursue at a later point.

To sum up, from a theoretical perspective it is plausible that legislative self-restraint in anticipation of judicial review grants the judiciary power over policymaking. However, from an empirical perspective the precise nature of autolimitation remains unclear. Hence, in order to understand the second face of judicial power, the question is: *To what extent do political actors anticipate judicial decision-making?*

In order to answer this question, I show theoretically that the governing majority anticipates a possible judicial review when drafting legislation. In particular, I argue that prior decisions by the highest court are used as legal signals by legislative committees to anticipate the judiciary's interest. Autolimitation occurs in response to a legal signal and encourages policymakers to modify their bills. Bills exposed to a legal signal are changed to meet the position of the court. In order to assess the argument empirically, I propose a research design mirroring an experiment analyzing the causal effect of legal signals on committee bargaining.

The idea of autolimitation has been transferred to bicameral bargaining between opposing parties. Manow and Burkhart (2007) find that in situations of divided government—defined as situations in which the federal government has no majority in the second chamber—open conflict between opposing parties rarely occurs. The authors argue that this is the result of the federal government's attempt not to present controversial legislation, knowing that the second chamber's approval is necessary. Instead, the federal government engages in autolimitation itself. Fortunato et al. (2013) argue that the authors overlook the uncertainty that exists in bargaining between opposing parties across chambers. Accordingly, the composition of the second chamber can change over the duration of a legislative proposal. Moreover, the government can rely on institutions to settle conflict between chambers and modify bills once it becomes necessary. This is why the federal government has no incentives to restrain itself when drafting bills.

Considering judicial decisions here, the government can never be certain if and when a law will be referred to the court. In this regard, the laws are more like proposals drafted under uncertainty. However, once a law is referred to the court, there are no institutions that allow a government to modify laws; instead, once involved, the court has the power to veto a law. Therefore, in analyzing legislative self-restraint regarding the judiciary, I generate findings for an additional bargaining situation complementing the ones considered in legislative bargaining.

In sum, the first face of judicial power is characterized by the court's ability to present a certain judicial choice choosing (1) not to justify a referral, (2) to justify a referral, or (3) to present a directive. The second face of judicial power leads to legislative self-restraint in anticipation of the court's ability to render decisions. Throughout this book, I analyze the conditions under which judges choose a specific judicial outcome and I identify the causal effect of a possible judicial veto on legislative behavior.

1.2 Approach of This Book

In order to assess judicial choices (the first face of judicial power) and the government's anticipation of possible judicial choices (the second face of judicial power), I present a formal model. The model extends existing separation of powers models (e.g., Vanberg 2001, 2005; Carrubba and Zorn 2010; Staton 2010) to incorporate the court's ability to present its own policy positions using directives. The theoretical approach is a general one, without the need to constrain considerations to particular democracies, political or legal systems. However, by focusing on decisions as collective judicial outcomes affecting the power relation between the court and the governing majority, I adopt an outside perspective and treat courts as unitary actors (Dyevre 2010, 304; Staton 2010). The assumption is further justified in Chapters 2 and 3.

The empirical analyses focus on centralized constitutional courts and in particular the German Federal Constitutional Court (GFCC). A comparative assessment among European countries shows that Germany is a representative case to study the two faces of judicial power (see Chapter 3). Constitutional courts are specialized higher courts empowered to review laws and acts based on constitutional norms (Kelsen 2008 [1931]; Shapiro and Stone 1994). In countries with constitutional review—like those in Table 1.1—only the specialized constitutional court is empowered to nullify laws and declare them void. In addition, constitutional courts allow for abstract judicial review of a law independently of a concrete legal dispute. These are major differences compared with countries with diffuse judicial review—like the United States—where regular courts are empowered to invalidate legislative acts, albeit only once concrete legal disputes occur (Epstein et al. 2001, 120–123; Stone Sweet 2000, Ch. 3). There are no obvious reasons why the two faces of judicial power should not occur in both systems. However, the centralized review powers of constitutional courts are an advantage for the analyses. All laws that are of constitutional concern are concentrated on one judicial level and in one court. Moreover, the constitutional court also reviews other acts by state authorities or decisions by regular courts. This allows for analyzing judicial choices between different types of referrals on one level (see Chapter 4). The legal tradition is of lesser relevance when studying the second face of judicial power. Instead, I focus on the behavior in legislative committees to study political reactions in anticipation of judicial review (see Chapter 5). The comparative assessment in Chapter 3 shows that Germany's committee system is equally representative of a large number of European countries.

Finally, I apply a quantitative approach to assess the power relations between the court and the governing majority. The analysis of the first face of judicial power requires an assessment of judicial choices while accounting for the political and societal arena, yet the analysis of the second face of judicial power requires an assessment of political choices while accounting for the judicial arena. This is why I present a novel database—the Constitutional Court Database (CCDB; Hönnige et al. 2015)—that provides for a data structure linking the judicial, political, and societal arenas. Moreover, the setup of the database allows me to extend the data structure to add necessary variables to the analysis (see Chapter 4).

The literature has developed three general models to explain judicial behavior (see Parcelle Jr. et al. 2011, 29–49; Wittig 2016, 5–16). First, according to the legal model judges make choices based on the written law and the jurisprudential methods that they acquired at law school (George and Epstein 1992; Parcelle Jr. et al. 2011, 29–34). Thus, the legal system constrains judges and they do not decide based on their own preferences. Second, attitudinalists argue that judges are unconstrained actors who cast sincere votes that reflect their policy interests (Schubert 1965; Rohde and Spaeth 1976; Segal and Cover 1989; Segal and Spaeth 1993, 2002; Parcelle Jr. et al. 2011, 34–39). Third, proponents of the strategic model argue that judges are constrained by other actors and the institutional setting. Hence, when they make decisions, they act strategically accounting for the constraints taking rational choices (Murphy 1964; Epstein and Knight 1998; Hammond et al. 2005; Parcelle Jr. et al. 2011, 39–49). The approach applied here follows the strategic model as it is argued that the court is part of a separation of powers system and makes decisions that strategically account for other actors and the institutional environment.

1.3 Chapter Outline

In this chapter, I have introduced the two faces of judicial power that highest courts show when making or threatening to make judicial decisions. In the following paragraphs, I conclude with an overview of the individual chapters.

In Chapter 2, I design the Judicial-Policy-Dialogue Game. The game outlines the interaction between the government and the court, assuming that both actors have preferred positions where they wish to see policies implemented. The government presents an initial policy that is referred to the court. The court is not only able to justify referrals or to not justify referrals but can also present directives. However, it is at the government's discretion to react to decisions. The actors' choices are not free of costs. The court has costs from an evasion of judicial decisions, while the government has costs to legislate in response to judicial decisions. Numerical examples help to outline implications of the game. Two sets of implications are relevant for the empirical tests: first, variations in the actors' costs affect the judicial choices, which addresses the first face of judicial power; and second, the government anticipates the final outcome of the interaction when presenting the initial policy. An arena to observe this behavior is legislative committees that consider previous court decisions. This addresses the second face of judicial power.

In Chapter 3, I argue that Germany is a suitable case to study the two faces of judicial power. For this purpose, I outline certain preconditions of judicial power. First, there are preconditions that are inherent to the design of courts. Procedural rules allow different actors to refer to courts and this allows courts to produce decisions. Second, there are preconditions as part of the separation of powers framework that define a court's role in the political process. Different institutionalized and noninstitutionalized features allow political actors to anticipate judicial behavior or react to judicial decisions. Third, the government and the court interact in an environment that can constrain or strengthen both actors. Measurable preconditions of judicial power are evaluated among European countries with constitutional courts and combined in two indices, which address each face of judicial power. Analyses reveal that Germany clusters with half of the European countries on the indices. Chapter 3 concludes with a case study assessing the judicial–political bargaining around Germany's parental custody reform of 1998. This provides first insights into how the GFCC exercises power and highlights variables of interest for the empirical analyses.

In Chapter 4, I assess the first face of judicial power using multinomial logistic regressions to explain changes in judicial choices with changes in the government's and court's costs. In order to do so I code judicial choices to compute the dependent variable. While commonly used choices—to justify and to not justify referrals—are easily identifiable, I also outline how to identify directives. Moreover, I operationalize the costs of the government to legislate and the costs for the court from an evasion, which are used to explain variation in the judicial choices. When do judges choose one judicial outcome over the other? The findings suggest that the GFCC behaves in a risk-averse manner anticipating the government's costs to legislate when making judicial choices. When the government faces high costs to legislate, then the court reduces the use of directives and often chooses not to justify referrals. However, once the government's costs change and the court's costs from an evasion increase, then the court chooses to present directives. The choice to only justify referrals is less well explained by changes in the actors' costs. Robustness assessments using meaningful subsamples confirm the patterns of relative changes in judicial choices. The findings suggest that the theoretical considerations best apply to decisions based on referrals that involve at least one law. The findings have implications for research on public opinion and judicial behavior, as well as for research on opinion clarity.

In Chapter 5, I assess the second face of judicial power using a difference-in-differences approach to isolate the causal effect of a legal signal on policy shifts in the direction of the court. For this purpose, I propose a text analysis approach that allows me to approximate those shifts. Legal signals are references to past decisions by the GFCC in reports of legislative committees. To what extent do political actors anticipate judicial decision-making? Robust findings show that autolimitation has minor effects on committees, but bills exposed to legal signals are drafted accounting for the court compared with bills that are not exposed to signals. The chapter concludes by discussing the implications of the findings. Self-restraint between opposing parties in intra-legislative bargaining follows different dynamics than legislative self-restraint in anticipation of judicial review. The findings suggest that we need to understand the ways in which legislation is drafted to account for the second face of judicial power.

In Chapter 6, I summarize the main findings and present the implications of this study for research on the judicialization of politics, highlighting the theoretical and social relevance of the presented research. Moreover, I argue that better spatial measures and analyses of compliance with judicial decisions provide for fruitful paths to extend the research on the two faces of judicial power.

Notes

1. These are not the only perspectives on power; for further debates see, for example, Debnam (1975), Isaac (1987), Digeser (1992), and Lukes (2005).
2. The definition is different from what Baum (1976) calls directives. He builds on organizational theory to assess the implementation of appellate decisions by subordinate courts. In this regard, a directive is a remand of a decision to a subordinate court by an appellate court (Baum 1976, 89).
3. In order to identify the highest court with review powers in a European country, information from the CIA's World Factbook (2017) was compared with information from Harutyunyan et al. (2011, 62–63). If both sources contradicted one another, country reports by Ismayr (2009, 2010) were reviewed and countries were grouped based on the additional information.

References

Bachrach, P., Baratz, M.S. (1962). Two Faces of Power. *American Political Science Review*, *56*(4), 947–952.

Baum, L. (1976). Implementation of Judicial Decisions. An Organizational Analysis. *American Politics Quarterly*, *4*(1), 86–114.

Brouard, S. (2009). The Politics of Constitutional Veto in France: Constitutional Council, Legislative Majority and Electoral Competition. *West European Politics*, *32*(2), 384–403.

Brouard, S. (2016). Constitutional Politics: The French Case and Theory-Building. In R. Elgie, E. Grossman, and A. G. Mazur (Eds.) *The Oxford Handbook of French Politics* (pp. 220–242). Oxford: Oxford University Press.

Brouard, S., Hönnige, C. (2017). Constitutional Courts as Veto Players: Lessons from the United States, France and Germany. *European Journal of Political Research*, *56*(3), 529–552.

Bueno de Mesquita, B. (2006). *Principles of International Politics. People's Power, Preferences, and Perceptions*. Washington, DC: CQ Press, 3rd ed.

Cameron, C.M. (2002). Judicial Independence: How Can You Tell It When You See It? And, Who Cares? In *Judicial Independence at the Crossroads: An Interdisciplinary Approach* (pp. 134–147). Thousand Oaks: Sage.

Carrubba, C.J., Zorn, C. (2010). Executive Discretion, Judicial Decision Making, and Separation of Powers in the United States. *Journal of Politics*, *72*(3), 812–824.

Central Intelligence Agency [CIA]. (2017). *The World Factbook*. Washington, DC: Central Intelligence Agency. https://www.cia.gov/library/publications/the-world-factbook/ (accessed February 21, 2018).

Christiansen, M.R., Eskridge Jr., W.N. (2014). Congressional Overrides of Supreme Court Statutory Interpretation Decisions, 1967–2011. *Texas Law Review*, *92*(6), 1317–1515.

Clark, T.S., Lauderdale, B. (2010). Locating Supreme Court Opinions in Doctrine Space. *American Journal of Political Science*, *54*(4), 871–890.

Corley, P.C., Wedeking, J. (2014). The (Dis)Advantage of Certainty: The Importance of Certainty in Language. *Law and Society Review*, *48*(1), 35–62.

Dahl, R.A. (1957). The Concept of Power. *Behavioral Science*, *2*(3), 201–215.

Davis, M.H. (1986). The Law/Politics Distinction, the French Conseil Constitutionnel, and the U.S. Supreme Court. *American Journal of Comparative Law*, *34*(1), 45–92.

Debnam, G. (1975). Nondecisions and Power: The Two Faces of Bachrach and Baratz. *American Political Science Review*, *69*(3), 889–899.

Digeser, P. (1992). The Fourth Face of Power. *Journal of Politics*, *54*(4), 977–1007.

Dyevre, A. (2010). Unifying the Field of Comparative Judicial Politics: Towards a General Theory of Judicial Behaviour. *European Political Science Review*, *2*(2), 297–327.

Epstein, L., Knight, J. (1998). *The Choices Justices Make*. Washington, DC: CQ Press.

Epstein, L., Knight, J., Shvetsova, O. (2001). The Role of Constitutional Courts in the Establishment and Maintenance of Democratic Systems of Government. *Law and Society Review*, *35*(1), 117–164.

Eusepi, G. (1995). Broadcasting system in Italy: Evolution and perspectives. *Public Choice*, *82*(3–4), 307–324.

Feld, L.P., Voigt, S. (2003). Economic Growth and Judicial Independence: Cross-Country Evidence Using a New Set of Indicators. *European Journal of Political Economy*, *19*(3), 497–527.

Fortunato, D., König, T., Proksch, S.-O. (2013). Government Agenda-Setting and Bicameral Conflict Resolution. *Political Research Quarterly*, *66*(4), 938–951.

George, T.E., Epstein, L. (1992). On the Nature of Supreme Court Decision Making. *American Political Science Review*, *86*(2), 323–337.

Gibson, J.L., Caldeira, G.A., Baird, V.A. (1998). On the Legitimacy of National High Courts. *American Political Science Review*, *92*(2), 343–358.

Ginsburg, T. (2003). *Judicial Review in New Democracies: Constitutional Courts in Asian Cases*. Cambridge: Cambridge University Press.

Ginsburg, T., Versteeg, M. (2014). Why Do Countries Adopt Constitutional Review? *Journal of Law, Economics, and Organization*, *30*(3), 587–622.

Hammond, T.H., Bonneau, C.W., Sheehan, R.S. (2005). *Strategic Behavior and Policy Choice on the U.S. Supreme Court*. Stanford: Stanford University Press.

Harutyunyan, G., Nussberger, A., Paczolay, P. (2011). Study on Individual Access To Constitutional Justice. *Venice Commission [European Commission for Democracy Through Law]*, *2009*(538), 1–172.

Hausegger, L., Baum, L. (1999). Inviting Congressional Action: A Study of Supreme Court Motivations in Statutory Interpretation. *American Journal of Political Science*, *43*(1), 162–185.

Helmke, G. (2002). The Logic of Strategic Defection: Court-Executive Relations in Argentina Under Dictatorship and Democracy. *American Political Science Review*, *96*(2), 291–303.

Hibberd, M. (2007). Conflicts of Interest and Media Pluralism in Italian Broadcasting. *West European Politics*, *30*(4), 881–902.

Hirschl, R. (2004). *Towards Juristocrarcy. The Origins and Consequences of the New Constitutionalism*. Cambridge: Harvard University Press.

Hirschl, R. (2008). The Judicialization of Politics. In G. A. Caldeira., D. R. Kelemen, and K. E. Whittington (Eds.) *The Oxford Handbook of Law and Politics* (pp. 119–141). Oxford: Oxford University Press.

Hönnige, C. (2008). Verfassungsgerichte in den EU-Staaten: Wahlverfahren, Kompetenzen und Organisationsprinzipien. *Journal for Comparative Government and European Policy*, *6*(3), 524–553.

Hönnige, C. (2009). The Electoral Connection: How the Pivotal Judge Affects Oppositional Success at European Constitutional Courts. *West European Politics*, *32*(5), 963–984.

Hönnige, C. (2011). Beyond Judicialization: Why We Need More Comparative Research About Constitutional Courts. *European Political Science*, *10*(3), 346–358.

Hönnige, C., Gschwend, T. (2010). Das Bundesverfassungsgericht im politischen System der BRD – ein unbekanntes Wesen? *Politische Vierteljahresschrift*, *51*(3), 507–530.

Hönnige, C., Gschwend, T., Wittig, C., Engst, B.G. (2015). *Constitutional Court Database (CCDB), V17.01 [Mar.]*.

Hufen, F., Nörr Stiefenhofer Lutz. (Eds.). (2008). *Beschränkung von Urteilswirkungen im Falle der Feststellung der Verfassungswidrigkeit von Rechtsnormen. Teil 2: Länderberichte*. Berlin: Bundesministerium der Finanzen.

Huntington, S.P. (1991). *The Third Wave. Democratization in the Late Twentieth Century*. Norman: Oklahoma UP.

Isaac, J.C. (1987). Beyond the Three Faces of Power: A Realist Critique. *Polity*, *20*(1), 4–31.

Ismayr, W. (2009). *Die politischen Systeme Westeuropas*. Wiesbaden: VS Verlag für Sozialwissenschaften, 4th ed.

Ismayr, W. (2010). *Die politischen Systeme Osteuropas*. Wiesbaden: VS Verlag für Sozialwissenschaften, 3rd ed.

Kelemen, K. (2013). Dissenting Opinions in Constitutional Courts. *German Law Journal*, *14*(8), 1345–1371.

Kelsen, H. (2008). [1931]. Wer soll der Hüter der Verfassung sein? In R. C. van Ooyen (Ed.) *Wer soll der Hüter der Verfassung sein? Abhandlungen zur Theorie der Verfassungsgerichtsbarkeit in der pluralistischen, parlamentarischen Demokratie*, (pp. 58–105). Tübingen: Mohr Siebeck.

Kommers, D.P. (1994). The Federal Constitutional Court in the German Political System. *Comparative Political Studies*, *26*(4), 470–491.

Krehbiel, J.N. (2016). The Politics of Judicial Procedures: The Role of Public Oral Hearings in the German Constitutional Court. *American Journal of Political Science*, *60*(4), 990–1005.

Landfried, C. (1985). The Impact of the German Federal Constitutional Court on Politics and Policy Output. *Government and Opposition*, *20*(4), 522–542.

Landfried, C. (1992). Judicial Policy-Making in Germany: The Federal Constitutional Court. *West European Politics*, *15*(3), 50–67.

Langer, L., Brace, P. (2005). The Preemptive Power of State Supreme Courts: Adoption of Abortion and Death Penalty Legislation. *Policy Studies Journal*, *33*(3), 317–340.

Linzer, D.A., Staton, J.K. (2015). A Global Measure of Judicial Independence, 1948–2012. *Journal of Law and Courts*, *3*(2), 223–256.

Luchterhandt, O., Starck, C., Weber, A. (Eds.). (2007). *Verfassungsgerichtsbarkeit in Mittel- und Osteuropa. Teilband I: Berichte*. Baden-Baden: Nomos.

Ludewig, P. (2012). *Die zeitliche Beschränkung der Wirkung von Urteilen des EuGH im Vorabentscheidungsverfahren*. Berlin: Ducker und Humbolt.

Lukes, S. (2005). *Power. A Radical View*. Houndmills: Palgrave Macmillan, 2nd ed.

Manow, P., Burkhart, S. (2007). Legislative Self-Restraint Under Divided Government in Germany, 1976–2002. *Legislative Studies Quarterly*, *32*(2), 167–191.

Martin, A.D., Quinn, K.M. (2002). Dynamic Ideal Point Estimation via Markov Chain Monte Carlo for the U.S. Supreme Court, 1953-1999. *Political Analysis*, *10*(2), 134–153.

Melton, J., Ginsburg, T. (2014). Does De Jure Judicial Independence Really Matter? *Journal of Law and Courts*, *2*(2), 187–217.

Murphy, W.F. (1964). *Elements of Judicial Strategy*. Chicago: Chicago University Press.

Parcelle Jr., R.L., Curry, B.W., Marshall, B.W. (2011). *Decision Making by the Modern Supreme Court*. Cambridge: Cambridge University Press.

Raffaelli, R. (2012). *Dissenting Opinions in the Supreme Courts of the Member States*. European Parliament: Directorate General for Internal Policies (PE 462.470). https://www.europarl.europa.eu/document/activities/cont/201304/20130423ATT64963/20130423ATT64963EN.pdf (accessed February 21, 2018).

Ramseyer, M.J. (1994). The Puzzling (In)Dependence of Courts: A comparative Approach. *Journal of Legal Studies*, *23*(2), 721–747.

Rios-Figueroa, J., Staton, J.K. (2014). An Evaluation of Cross-National Measures of Judicial Independence. *Journal of Law, Economics, and Organization*, *30*(1), 104–137.

Rohde, D.W., Spaeth, H.J. (1976). *Supreme Court Decision Making*. San Francisco: Freeman.

Salzberger, E.M. (1993). A Positive Analysis of the Doctrine of Separation of Powers, or: Why Do We Have an Independent Judiciary? *International Review of Law and Economics*, *13*(4), 349–379.

Santoni, M., Zucchini, F. (2004). Does Policy Stability Increases the Constitutional Court's Independence? The Case of Italy During the First Republic (1956–1992). *Public Choice*, *120*(3–4), 439–461.

Schlaich, K., Korioth, S. (2015). *Das Bundesverfassungsgericht. Stellung, Verfahren Entscheidungen*. München: C.H. Beck, 10th ed.

Schubert, G.A. (1965). *The Judicial Mind. Attitudes and Ideologies of Supreme Court Justices, 1946–1963*. Evanston: Northwestern University Press.

Segal, J.A., Cover, A.D. (1989). Ideological Values and the Votes of U.S. Supreme Court Justices. *American Political Science Review*, *83*(2), 557–565.

Segal, J.A., Spaeth, H.J. (1993). *The Supreme Court and the Attitudinal Model.* Cambridge: Cambridge University Press.

Segal, J.A., Spaeth, H.J. (2002). *The Supreme Court and the Attitudinal Model Revisited.* Cambridge: Cambridge University Press.

Shapiro, M., Stone, A. (1994). The New Constitutional Politics of Europe. *Comparative Political Studies, 26*(4), 397–420.

Shapiro, M., Stone Sweet, A. (2002). *On Law, Politics and Judicialization.* Oxford: Oxford University Press.

Simon, H.A. (1953). Notes on the Observation and Measurement of Political Power. *Journal of Politics, 15*(4), 500–516.

Spiller, P.T., Tiller, E.H. (1996). Invitations to Override: Congressional Reversals of Supreme Court Decisions. *International Review of Law and Economics, 16*(4), 503–521.

Spriggs, J.F., II. (1996). The Supreme Court and Federal Administrative Agencies: A Resource-Based Theory and Analysis of Judicial Impact. *American Journal of Political Science, 40*(4), 1122–1151.

Starck, C., Weber, A. (Eds.). (2007). *Verfassungsgerichtsbarkeit in Westeuropa. Teilband I: Berichte.* Baden-Baden: Nomos, 2 ed.

Staton, J.K. (2010). *Judicial Power and Strategic Communication in Mexico.* Cambridge: Cambridge University Press.

Staton, J.K., Vanberg, G. (2008). The Value of Vagueness: Delegation, Defiance, and Judicial Opinions. *American Journal of Political Science, 52*(3), 504–519.

Stephenson, M.C. (2003). "When the Devil Turns ...": The Political Foundations of Independent Judicial Review. *Journal of Legal Studies, 32*(1), 59–89.

Sternberg, S., Gschwend, T., Wittig, C., Engst, B.G. (2015). Zum Einfluss der öffentlichen Meinung auf Entscheidungen des Bundesverfassungsgerichts: Eine Analyse von abstrakten Normenkontrollen sowie Bund-Länder-Streitigkeiten 1974–2010. *Politische Vierteljahresschrift, 56*(4), 570–598.

Stone, A. (1992). *The Birth of Judicial Politics in France. The Constitutional Council in Comparative Perspective.* Oxford: Oxford University Press.

Stone Sweet, A. (1998). A Comment on Vanberg: Rules, Dispute Resolution, and Strategic Behavior. *Journal of Theoretical Politics, 10*(3), 327–338.

Stone Sweet, A. (2000). *Governing with Judges: Constitutional Politics in Europe.* Oxford: Oxford University Press.

Tate, C.N., Vallinder, T. (1995). *The Global Expansion of Judicial Power. The Judicialization of Politics.* New York: New York University Press.

Vanberg, G. (1998a). Abstract Judicial Review, Legislative Bargaining, and Policy Compromise. *Journal of Theoretical Politics, 10*(3), 299–326.

Vanberg, G. (1998b). Reply to Stone Sweet. *Journal of Theoretical Politics, 10*(3), 339–346.

Vanberg, G. (2001). Legislative-Judicial Relations: A Game-Theoretic Approach to Constitutional Review. *American Journal of Political Science, 45*(2), 346–361.

Vanberg, G. (2005). *The Politics of Constitutional Review in Germany*. Cambridge: Cambridge University Press.
Vanberg, G. (2015). Constitutional Courts in Comparative Perspective: A Theoretical Assessment. *Annual Review of Political Science*, *18*(1), 167–185.
Voigt, S., Gutmann, J., Feld, L.P. (2015). Economic Growth and Judicial Independence, a Dozen Years On: Cross-Country Evidence Using an Updated Set of Indicators. *European Journal of Political Economy*, *38*, 197–211.
Whittington, K.E. (2005). "Impose Your Friendly Hand:" Poitical Supports for the Exercise of Judicial Review by the United States Supreme Court. *American Political Science Review*, *99*(4), 583–596.
Wittig, C.E. (2016). *The Occurrence of Separate Opinions at the Federal Constitutional Court: An Analysis with a Novel Database*. Berlin: Logos Verlag Berlin GmbH.

CHAPTER 2

The Judicial-Policy-Dialogue Game

In this chapter, I present the theoretical considerations to assess the two faces of judicial power. For this purpose, I design the *Judicial-Policy-Dialogue Game* (JPD game). Implications of the game theoretic model are assessed using a numerical simulation. The findings from the assessment are helpful to derive hypotheses, which I test in the following chapters.

In general, a model "aims not at replicating the world, but at artificially isolating features in order to study their potential or dynamics" (Chwaszcza 2008, 139; similar Shepsle 2010, 7–9). In line with this definition, the formal model presented here will focus on the necessary elements to assess the mechanisms that characterize a court's opportunity to exercise any form of the two faces of power. Power is a relational concept and it can only exist between actors (Dahl 1957b; Bueno de Mesquita 2006, Ch. 7). The power relation of interest here is between the court and the political majority, which will be set equal to the government. This is why it is not necessary to model the intra-court deliberation between judges; instead, it is necessary to analyze the choices the court and the government take while interacting with each other. In other words, I take an external perspective on the court (Dyevre 2010, 304). Therefore, it is appropriate to treat courts as unitary actors for the purpose of this study. Power as assessed here is the result of the court's opportunity to render decisions and engage in judicial policymaking. It holds less concern how intra-court bargaining will lead to a certain decision, but rather how environmental

B. G. Engst, *The Two Faces of Judicial Power*,
https://doi.org/10.1007/978-3-030-46016-7_2

factors influence decision-making. The court makes one binding decision. In other words, I acknowledge that courts are composed of individual judges (Forrest et al. 2000), although by taking an outward-oriented perspective here it is appropriate to treat them as unitary actors (Staton 2010, 17–18).

Finally, using a formal model the method applied here follows the tradition of positive political theorists (Epstein and Knight 2000). Respective scholars derive scientific statements rigorously applying methods based on similar foundations as used by the natural sciences, such as mathematics (Amadae and Bueno de Mesquita 1999, 270; Riker 1990). Schubert (1958) was among the first to argue that "the judicial process is tailor-made for investigation by the theory of games" since the actors involved in judicial interactions "frequently play the role of competing gamesmen" (Schubert 1958, 1022). Indeed, "game theory aims to help us understand situations in which decision-makers interact" (Osborn 2004, 1). Following Schubert (1958), a few scholars began to take a strategic perspective on judicial behavior, especially as the rational choice paradigm entered political science in the mid-1960s (Epstein and Knight 2000, 627–635; Riker 1990; Amadae and Bueno de Mesquita 1999, 270). Nevertheless, it was the unpublished dissertation by Marks from 1989 that helped game theory to reach a breakthrough in the study of law and courts (Epstein and Knight 2000, 635; Cameron 1993, 1). An article published by the "Journal of Law, Economics, and Organization" (Marks 2012 [1988]) summarizes his separation of powers game used to assess the interaction between the United States Supreme Court and Congress. Since then, games assessing the interaction between a court and its institutional environment have become increasingly popular (Dyevre 2010, 304–310). Scholars have repeatedly assessed the interaction between the judiciary and political actors, using formal models in the context of the United States Supreme Court (Ferejohn and Shipan 1990; Eskridge Jr. 1991; Segal 1997; Rogers 2001; Rogers et al. 2006; Clark 2011) as well as regarding courts outside the United States (Vanberg 2001, 2005; Helmke 2002; Carrubba 2005; Staton 2010).

The two faces of power assessed here require analyzing the interaction between the court and the government. Hence, I regard a game theoretic model as appropriate for the analysis. Nonetheless, I do not claim that this is the only approach to address my research questions, but rather that it is one feasible approach (see Staton 2008). In the next sections, I will present the JPD game and wish to show that formal theories "contribute to the clarity and internal consistency of particular arguments" (Staton 2008, 10).

Table 2.1 Summary of the notation and the modeling choices

Notation	*Meaning [and the particular specification when defined]*
G	Ideal point of the governing majority [fixed to 0]
l	The governing majority legislates
$\neg l$	The governing majority does not legislate
C	Ideal point of the court
j	The court justifies a referral
jd	The court justifies a referral and presents a directive
$\neg j$	The court does not justify a referral
x_{sq}	The spatial position of the status quo [fixed to 1]
x_{g1}	The spatial position of the law passed by the governing majority in the *initial* move of the game
x_{g2}	The spatial position of the law passed by the governing majority in the *final* move of the game
x_d	The spatial position of the directive presented by the court
α	The costs the government has when legislating again [bounded to $\alpha > 0$]
γ	The costs the court has when being evaded [bounded to $\gamma > 0$]

2.1 The Sequences of the Judicial-Policy-Dialogue Game

The JPD game comprises two actors: the governing majority in the legislature—which I set equal to the government G—and the court C. The model is a general one, independent of any (democratic) political system, and G is not restricted to the government but equivalent to any possible actor empowered to evade judicial decisions. Each actor has an individual ideal point in a unidimensional policy space, X, and I assume that the policy proposal, the judicial decision, and the policy outcome can be represented on the same policy space. Therefore, the ideal points of the government and the court are both $G \in X$ and $C \in X$.

Table 2.1 summarizes the model's notation and modeling choices. The table is presented in advance to allow the reader to follow all subsequent discussions.

Bargaining models often assume a unidimensional policy space (Krehbiel 1998; Cameron 2000), although it is debated whether this is appropriate (Anderson IV. and Tahk 2007). While some studies generate findings that justify the reduction of policy choices to one dimension (Poole and Rosenthal 1991, 2007), others speak in favor of multiple dimensions (Koford 1989; Roberts et al. 2016). Judicial decisions addressing specific policies are at the center of the model presented here. This focus justifies the simplification that the bargaining between the government and the court occurs in a unidimensional policy space. Courts often consider only parts of a policy and legal controversies are reduced to particular provisions. This leads to very specific questions that courts address. For example, the general read on *King v. Burwell* (576 U.S. 988 [2015]) is that Obamacare survived the challenge at the United States Supreme Court (Barnes 2015). However, the actual question that the judges answered was "whether the [Patient Protection and Affordable Care] Act's tax credits are available in States that have a Federal Exchange" (576 U.S. 988 [2015], 5). Similarly, when legislators draft a policy and anticipate judicial decision-making, they rarely question the constitutionality of the whole bill but rather only single provision. For example, when committee members of the German legislature discussed the parental custody reform of 1998—which introduced a total of 162 changes to 25 laws (own count; BT 13/4899)—they did not question the whole reform, but rather modified a single paragraph to bring this paragraph in line with past decisions by the Federal Court of Justice and the German Federal Constitutional Court (see BT 13/851, 74).[1] In other words, the dimension relevant to the interaction between the court and the government is a narrow one, driven by legal specifics. This is why the simplifying assumption of a unidimensional policy space is appropriate for the JPD game.

The government moves first and chooses to legislate (l) or not legislate ($\neg l$). If G chooses not to legislate, a preexisting status quo (x_{sq}) will prevail (with $x_{sq} \in X$) and the game ends. If G chooses to legislate, then G proposes some initial policy x_{g1} (with $x_{g1} \in X$). Afterwards, I assume that x_{g1} is referred to the court for review.

The court moves second, having three options to respond to the proposal x_{g1}. If C does not justify a referred law on legal grounds ($\neg j$), then x_{g1} will prevail and the game ends.[2] However, if the court chooses to justify a referral (j), then x_{g1} is not in accordance with the constitution and as a result x_{sq} is restored. Finally, the model allows for a judicial directive (jd). If the court announces a justification including a directive this directive is equivalent to taking a position in the unidimensional policy space. Put simply, a directive is a new policy x_d with $x_d \in X$ presented by C.

If C chooses to justify a referral or justify a referral and to present a directive then the government moves again. In this third step, G can choose to legislate (l) one more time or not to legislate ($\neg l$). On the one hand, if G chooses not to legislate but to accept the court's decision, then the original

Setup
$I = G, C$
$S = S_G \times S_C$
$S_G \in \{\neg lll, \neg l\neg ll, \neg ll\neg l, \neg l\neg l\neg l | lll, l\neg ll, ll\neg l, l\neg l\neg l\}$ and $S_c \in \{\neg j, j, jd\}$

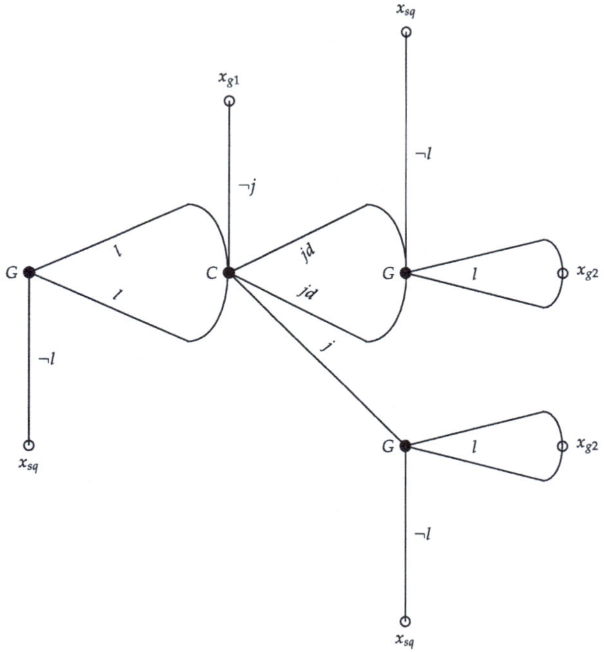

Fig. 2.1 Setup, sequences, and outcomes of the Judicial-Policy-Dialogue Game in extensive form. Note: G = Governing majority in the legislature set equal to the government, C = Constitutional court, l = Legislate, $\neg l$ = Not legislate, $\neg j$ = Not justified, j = Justified, jd = Justified with directive

status quo x_{sq} is restored. On the other hand, if G chooses to legislate, then G will present a new policy x_{g2} with $x_{g2} \in X$. After this final move by G, the game ends.

Figure 2.1 summarizes the setup of the outlined sequential game in extensive form and the possible outcomes x_{sq}, x_{g1}, or x_{g2}. It is interesting to see that the directive of the court x_d is not a possible outcome. This highlights that the court is unable to enforce x_d itself. Instead, the governing majority in the legislature has to legislate to implement x_d. Therefore, if the government has an interest in implementing x_d, it may do so presenting a respective x_{g2} (with $x_{g2} = x_d$), but it does not have to. Instead, the government can pass new legislation x_{g2} different to the directive and this evades the court's proposal. Why does the court take the risk of an evasion and choose to invest resources in justifying a referral or presenting a directive? In the next section, I will outline the utilities that actors gain from playing the game and the strategies available to each player to maximize the respective utilities.

2.1.1 The Government as an Actor

The literature on legislative research has identified three major goals of political actors (see Strøm 1990 for a review). Accordingly, legislators or any other political actors are either vote-seeking, office-seeking, or policy-seeking (Downs 1957; Riker 1962; Strøm 1990; Müller and Strøm 1999). It is plausible to argue that these motivations are linked to one another. A certain number of votes is necessary to ensure office. In other words, political actors will pursue any necessary interest to ensure votes, given that this will secure office. In turn, this motivation for votes should also lead to a certain policy motivation among legislators. They should be encouraged to position themselves and their policies close to their respective electorate. Having a visible position and presenting policy close to this position will ensure respective lasting electoral support. The policy motivation thus becomes a compliment to vote-seeking and office-seeking (De Swaan 1973; Strøm 1990, 567; Laver and Shepsle 1996, 8–9). Attractive policy will ensure votes and allow legislators to solidify their position in office. Therefore, playing the JPD game, the government is strictly policy motivated.

This is why the government will receive the general policy gain based on the outcome in relation to its own ideal point. Hence, when proposing an initial policy x_{g1} the government wants to maximize $-(x_{g1} - G)^2$ where G is the ideal point of the government. However, once a law is referred to the court for review and the court chooses to justify a referral, the government will lose x_{g1}. Instead, the court's decision to justify a referral implies a return to the status quo x_{sq} and the government receives the gain $-(x_{sq} - G)^2$. If the government is not satisfied with this decision, then it can engage in a new legislative effort and respond to the decision with a new (second) bill x_{g2}. Accordingly, the government receives a final policy gain from the second bill in relation to its own ideal point with $-(x_{g2} - G)^2$.

Table 2.2 Utility functions of the government

Outcome	*History*	*Policy gain*	*Costs new effort*
x_{sq}	$U_G(\neg l, \emptyset)$	$-(x_{sq} - G)^2$	
x_{g1}	$U_G(l, \neg j)$	$-(x_{g1} - G)^2$	
x_{sq}	$U_G(l\neg l, j)$	$-(x_{sq} - G)^2$	
x_{g2}	$U_G(ll, j)$	$-(x_{g2} - G)^2$	$-\alpha(x_{g2} - x_{sq})^2$
x_{sq}	$U_G(l\neg l, jd)$	$-(x_{sq} - G)^2$	$-\alpha(x_{sq} - x_d)^2$
x_{g2}	$U_G(ll, jd)$	$-(x_{g2} - G)^2$	$-\alpha(x_{g2} - x_d)^2$

In addition, once a law is referred to the court for review and the court chooses to justify a referral and presents a directive, then the government will also lose x_{g1}. The court's directive implies a response by the government to implement the judicial decision. However, if the government chooses not to legislate ($\neg l$), then the directive will not be implemented. Hence, the original status quo will be restored and the government's benefit is $-(x_{sq} - G)^2$. If the government chooses to legislate (l) in response to a directive and to present a new (second) bill x_{g2}, then it is free to design this new bill. The policy gain is thus $-(x_{g2}-G)^2$. This illustrates once again that the court is able to present directives albeit unable to enforce them. The government can deviate from the directive. The final policy is completely at the government's discretion.

In sum, the policy gains that the government receives from the JPD game are $-(x_{g1} - G)^2$, $-(x_{sq} - G)^2$, or $-(x_{g2} - G)^2$ dependent on the game's history. The third column of Table 2.2 summarizes this information.

Nevertheless, an action to respond to a judicial decision is costly. First, if the government chooses to present new legislation in response to a justified referral, then it faces the costs from the deviation from the court's request to implement the status quo, $-\alpha(x_{g2} - x_{sq})^2$. Second, if the government chooses not to legislate in response to a judicial directive, then it faces the costs from the deviation from the court's directive, $-\alpha(x_{sq} - x_d)^2$. Third, if the government chooses to deviate from a judicial directive presenting new legislation not equal to the directive, then it faces the costs from this deviation, $-\alpha(x_{g2} - x_d)^2$. The final column in Table 2.2 summarizes the cost components of the government's utility functions. What is decisive about these costs is the weight that the government places on them. This is summarized in the term α. For example, if the weight placed on the costs is low, then the effect of the spatial loss from a cost component on the general policy gain will be minor compared to when the weight is high.

The assumption is that changes in the costs are proportional to the squared policy changes. This is the simplest assumption one can make, accounting for the fact that every other modeling choice would require profound knowledge of how policymakers perceive the costs. There are no obvious ways to gain such knowledge. Instead, such an alternative approach would require more, possibly even stronger assumptions. Therefore, the assumption of proportionality appears as the weakest one can make. What drives the government's costs α to react to judicial decisions in a new legislative effort?

The drivers of the costs from a new effort (α). There are many factors that appear plausible to drive the costs. I will briefly discuss three factors but operationalize the costs later.

First, the costs can be driven by the government's ability to mobilize legislators to respond to a judicial decision. Carey (2009) assessed the willingness of individual legislators to follow the party line. He finds that when opinions on legislation among legislators are sufficiently divided, then the legislators are unwilling to blindly follow the party line; instead, individual legislators wish to ensure that their constituents can discern their specific position on an issue. Assuming that court decisions are often controversial—at least somebody felt the need to file a lawsuit—then Carey's (2009) findings imply that the government will have to invest resources to mobilize legislators to respond to a court decision. Hence, the costs from a new legislative effort to respond to a decision are driven by the necessary effort to mobilize legislators.

Second, the government's reaction to a court decision can cause a public backlash. It is one of the most robust findings in social science research that courts experience high levels of public support with low variation compared to the political branches (Gibson et al. 1998; Epstein and Knight 1998, 157–159; Vanberg 2005, 197; Sieberer 2006). Thus, it is plausible that parts of the public are in favor of the government and still feel a moral obligation towards compliance with legal decisions. The size of the public in favor of the court can increase the costs for the government to go against the court. In democracies, the government is dependent on the public's discretion. In line with this reasoning, it is plausible that the government has an interest in preventing conflict with the court during an election year (Ignagni and Meernik 1994, 359; Vanberg 1998a, 313; Brouard 2009).

This is why public opinion influences the weight placed on the costs to react to a judicial decision.

Third, governments in office are not necessarily faced with court decisions aimed at their agenda. The topic raised in a decision can be pressing or less important to the government. It is plausible to assume that the weight that the government places on the loss of a policy agenda is lower when the issue is not at the heart of its party ideology compared to when the issue holds major importance. This is implicitly connected to the timeliness of a topic addressed in a court decision. A ruling affecting a topic that is already outdated holds less relevance to the government than the need to respond to a pressing, contemporary issue (Ignagni and Meernik 1994, 362). Therefore, the relevance of a topic under consideration drives the costs to respond to a decision.

The three factors that drive the costs of a new legislative effort (α) are not necessarily distinct, but it is evident that—for example—electoral considerations and the policy agenda reinforce one another. Summarizing the utility functions of the government in Table 2.2, I now turn to the court as an actor.

2.1.2 The Court as an Actor

The motives for judicial behavior were at the center of judicial politics in the early 1990s. Posner (1993) was among the first to ask provocatively: "What do judges and justices maximize?" He argues that judges are rational actors responding to an incentive structure in a way that is similar to anyone else. Hence, judges follow their self-interest rather than the constraints set by the legal system. Therefore, judges do not regard the law as a dominant factor when rendering decisions, as proponents of the legal model of judicial review would argue. Instead, such a model is a normative ideal rather than an accurate empirical description of judicial behavior (Parcelle Jr. et al. 2011, 29–34). Moreover, Segal and Cover (1989) as well as Segal and Spaeth (1993, 2002) have come to design the attitudinal model following Schubert (1965), who first proposed that judges choose ideal points in an ideological space. This behavioral view is widely accepted by now but has been criticized for overlooking the external factors that constrain judicial activities. Therefore, Epstein and Knight (1998) further enhanced the behavioral approach, arguing that judges anticipate external constraints as well as constraints within the panel of judges. This led to the strategic model of judicial behavior, which is the dominant paradigm of judicial politics today. What all models have in common is that judges are seen as ideologically driven with respective ideal points in the policy space. Hence, following these approaches and the empirical evidence of various studies (Parcelle Jr. et al. 2011, 29–50; Segal 1997), I assume that judges are policy driven to the extent that they prefer policy that is as close as possible to their ideal point.

Therefore, the gain that the court will receive from the JPD game is a policy gain based on the outcome in relation to its own ideal point C. Hence, as long as the government does not legislate, the court is not involved and will only receive the benefits from the existing status quo, which is $-(x_{sq} - C)^2$. If the government legislates, I assume that the law will be referred to the court for review. It has been mentioned that the court can choose among three actions to respond to a referral. When the judges regard a referral as not justified, they reject a plaintiff's request on legal grounds. In this case, the court's decision will lead to the government's initial law x_{g1} being implemented. The benefits for the court are those dependent on the position of this initial law compared to the court's ideal point and given by the utility function $-(x_{g1} - C)^2$. Nevertheless, the court might decide that a plaintiff's referral is justified and that a public act or a referred law is not in accordance with the constitution. By justifying a referral, the court implicitly restores the original status quo x_{sq}. Hence, if the government accepts a justification, the court will receive the utility $-(x_{sq} - C)^2$. However, it is the government's right to respond to a court's decision. If the government chooses to legislate again, then the court can only gain from the location of the government's final (second) policy x_{g2} compared to the court's ideal point $-(x_{g2} - C)^2$. The utilities $-(x_{sq} - C)^2$ and $-(x_{g2} - C)^2$ are also those that the court will receive when justifying a referral with a directive. It has been mentioned multiple times that the court is unable to enforce a decision. If the government does not implement a directive, then the court's decision will imply a return to the status quo. If the government chooses to legislate again, the court will receive a benefit based on the second policy x_{g2} in comparison to the own ideal point. This second policy may reflect the judicial directive, but it does not have to.

In sum, the policy gains that the court receives from the JPD game are $-(x_{g1} - C)^2$, $-(x_{sq} - C)^2$, or $-(x_{g2} - C)^2$ dependent on the game's history. The third column of Table 2.3 summarizes this information.

In addition, the evasion of a judicial decision will be costly. Under such circumstances, the court will only receive a limited benefit. If the

Table 2.3 Utility functions of the court

Outcome	*History*	*Policy gain*	*Costs evasion*
x_{sq}	$U_C(\emptyset, \neg l)$	$-(x_{sq} - C)^2$	
x_{g1}	$U_C(\neg j, l)$	$-(x_{g1} - C)^2$	
x_{sq}	$U_C(j, l\neg l)$	$-(x_{sq} - C)^2$	
x_{g2}	$U_C(j, ll)$	$-(x_{g2} - C)^2$	$-\gamma(x_{sq} - x_{g2})^2$
x_{sq}	$U_C(jd, l\neg l)$	$-(x_{sq} - C)^2$	$-\gamma(x_d - x_{sq})^2$
x_{g2}	$U_C(jd, ll)$	$-(x_{g2} - C)^2$	$-\gamma(x_d - x_{g2})^2$

government chooses to implement a new policy despite the fact that the court prefers the status quo, the loss is $-\gamma(x_{sq} - x_{g2})^2$. Moreover, if the government chooses not to react to a judicial directive, then the court's loss is the difference between the position of the presented directive and the reenacted status quo $-\gamma(x_d - x_{sq})^2$. Finally, the court also experiences a loss when the government's response to a directive is imperfect. This loss is $-\gamma(x_d - x_{g2})^2$. These later costs reduce to zero once the government chooses to perfectly implement the directive ($x_d = x_{g2}$). The weight that the court places on any judicial evasion is decisive and illustrated by γ.

The assumption that changes in the costs are proportional to the squared policy changes is the same as made for the government's costs. Any other assumption would require profound knowledge of how the judges perceive the costs. There are no obvious ways to gain such knowledge which makes the alternative approach not feasible. Therefore, the assumption of proportionality appears as the weakest one can make. The cost components are summarized in the final column of Table 2.3. What drives the weight placed on the costs from an evasion?

The drivers of the costs from an evasion (γ). There are a number of plausible factors that can drive the costs from an evasion. I will discuss two factors here to develop an understanding of the concept but leave the operationalization for later.

First, it is necessary for the court to ensure public support. Scholars have argued that the court requires the public's support to pressure the government to implement decisions (Vanberg 2001, 2005; Carrubba and Zorn 2010). Hence, judges need to anticipate the public's support on an issue addressed in a decision. Sternberg et al. (2015) present evidence that the court accounts for the public's interest when faced with a referral. In line with these findings, one may assume that if the court presents a decision unfavorable to the public, then the costs of an evasion of a decision may increase. The costs are lower when the court enjoys public support. It is important to note that the exact level of public support does not matter; instead, the level of support perceived by the court is important. For example, the popular German Federal Constitutional Court encountered a crisis early in the 1990s when deciding on electoral rights for immigrants, the right to have an abortion or not to display a crucifix in a classroom, losing public support (Wesel 2004, Ch. 7; Sternberg et al. 2015, 571). The levels of support were still high, but the feeling of a "crisis" influenced the costs received from every evasion.

Second, the weight placed on an evasion is influenced by the relevance of the issue under consideration. If the issue holds less importance to the court, then an evasion is less costly compared to an issue of major importance. A possible mechanism is that a court's decisions have implications for the perceived standing of the court among the legal community. Judges are selected based on a prior legal career at the highest courts in Europe (Hönnige 2007, 115–119). There are also legal topics for which judges are known. Accordingly, an evasion in such legal areas is costlier than an evasion in legal areas that hold less importance to the standing of the court. In other words, the relevance of the issue under consideration influences the weight that the court places on the costs of an evasion.

The two factors that influence the costs of an evasion (γ) are most likely to occur jointly. Summarizing the utility functions of the court in Table 2.3, I will outline additional modeling choices now. Subsequently, I present strategies and solutions to the JPD game.

2.1.3 Additional Modeling Choices

The model is based on some simplifying assumptions. Primarily, I assume complete information, meaning that all actors are informed about each other's preferences and actions when taking decisions (McCarty and Meirowitz 2007, 7). While this is a particularly strong assumption, there is support for this modeling choice.

First, there is reason to believe that political actors and legal professionals can anticipate judicial behavior to a certain extent (see Schlink 2007, 162). At least it is known that political actors frequently invite legal experts to help them to foreshadow possible judicial action (Landfried 1992, 56–58; Kommers 1994, 475–476). Moreover, ministries have special legal divisions that monitor judicial decision-making (Gawron and Rogowski 2015, 159).

In this regard, former decisions by highest courts are helpful as courts develop a certain doctrinal path over time (Clark and Lauderdale 2010). Finally, while judges are silent on current judicial action, they comment on older decisions and we know of background talks between the media and the courts (see Rath 2015). All of these different options allow political actors to gain a sense of possible judicial behavior.

Second, designed as a sequential game, each actor playing the JPD game can monitor prior behavior by the other actor, which provides information on the character of that actor throughout the game. In particular, the government's final move follows once the court has revealed its interests.

Third, the judges are also able to fully monitor the political process, ongoing public debates, and the passage of bills in the legislature. Moreover, most documents discussed during the legislative process are publicly accessible. This is why it is plausible to assume that judges can anticipate political interests. Furthermore, by moving after the government has revealed its legislative aim, the courts can anticipate at least these interests.

Besides these theoretical assumptions, the model simplifies institutional features to focus on the dialogue between the judiciary and the government. First, for now I assume that the judiciary is actively involved when a bill is passed and becomes law. This assumption will be relaxed when assessing the second face of judicial power which implies no judicial involvement. However, even if the judiciary is not actively involved, the institution exists and an indirect anticipation of judicial behavior is plausible (Landfried 1992; Stone Sweet 2000; Vanberg 2001). Second, while the design features of the judiciary widely vary in an international comparison (Hönnige 2008; Engst 2017), the model presented here is reduced to the basic feature inherent in every judicial system, namely that judges have to come to some decision. By focusing only on this outcome, the model is parsimonious and uses an internationally comparable feature. Hence, the model is a general one designed to address the question of interest here: when do judges choose one judicial outcome over the other?

The model is designed as a one-shot game for three reasons. First, while the institutions interacting are stable across time, the actors shaping the institutional behavior vary over time. In particular, judges and political actors serve different alternating terms (see e.g., Hönnige 2007, 191–192) and thus the actors playing the game have no endless shadow of the future; instead, with each case referred to the court, particular actors play the game. Second, according to the legal philosophy taught in law schools and according to judicial practice, constitutional courts will decide on a matter only once. Hence, every case is based on an individual scenario that will be addressed once. While the court might decide on an issue area multiple times, the particular case itself has to be regarded as one single-shot game. Third, every case addresses one particular administrative act or law. This illustrates that every case should be regarded as a particular scenario always leading to a new dialogue between the judiciary and the political branches.

Finally, it is plausible to assume that the weights placed on the costs that the government (α) and the court (γ) face are only positive. This is obvious once one considers the substantive meaning of such weights. For example, the public's interest in the court may be low or high but will never be completely absent. Similarly, political actors or the media may pay attention to the court to varying degrees but they never ignore the court completely. In other words, there are worlds in which the court faces less attention leading to low costs of an evasion and there are worlds in which the court faces strong backlash leading to high costs of an evasion. Hence, the weight placed on the costs may be small or large but never nonexistent. The same logic also holds true for the government's costs. Hence, $\alpha > 0$ and $\gamma > 0$. In addition, the positions of two ideal points are normalized. I fix the ideal point of the government at $G = 0$ and assume that the status quo is larger than 0, fixed at $x_{sq} = 1$. This is without the loss of generality. Symmetry implies that points to the right of the government are simply mirror images of points to the left of G (Cameron 2000, 90).

In sum, the outlined assumptions simplify the JPD game to isolate the interaction of interest. However, the game fulfills the major requirements of a model. The idea of a model is not to appeal "to some abstract ideal of 'reality"' but rather to add to our understanding of one aspect in a complex interaction (Morrow 1994, 58; similar Chwaszcza 2008). This study claims nothing more than to understand when the judiciary and the government follow one particular form of dialogue. In particular, I will isolate when judges choose one judicial outcome over the other.

Knowing the structure of the game (Fig. 2.1), the utility that the government (Table 2.2) and the court (Table 2.3) can gain when playing different histories of the game and having summarized additional modeling assumptions, it is possible to identify the actors' strategies in equilibrium.

2.2 Strategies in Equilibrium

Figure 2.2 summarizes all considerations made regarding the JPD game in extensive form. The general utility functions are shown in gray in a smaller

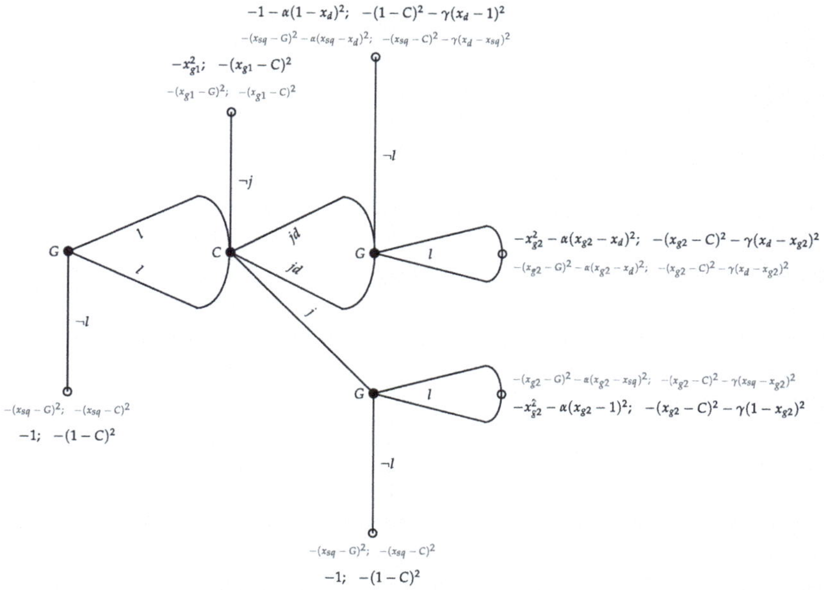

Fig. 2.2 The Judicial-Policy-Dialogue Game in extensive form with utility functions

typeset, while the black utility functions are simplifications based on the modeling choices ($G = 0$; $x_{sq} = 1$). In what follows, I focus on these simplified utility functions.

In order to solve the game, I apply optimization and backward induction to identify subgame perfect Nash equilibria (see Osborn 2004; McCarty and Meirowitz 2007). Optimization will help to identify the ideal policies of interest to the government under the various outcomes of the game. Moreover, optimization helps to determine the court's optimal judicial directive. Backward induction is applied to identify the behavior of the government and the court in each step, accounting for the optimal policies. The idea of backward induction is that "the last player to act at each node chooses the action that maximizes her utility. The second to last player then chooses his action optimally, knowing that the last player chooses optimal actions at each node. This process continues until each player has chosen optimally under the assumption that all future players make optimal choices" (McCarty and Meirowitz 2007, 175). In other words, the court and the government aim to follow subgame perfect strategies. A strategy profile in the JPD game—in extensive form with perfect information—is subgame perfect if the utility that the court or the government receive by following their respective equilibrium strategy after every nonterminal move is at least as high as the utility that the court or the government could gain from any other strategy played (given the belief that the other actor will play the strategy required by the strategy profile).[3]

Applying backward induction, the next step is to identify the government's behavior in the final move of the game. Thereafter, it is necessary to understand the judicial action in anticipation of the government's behavior in the final move. Subsequently, it is possible to identify whether the government ever legislates in the first step of the game.

2.2.1 *The Government's Final Choice*

In the final move of the JPD game, the government is able to respond to the court's decision to (1) justify a referral or (2) justify a referral and present a directive. The government will choose to either legislate (l) or not legislate ($\neg l$). If the government legislates, it presents an optimal policy (x^*_{g2}) maximizing its own benefits. This optimal policy can be identified by optimization. The unconstrained optimal policy following a court's choice to justify a referral and present a directive ($U_G[ll, jd]$) is[4]

$$\max_{x_{g2}} = -x_{g2}^2 - \alpha(x_{g2} - x_d)^2$$

$$x_{g2}^{*1} = \frac{\alpha x_d}{\alpha + 1} \tag{B1.1}$$

and following a judicial decision to only justify a referral ($U_G[ll, j]$) the optimal policy is

$$\max_{x_{g2}} = -x_{g2}^2 - \alpha(x_{g2} - 1)^2$$

$$x_{g2}^{*2} = \frac{\alpha}{\alpha + 1} \tag{B1.2}$$

The substantive interpretations of these rational functions are dependent on the weights (α) placed on the legislative or public costs. To illustrate this, I refer to Fig. 2.3 with the position of hypothetical directives (x_d) on the x-axis and ideal policies (x^*_{g2}) on the y-axis. The bold lines illustrate different degrees of the costs (α). Hence, read the figure as follows: if the

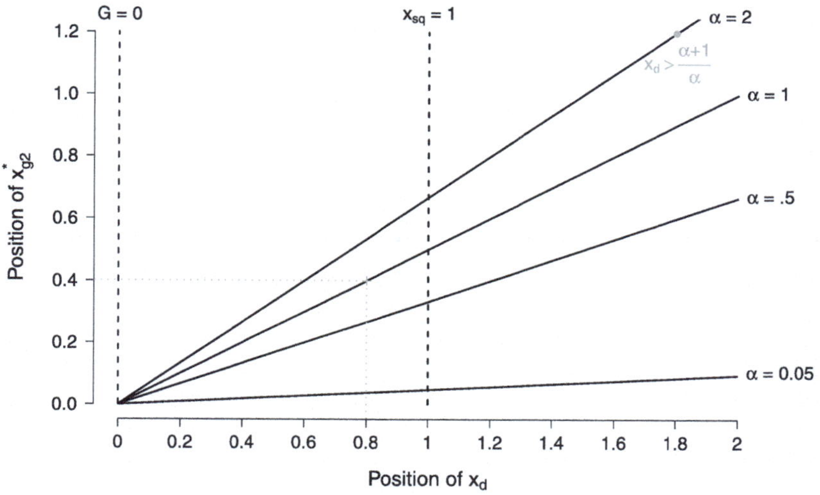

Fig. 2.3 Optimal government policies in response to different directives and costs

court presents a directive at ($x_d =$) 0.8 and the costs that the government has to convince fellow legislators to respond to the directive are ($\alpha =$) 1, then the optimal policy is ($x^*_{g2} =$) 0.4. The dotted gray lines in Fig. 2.3 highlight the example. The figure allows deriving further conclusions. First, when the costs to present an optimal policy are very low ($\alpha = 0.05$), then the government will move an ideal policy x^*_{g2} close to the own ideal point at 0. If the government has a chance to evade a directive at nearly no costs then it would not be rational to implement a directive. In addition, as the costs increase, the government has to become more accommodating to the court and an ideal policy will be placed closer to the position of a directive. For example, if the court presents a directive at ($x_d =$) 0.8 but the costs increase to ($\alpha =$) 2, then the optimal policy is located at ($x^*_{g2} =$) 0.533. This logic also applies if the court chooses to only justify a referral. Remember that as a result of a justified referral without a directive, the original status quo at ($x_{sq} =$) 1 will prevail. The dashed vertical line at ($x_d =$) 1 in Fig. 2.3 illustrates that one can think about a justified referral as a directive at the status quo. Again, if the costs are ($\alpha =$) 0.05, an optimal policy x^*_{g2} will be presented close to ($G =$) 0 and the judicial decision will mostly be ignored. However, as α increases, implementing the judicial decision becomes costlier and an optimal policy will be designed accounting for these costs, presenting the policy closer to the status quo. Nevertheless, regardless whether facing a judicial directive or a justified referral, the ideal policy will never be presented to exactly meet the court's demands. Instead, the costs only define the extent to which the government will accommodate the court's interests.

Equations B1.1 and B1.2 and Fig. 2.3 present insights into the government's optimal policy at the final move of the JPD game. This does not imply that the government will always present this ideal policy; instead, the government can choose between the two options—i.e., to legislate or not legislate—and will account for the benefits from the optimal policy. The government will need to take this decision in either of the subgames following (1) a judicial directive or (2) a court's decision to only justify a referral. Hence, the government will only legislate when $U_G(ll, jd) \geq U_G(l\neg l, jd)$ with x^{*1}_{g2} (from Eq. B1.1) and $U_G(ll, j) \geq U_G(l\neg l, j)$ with x^{*2}_{g2} (from Eq. B1.2). Indeed, in any given subgame perfect Nash equilibrium, the government's strategy (s_G) is (*Lemma 1*):

$$G^*(s_G) = \text{always } l \text{ with} \begin{cases} \frac{\alpha x_d}{\alpha+1} \text{ following } jd \\ \frac{\alpha}{\alpha+1} \text{ following } j \end{cases} \quad \text{(B2.1 \& B2.2)}$$

Therefore, in a one-shot game with complete and perfect information, legislating in the final move is the rational strategy pursued by the government. Complete information is not an exaggerated assumption at this point of the game. Given that the government's move follows that of the judicial move, the government is able to observe the prior moves. Moreover, the finding that the government will legislate in the equilibrium is in accordance with empirical findings that courts are sometimes evaded (Epstein and Knight 1998, 140; Dahl 1957a, 288–289) and while judicial decisions might be implemented, implementation is sometimes incomplete (Staton and Vanberg 2008, 504). Instead, the government engages in legislative activities that appear as the government reacts to a judicial decision but in fact the government skillfully circumvents the judicial choice (Vanberg 2001, 347–348). In sum, the government always legislates in the final move of the JPD game.

While these interesting implications confirm expectations discussed among scholars, these findings are not at the center of this book. Instead, to answer the question regarding when judges will choose one judicial outcome over the other, we need to focus on the court's subgame prior to the final choice made by the government. This is when the judges exert their power directly showing the first face of judicial power.

2.2.2 *The Court's Choice*

The court has three options. First, it has the option to not justify a referral ($\neg j$). If the court chooses not to justify a referral, then it will receive a payoff based on the original policy (x_{g1}) in relation to its own ideal point (C). Second, the court has the option to justify a referral (j) but will have to anticipate the government's response. The preceding section shows that the government will always legislate in the final move, which affects the payoff that the court eventually receives. Therefore, the court will account for the government's optimal policy (x^{*2}_{g2} from Eq. B1.2) when justifying a referral. Third, the court can choose to justify a referral and present a directive (jd). By presenting a directive, the court will anticipate the government's optimal policy following such a directive (x^{*1}_{g2} from Eq. B1.1). Based on this knowledge, the court will present an optimal directive (x^*_d) as

$$\begin{aligned} \max_{x_d} &= -(x^{*1}_{g2} - C)^2 - \gamma(x_d - x^{*1}_{g2})^2 \\ x^*_d &= x^{*1}_{g2} \end{aligned} \tag{B3.1}$$

Hence, the court's judicial directive is equal to the government's policy in the final move. This finding is unsurprising to the extent that an optimal directive is only plausible to the court if the government will also implement this directive. Moreover, the court will want to increase its own benefits when presenting a directive. Hence, the benefits from the ideal judicial directive will be compared with those gained as a result of the outcome following any other judicial choice. The decision to choose one judicial outcome over the other is the result of a thought experiment: based on my own position (C), will any (legislative) outcome as a result of my (judicial) choice be equally beneficial to me? The answer to this question is dependent on the anticipated outcome of the game and the cost parameters. Therefore, in any subgame perfect Nash equilibrium, the court's strategy (s_C) is (*Lemma 2*)

$$C^*(s_C) = \begin{cases} jd \text{ if } \begin{cases} x_d > x_{sq} \cap C \geq \frac{\alpha^2(x_d-1)-\gamma}{2\alpha(\alpha+1)(x_d-1)} \cap C \geq \frac{\alpha x_d}{2\alpha+2} \\ G < x_d < x_{sq} \cap C \leq \frac{\alpha^2(x_d-1)-\gamma}{2\alpha(\alpha+1)(x_d-1)} \cap C \geq \frac{\alpha x_d}{2\alpha+2} \\ x_d < G \cap C \leq \frac{\alpha^2(x_d-1)-\gamma}{2\alpha(\alpha+1)(x_d-1)} \cap C \leq \frac{\alpha x_d}{2\alpha+2} \end{cases} \\ j \text{ if } C \geq \frac{\alpha^2+\gamma}{2\alpha^2+2\alpha} \\ \neg j \text{ otherwise} \end{cases}$$

(B3.2 – 3.4)

Lemma 2 is the (theoretical) answer to the question of when judges will choose one judicial outcome over another, and it is read as follows. First, assess whether one condition in the sets that define jd is true. If a condition is fulfilled, the court will justify a referral and present a directive. If none of the conditions is met, then turn to the condition for j. If this condition is met, then the court will justify a referral. Finally, if neither the conditions that lead to jd nor the condition that leads to j are met, then the court will not justify a referral ($\neg j$).

Two conditions related to a court's choice to present a judicial directive are evident in Lemma 2. Accordingly, the court will only present a directive if this directive is $x_d > x_{sq}$ or $x_d < x_{sq}$ and $x_d > G$ or $x_d < G$. In other words, the directive will not be equal to the position of the status quo ($x_d \neq 1$) nor to the position of the government ($x_d \neq 0$). Presenting a directive would not be rational if the court preferred either of these positions. Instead, the court could only justify a referral, which implies a return to the status quo (x_{sq}). In addition, the court can choose not to justify a referral, which will lead to an implementation of the initial policy suggested by the government. The next section will show that the government presents its ideal point when legislating in the initial move. Hence, once the court chooses not to justify a referral, the court's decision will lead to an implementation of the government's ideal point. Therefore, a judicial directive at the position of the status quo or at the government's ideal point is not rational.

Instead, the court will decide between the two options to only justify a referral or not justify a referral, as shown in Fig. 2.4. The figure illustrates that based on its own position C—shown on the y-axis—the court will take a judicial decision accounting for the costs that the government faces to respond to a judicial decision (α; shown on the x-axis) and the costs that the court receives from an evasion. The latter costs are those included

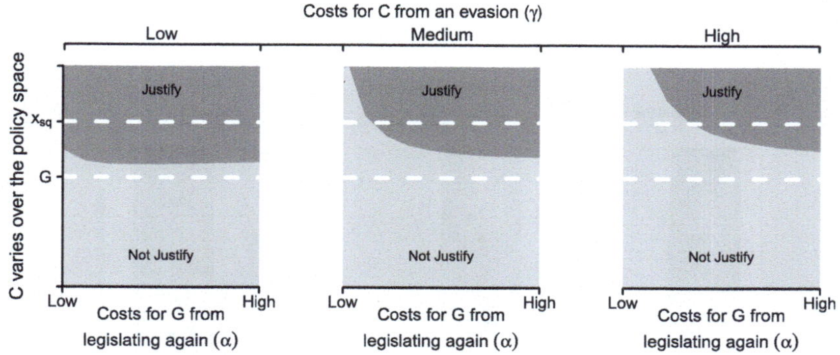

Fig. 2.4 Judicial behavior when the court presents no directive

in γ. An increase in these costs is visualized by the different illustrations in Fig. 2.4. The figure shows that the easier it is for the government to respond to a decision (lower values of α), the more likely that the court will not justify a referral. This is particularly true as the costs of an evasion (higher levels of γ) increase. The size of the light gray shaded area increases once γ increases while α decreases. Put simply, the court will justify a referral the more likely it is that the court's decision will not be evaded. Moreover, it is unsurprising that the court will always not justify a referral when located below the ideal point of the government ($C < G$) and away from the status quo ($C < G < x_{sq}$). It has been mentioned that the government will propose an initial policy at its ideal point. Hence, a court closer to the government than to the status quo will not justify a referral to ensure that the government's policy will be implemented. This policy holds stronger interest to the court than a return to the status quo. In what way do these outcomes change for a court that uses directives?

Lemma 2 highlights that the costs α and γ also drive the judicial choice to present a directive. Figure 2.5 summarizes the court's behavior regarding all three judicial choices: present a directive, only justify a referral, or do not justify a referral. The figure is read as follows: in each row, the position of a directive is fixed with $x_d > x_{sq}$ in the top row, to $x_d < x_{sq}$ but $x_d > G$ in the middle row, and $x_d < G$ in the bottom row. In addition, the size of the costs γ is fixed per column but varies across the columns. Hence, γ is low (fixed at 0.1) in the left column, medium sized in the middle column (fixed at 0.5), and high in the right column (fixed at 1). The size of the

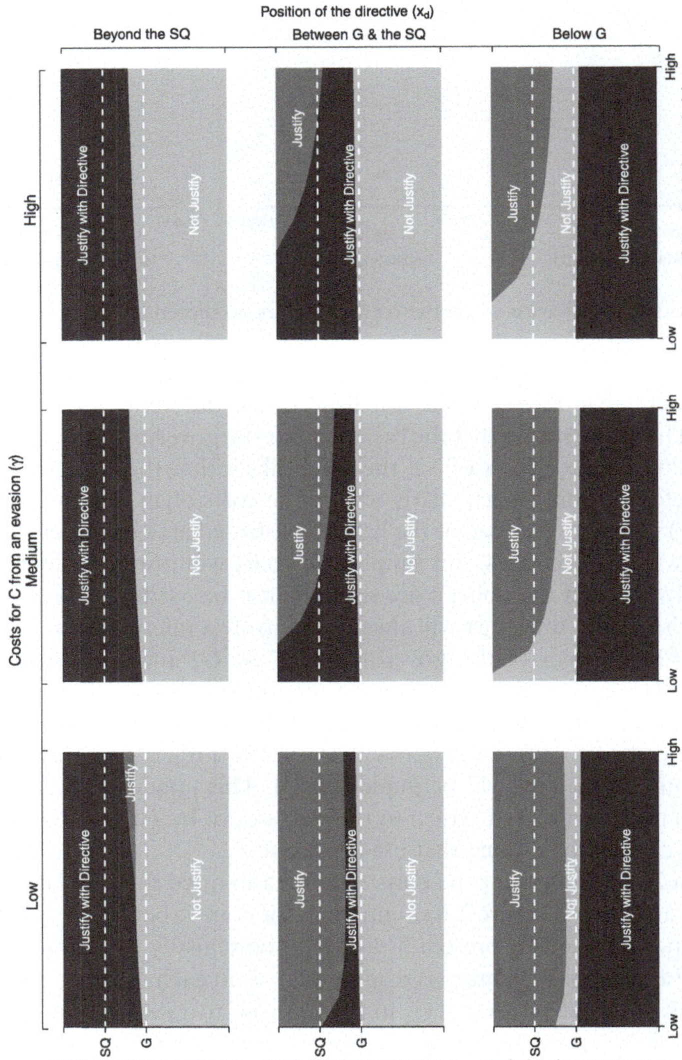

Fig. 2.5 Judicial behavior in the Judicial-Policy-Dialogue Game

costs α varies over the x-axis of each plot and the position of C varies over the y-axis. Finally, the labeled shaded areas highlight the judicial choices.

For example, the first illustration in the upper left corner of Fig. 2.5 shows that if the costs for a judicial evasion are low, the court will present a judicial directive beyond the status quo as long as the government faces low costs (α) to respond to the directive (black area in the figure). The court will not justify a referral once positioned outside the range of the government and the status quo ($C < G < x_{sq}$; light gray area in the figure). Interestingly, as the costs for a government's response to a judicial decision increase, the likelihood that the court will only justify a referral partially increases once the court is positioned between the government and the status quo ($G < C < x_{sq}$; dark gray area in the figure). However, compare all illustrations in the top row of Fig. 2.5. As the costs from an evasion of a judicial decision increase, the likelihood of a justified referral diminishes. In other words, the higher the costs of an evasion, the more likely that the court will present a judicial directive.

This behavior is plausible to the extent that one may argue that a directive draws attention towards a judicial decision. This will increase the likelihood that an evasion by the government will be uncovered. At least a directive may draw stronger media attention and requires more explanation than a referral justified only. Hence, the court may use a directive to enhance its own position in a conflict with the government by bringing this conflict to the public's attention. Such a strategy is not uncommon but confirms the argument by Staton (2010) on strategic communication by the Mexican *Suprema Corte de Justicia de la Nación*. Accordingly, the court publishes press releases to draw public attention and promote judicial independence. The court's aim is to strategically enhance its own position in a conflict with other actors.

This is one example of how Fig. 2.5 can be interpreted. The key hypotheses will be derived in a later section, but prior to this discussion it is helpful to finish solving the model to understand all dynamics of the game. In accordance with backward induction, I will assess the first step of the game now, namely the initial move by the government.

2.2.3 *The Government's Initial Choice*

For the government, it is only rational to legislate in the first move if the gains from the outcome at the final node are at least as large as those from a decision not to legislate at all. If the government chooses to present a policy, it will do so with the aim of placing the final policy as close as possible to its own ideal point. The actual gains are received at the end of the game. Accordingly, the government will compare the utility from the history not to legislate (which is −1, see Fig. 2.2) to the different utilities that the government will receive when choosing to legislate. These latter utilities are the ones (1) following a court's decision not to justify a referral, (2) following the government's response to a judicial directive, and (3) following the government's response to a justified referral. These comparisons lead to the following strategy (s_G) in an equilibrium (*Lemma 3*)

$$G^*(s_G)\begin{cases} \neg l \text{ if } x_d > \frac{\alpha+1}{\alpha} \cup x_d < -\frac{\alpha+1}{\alpha} \\ l \text{ otherwise with } x^*_{g1} = G \end{cases} \qquad \text{(B4.1 − 4.3)}$$

In order to understand this strategy, remember that the government receives its benefits from the policy that is eventually enacted. The initial policy x_{g1} will only be enacted if the court does not justify a referral. If the court chooses not to justify a referral, then it is rational for the government to legislate and present the initial policy at its own ideal point ($x^*_{g1} = G$).

Moreover, if the court only justifies the referral, it is also rational to present the initial policy at its own ideal point. Why? It has been outlined above that the government will always legislate in response to a judicial decision to justify a referral with or without a directive. This is why in the first move the government has nothing to lose from presenting a policy at its own ideal point. Following a decision to justify a referral, the government will legislate (as outlined in Sect. 2.2.1) and maximize its benefits from the final policy x^{*2}_{g2} (Eq. B1.2) compared to the status quo and independent of the initial move.[5]

These considerations change slightly once the court justifies a referral and presents a directive. The government will not legislate if a response to a judicial directive would move a policy further away from the government's ideal point than the status quo. This is similar to what the model by Vanberg (2001) yields. "If the legislature can anticipate that it will comply with an unfavorable ruling, it would therefore prefer not to pass the bill in the first place" (Vanberg 2001, 351). According to the JPD game, this is the case once a directive is $x_d > \frac{\alpha+1}{\alpha}$ (or $x_d < -\frac{\alpha+1}{\alpha}$ due to the policy space's symmetry). The gray dot in Fig. 2.3 illustrates this with a court's directive presented at ($x_d =$) 1.8, assuming that the government's costs to respond to the directive are ($\alpha =$) 2. The government would only be able to respond with an ideal policy at ($x^*_{g2} =$) 1.2. In other words, the government's benefits from the status quo at 1 is higher than the benefits from the possible final policy at 1.2. This is why under these conditions the government will not legislate and not initiate the JPD game; instead, the status quo will prevail. By contrast, Lemma 3 implies that the government will legislate if the directive is at least equal to $\frac{\alpha+1}{\alpha}$ (see also Appendix B—Step 4.3). Hence, for $\alpha = 2$, this is the case once the court presents a directive at ($x_d =$) 1.5. A glance at Fig. 2.3 shows that in this scenario the outcome would be equal to the status quo at ($x^*_{g2} =$) 1. Under these conditions, the choice to legislate is an equilibrium strategy. By presenting the initial policy at its own ideal point, the final policy is at least as good as the benefits received from the status quo.

In sum, if the benefits from the outcome are at least as good as those from the status quo, then the government always presents an initial policy at its own ideal point. The government will choose not to legislate if a response to a judicial directive would make it worse off.

With the model solved in this section, the next step is to discuss the implications of the JPD game and derive hypotheses. This is achieved by using a numerical simulation to confirm the presented solutions and to simulate different dynamics in the interaction between the government and the court.

2.3 Implications and Hypotheses

To present the model's implications, I illustrate the actors' behavior when facing different spatial scenarios. For this purpose, I work through numerical examples (similar to Cameron 2000, 114). This allows identifying the model's driving parameters to derive hypotheses, which are tested in the following chapters. The numerical computer simulation fulfills an important aspect in theory building. The simulation helps to assess the premises outlined in the JPD game. This allows deducing implications from the model and deriving hypotheses (see Toshkov 2016, 63). In general, the simulation assigns values to the actors' positions and the various policies proposed, thus creating a number of random variables. This leads to a large number of different spatial settings under the influence of different costs. The simulation is used for three purposes: first, to confirm the solutions previously presented regarding the actors' strategies in equilibrium; second, the simulation allows to present outcomes of the JPD game in an ideal world, whereby the numerical simulation also allows manipulating variables simulating various different scenarios; and third, findings from an ideal world allow deriving hypotheses to be tested against real-world data.

2.3.1 *Simulating the Judicial-Policy-Dialogue Game*

The numerical computer simulation assigns values to the parameters of the JPD game. The ranges of these values are based on a number of informed assumptions. It has been mentioned that without any loss of generality the ideal position of the government can be fixed to (G =) 0 and the status quo to (x_{sq} =) 1. While these ideal points are specified, the ideal point of the court (C) and the judicial directive (x_d) are not specified. For the simulation, both positions are defined over the range of [−2.1; 2.1]. The interval covers points inside and beyond the equivalence point of the status quo in relation to the ideal point of the government. This ensures that the court can hold extreme positions outside the range of the government and the status quo.[6] In other words, these boundary values ensure that all spatial configurations—moderate as well as extreme—among the actors and polices are simulated.

The ideal policies the government presents are calculated using Eqs. B1.1 and B1.2, while the ideal initial policy x^*_{g1} will be presented at (G =) 0. Finally, the costs from an evasion of a judicial decision are set to $\gamma > 0$. The same is true for the government's costs to legislate in response to a judicial decision ($\alpha > 0$). Hence, for the simulation I draw the values for both variables from the interval (0; 1]. In sum, while I draw the values for α, γ, C and x_d from a continuous uniform distribution with the mentioned boundary values, the other parameters have assigned values.[7] Table 2.4 summarizes the specifications used to simulate 100,000 different spatial settings in which the government and the court play the JPD game..[8]

The simulation allows verifying the mathematical findings on the strategies in equilibrium (from Sect. 2.2). The question to answer is whether the government and the court follow the outlined strategies. In line with backward induction, the first step is to assess whether the government always legislates in the final move following a court's decision to justify a referral with or without a directive. In other words, using the simulated values, does the government follow the strategy summarized in Lemma 1? Indeed, the findings from the computed simulation show that the government always legislates, confirming Lemma 1.

However, the court's choice is of stronger interest for this study. The court chooses one of the three judicial actions that maximizes its own

Table 2.4 Summary of the specifications used to draw 100,000 numerical computer simulations

Variable	Definition	Theoretical range	Fixed range	Implementation in R
G	Ideal point government	$G = 0$	0	`data < - data.frame(rep(0, 100000));` `colnames(data)[1] <- "G"`
C	Ideal point court	$C \in \mathbb{R}$	[−2.1; 2.1]	`numcases <- dim(data)[1];` `data$C <- runif(numcases, -2.1,2.1)`
x_{sq}	Status quo	$x_{sq} = 1$	1	`data$sq <- 1`
x_{g1}	Initial policy	$x_{g1} = G$	0	`data$g1 <- mydata$G`
x_d	Judicial directive	$x_d \in \mathbb{R}$	[−2.1; 2.1]	`data$d <- runif(numcases, -2.1,2.1)`
x^{*1}_{g2}	Ideal policy to a directive	$\frac{\alpha * x_d}{\alpha+1}$	$\frac{\alpha * x_d}{\alpha+1}$	`data$g21 <- (data$alpha * data$d) /(data$alpha + 1)`
x^{*2}_{g2}	Ideal policy to a justified referral	$\frac{\alpha}{\alpha+1}$	$\frac{\alpha}{\alpha+1}$	`data$g22 <- data$alpha / (data$alpha + 1)`
α	Costs for G to evade C	$\alpha > 0$	(0; 1]	`data$alpha <- runif(numcases, .00000000001,1)`
γ	Costs C has from an evasion	$\gamma > 0$	(0; 1]	`data$gamma <- runif(numcases, .00000000001,1)`

Note: The simulations and all estimations hereafter are computed using R-Version 3.5.1 (R Core Team 2018)

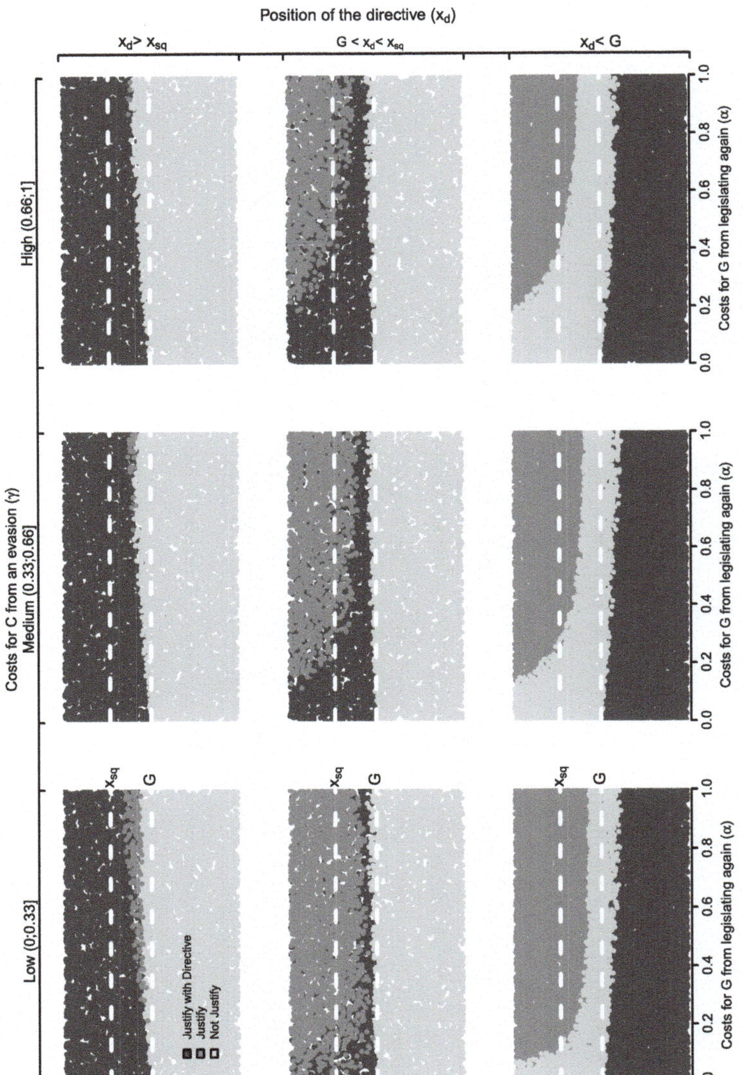

Fig. 2.6 Simulated judicial behavior in the Judicial-Policy-Dialogue Game

utility the most. In order to assess the final judicial choice when using the simulated values, I refer to Fig. 2.6. The figure is similar to Fig. 2.5 and interpreted in similar ways. However, it is important to note that Fig. 2.6 is not obtained by plotting the functions summarized in Lemma 2 with the simulated values. While Fig. 2.5 is a visualization of Lemma 2 highlighting the *theoretical expectations*, the illustrations in Fig. 2.6 are *based on the simulated outcomes*. Accordingly, the court will engage in the three comparisons between $U_C(jd, ll) \geq U_C(j, ll)$, $U_C(jd, ll) \geq U_C(\neg j, l)$ and $U_C(j, ll) \geq U_C(\neg j, l)$. Taking a decision, in each step the court will eventually follow the strategy that allows for the largest benefits over all three comparisons. Figure 2.6 illustrates the judicial choices for the different randomly drawn ideal positions of the court plotted over the simulated costs that the government has from responding to a choice. In addition, the illustrations are separated by the different degrees of the simulated costs that the court has from an evasion and the different simulated placements of a judicial directive. The similarities between Figs. 2.5 and 2.6 are intriguing. Therefore, the numerical simulation confirms the court's strategy from Lemma 2.

Finally, it has been argued that the government does not present an initial policy if a judicial directive would force a final outcome further away from the government than the status quo. According to the simulation, the government does not legislate in the first move in 77 scenarios. The analysis reveals that in all such scenarios the ideal response to a judicial directive would have required a policy further away from the government than the status quo. These findings confirm Lemma 3.[9] To sum up, the numerical simulation confirms the solutions presented in Sect. 2.2. The government and the court follow the outlined strategies.

The applied approach allows assessing further dynamics of the JPD game. First, I can plot additional results from the simulation. Second, I can run controlled simulations with specific scenarios setting the values of certain variables. The former approach is used to assess the final outcome of the game.

Figure 2.7 summarizes the final outcome of the game (x_{g2} on the y-axes) following a court's choice to justify a referral with or without a directive. The figure highlights the dynamics with a special emphasis on the costs that the government has to respond to a judicial directive (compare x-axes) and that the court has from an evasion (compare across columns). It is not necessary to plot the scenario when the court chooses not to justify a referral. On the one hand, the government has no need to legislate

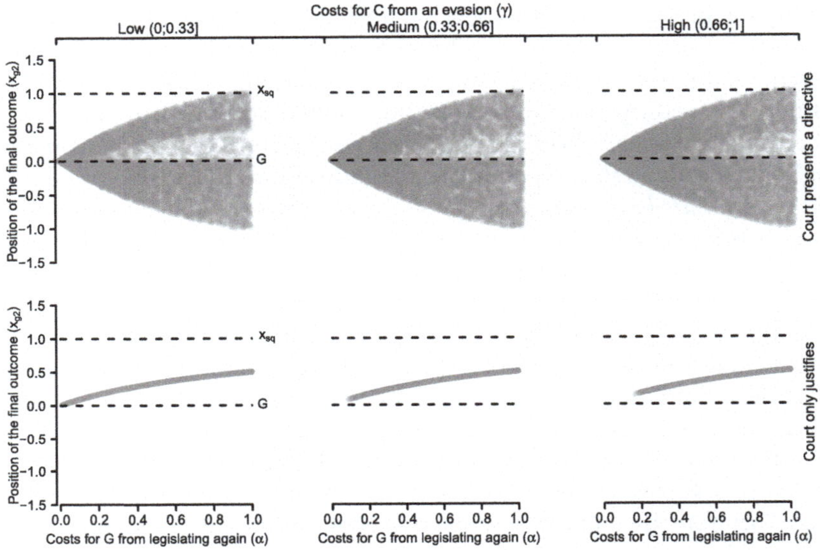

Fig. 2.7 Simulated outcomes of the Judicial-Policy-Dialogue Game accounting for the costs

again and thus faces no costs; instead, the final policy is implemented at the government's ideal point. On the other hand, the court's decision not to justify a referral does not become evaded, which is why the court also has no costs. The game tree in Fig. 2.2 also highlights this. The costs α and γ are not part of the utility functions at the histories $U_G(l, \neg j)$ and $U_C(\neg j, l)$. In other words, the costs are decisive when the court chooses to justify a referral with or without a directive. Moreover, the government always legislates in the final move (Lemma 1). This is why Fig. 2.7 yields implications about the government's behavior.

The figure provides a number of insights. First, in neither illustration is any final policy located outside the range of $[-1, 1]$. Hence, the government never accepts a final policy further away from the ideal point than the status quo or the indifference point of the status quo. This is evidence confirming Lemma 3. Second, once the court presents a directive (upper row of Fig. 2.7), the possible outcomes form a funnel with the wider end at higher costs of the government to legislate. In other words, if the costs to respond to a judicial decision are high, it is less possible for the government to respond to a directive with a policy close to its own ideal point. This makes intuitive sense and confirms the theoretical discussion on the government's final choice (see Sect. 2.2.1). Third, the lower row of Fig. 2.7 illustrates the same governmental behavior in response to a court's decision to only justify a referral. The higher the costs to legislate, the closer the government places the final policy to the status quo. Why do the outcomes form a curve in the lower row but a cloud in the upper row? Remember that a court's decision to only justify a referral implies a return to only one point, namely the original status quo. Hence, the policies passed by the government follow a curve, narrowing into the status quo with increasing costs to legislate. In the upper row of Fig. 2.7, the court defines the location of the directive. The government narrows in towards the directive in the same way that it narrows in to the status quo. However, the court presents the directive and the directive may be placed anywhere in the policy space. This is why we observe the funnels in the upper row of Fig. 2.7.

Interestingly, the funnels' densities are lower in the spatial area between the government and the status quo. The borderline along these reduced densities reflects the curves from the court's choice to only justify a referral. In other words, the lower the costs of a judicial evasion, the less likely that a policy outcome is located in the area below these curves. This is an implication of the finding that it is more likely that the court only justifies a referral when the costs of an evasion are low. Moreover, it is interesting that the variation in the final policy outcomes increases as the costs of a judicial evasion increase. This observation also explains why at higher judicial costs there are fewer outcomes on the curve, which summarizes the policy result once the court chooses to only justify a referral (lower row of Fig. 2.7). With higher costs from an evasion, the court chooses to justify a referral and present a directive. This leads to an increased variation in policy outcomes.

Finally, the numeric simulation allows for the computing of specific scenarios. The previous figures assume that the court does not necessarily present the directive at its own ideal point. C and x_d are drawn independently. It is also compelling to assess scenarios where the court presents a directive at its own ideal point. Hence, I compute the simulation again and set the position of the directive equal to the position of the court. While the latter scenario sounds more plausible than the former, this is not necessarily true. Instead, the theories on judicial behavior allow for both perspectives. On the one hand, advocates of the strategic model argue that courts make decisions anticipating other actors and external constraints (Epstein and Knight 1998; Hammond et al. 2005; Parcelle Jr. et al. 2011,

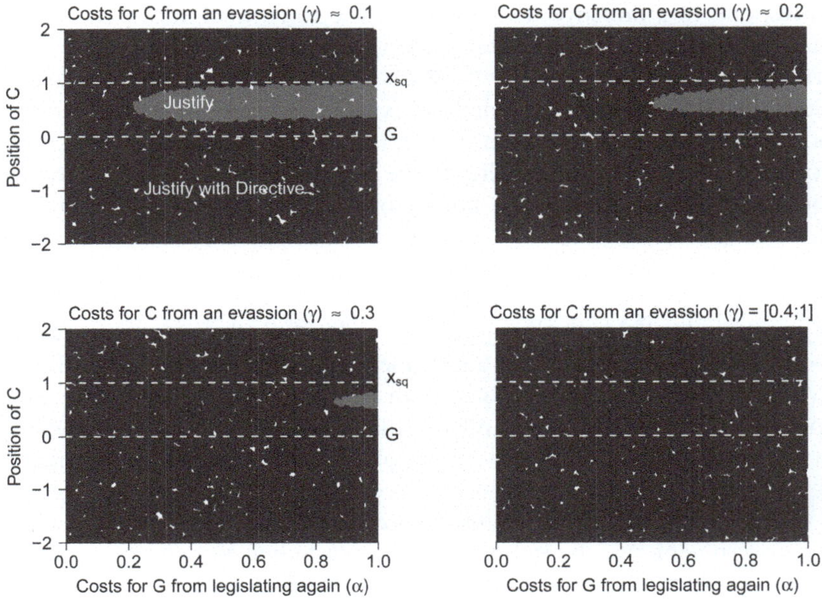

Fig. 2.8 Simulated judicial behavior when directives are equal to the court's position

39–49). Therefore, it is plausible to assume that the constraint does not allow courts to always present x_d at the own ideal point C. On the other hand, attitudinalists argue that the court is able to present sincere policy preferences (Segal and Cover 1989; Segal and Spaeth 1993, 2002). Hence, x_d is presented at the own ideal point C. The evidence in favor of both theories is mixed (see the summary by Parcelle Jr. et al. 2011, 28–49; Segal 1997). This is why one perspective on the relationship between C and x_d should be compared to the other perspective. While the former figures assume that the court cannot always present x_d at the own ideal point, the following assessment assumes that if the court presents directives it does so at the own ideal point ($x_d = C$). Figure 2.8 summarizes this latter scenario.

The figure presents the judicial decision following the same logic as the other figures, but with more fine-grained levels of the costs from an evasion in the first three illustrations. Simulating different scenarios revealed that holding the costs from an evasion constant at lower levels (with $\gamma \approx 0.1, 0.2, 0.3$) allows for the most appropriate way to depict the court's action. The court's behavior no longer changes once the costs form an evasion reach higher levels (e.g., in the interval $\gamma \in [0.4, 1]$). According to Fig. 2.8, the court never chooses not to justify a referral; instead, the court either justifies a referral to request a return to the status quo (gray dots) or it presents a directive to request a policy change (black dots). While Fig. 2.8 illustrates an ideal world, the illustration highlights two implications of the JPD game: first, the court does not only follows one strategy, but instead the choice of one judicial action over the other is driven by the costs that the court receives from an evasion; and second, the court chooses between the options to only justify a referral or present a directive only at lower levels of the costs from an evasion. As the costs increase, the court only presents directives. Hence, in a court's ideal world—where directives are always presented at the own ideal point—the likelihood of presenting a directive increases with the costs that the court receives from an evasion.

In sum, simulating the interaction between the government and the court allows obtaining observable implications from the JPD game. The next step is to use these implications to formulate hypotheses to be tested in the empirical chapters.

2.3.2 *Hypotheses from the Judicial-Policy-Dialogue Game*

The model's specifications are based on (1) costs, (2) actors, and (3) outcomes. The theoretical discussion has already outlined how these specifications drive the interaction in the JPD game. Therefore, it is plausible to derive the hypotheses regarding these three groups of parameters. In line with the question concerning when judges choose one judicial outcome over the other, I will develop the hypotheses focusing on the court. Hence, the hypotheses are derived from Lemma 2 and the visualizations from the preceding sections.

The numeric simulation highlights that the costs from an evasion and the costs of the government to respond to a judicial decision are decisive for the court's action. Lemma 2 highlights that the weight placed on both of these costs (α and γ) influences the court's strategy. Hence, in order to assess when the court chooses one judicial action over the other, I derive *hypotheses about the judicial choices accounting for the costs.* In order to understand the influence of the government's costs on judicial choices, it is necessary to consider each panel in Fig. 2.6 separately, as α increases from low to high over the x-axis within each panel. The comparison allows identifying two patterns: first, the area in which the court chooses to present directives is larger at low costs for the government compared with high costs within each panel; and second, the area in which the court justifies referrals is smaller when the government's costs are low compared with when the government's costs are high. This leads to two hypotheses in the first group of hypotheses.

> *H1a*: If the costs of the government to legislate in response to a judicial decision are low, then the likelihood that the court will justify a referral and present a directive is higher than when the government's costs to legislate again are high.

> *H1b*: If the costs of the government to legislate in response to a judicial decision are low, then the likelihood that the court will only justify a referral is lower than when the government's costs to legislate again are high.

Based on the government's costs alone, it is not possible to derive a hypothesis regarding the choice not to justify referrals. This matter is further addressed below. Nevertheless, comparing the panels in Fig. 2.6 across columns allows deriving two hypotheses as the costs for the court from an evasion increase. Accordingly, two patterns have been identified throughout the discussion: first, the area in which the court chooses to present directives is larger at high costs from an evasion compared with low costs; and second, the area in which the court justifies referrals is lager when the court's costs from an evasion are low compared with when the costs are high.[10] This leads to two additional hypotheses in the first group of hypotheses.

> *H1c*: If the costs of a judicial evasion increase, then the likelihood that the court will justify a referral and present a directive also increases.

> *H1d*: If the costs of a judicial evasion increase, then the likelihood that the court will only justify a referral decreases.

The first group of hypotheses address complex judicial behavior. For example, it is compelling that the court presents a directive when the costs from an evasion increase. Assuming that the court wishes to draw attention to a decision when an evasion is costly, then directives are a useful tool. News agencies frequently cover judicial decisions made by the highest courts. It is plausible to assume that a decision with a directive requires more explanation and coverage. The government's response to a decision with a directive can also be more easily monitored. This makes reoccurring news coverage more likely and the decision becomes more accessible to the public. Finally, plaintiffs at lower courts may use directives to justify a certain constitutional interpretation. At least lower courts need to pay attention to a directive presented by a constitutional court. Rational political actors need to pay attention to the court's decisions, especially as constitutional courts receive much stronger public support than the political branches (Gibson et al. 1998; Vanberg 2001; Sternberg et al. 2015). From this perspective, judicial directives are a strategic tool to draw public attention and reduce the likelihood of an evasion.

Other studies have also identified strategic judicial behavior to ensure compliance with decisions. Staton (2010) finds evidence of the strategic use of press releases by the Mexican Supreme Court. The court uses press releases to draw public attention and promote judicial independence to eventually enhance its own position vis-à-vis the government. Similarly, Hale (1978) outlines how press releases by the California Supreme Court influence which decisions receive news coverage and public attention. A number of other studies outline case characteristics that judges use to strategically draw attention to judicial decisions (see Stoutenborough et al. 2006; Yanus 2009; Linos and Twist 2016). Moreover, Krehbiel (2016) has shown that the German Federal Constitutional Court uses public oral hearings to address possible noncompliance with the court's decisions. Based on these findings, it is plausible to argue that judicial directives are an additional tool to enhance compliance with legal decisions when evasion is costly for the court. Nevertheless, it is plausible that the court presents more directives in a setting where it is still not too costly for the government to respond to a decision (see H1a). If it is less costly for the government to legislate again, then this also gives the court a higher possibility to see a response from the government.

In sum, the hypotheses based on the different costs outline sophisticated choices by the court, which speaks to the literature on strategic judicial behavior (Epstein and Knight 1998; Vanberg 2005; Staton 2010; Krehbiel 2016).

Obtaining hypotheses based on the actors' policy positions is challenging as their falsification reaches methodological boundaries. Assessing the location of the court, the government, the different policies, and the status quo on one common dimension is not feasible, albeit necessary to test the hypotheses. First, satisfying spatial position measures are not yet available for most constitutional courts. Existing measures are mainly based on judicial votes by supreme court judges, which reveal their preferences

(Martin and Quinn 2002, 2007; Hanretty 2014). However, the publication of votes is by no means standard and procedures strongly vary (Raffaelli 2012, 30), with some countries explicitly forbidding judges from publishing votes (Kelemen 2013, 1345). Second, measuring the positions of courts with judicial votes poses a theoretical challenge. The aim of this study is to assess when the court will choose one judicial outcome over the other. Hence, judicial votes that define the outcome cannot become part of the variables used to predict outcomes; otherwise, the measure used to predict a judicial choice is the result of that choice (similar Carrubba and Zorn 2010, 816; Segal and Cover 1989, 558) which leads to an endogeneity problem. Some scholars approximate the court's position based on the position of the political actors selecting the judges (Hönnige 2007), while others use process tracing to approximate the position of a court (Epstein et al. 2001). In my own work, I use WordFish (Slapin and Proksch 2008) to approximate the position of the court based on laws from referrals that the judges did not justify. The underlying assumption is that judges support those laws that they uphold (Engst 2016). In addition, we assessed networks at the German Federal Constitutional Court based on a few identifiable judicial votes and applied multidimensional scaling to assess the intra-court cooperation between judges (Engst et al. 2017). All of these approaches only lead to rough estimates of the position of a court and none of the approaches allow us to measure the legislative status quo. However, the position of the status quo is essential when testing hypotheses about the bargaining between the court and the government over a possible change in the legislative status quo. Hence, falsifying hypotheses based on common positions of the court, the government, and the status quo is not yet possible. This is why I only derive respective hypotheses but leave assessments to further research.

One such hypothesis addresses the court's choice not to justify a referral accounting for the government's costs. The first two rows of Fig. 2.6 show that the area in which the court chooses not to justify a referral increases as the government's costs increase. However, the final row of the figure shows the opposite effect. Hence, the position of the government vis-à-vis the status quo and the area in which the court is able to present directives define the choice not to justify referrals. Therefore, it is possible to derive two competing hypotheses.

> *H2a*: If the costs of the government are low and the government is positioned between the area in which the court can present a directive and the status

quo, then the likelihood that the court does not justify a referral is higher than when the government's costs are high under the same spatial setting.

H2b: If the costs of the government are low and the government is not positioned between the area in which the court can present a directive and the status quo, then the likelihood that the court does not justify a referral is lower than when the government's costs are high under the same spatial setting.

For the aforementioned reasons, these hypotheses are not tested here, although they illustrate that the JPD game can be used to generate further hypotheses addressing strategic judicial behavior.

Finally, a third group of *implications can be developed regarding the outcome of the game*. The court will not present the final policy of the JPD game; rather, this policy is passed by the government. However, the court will prestructure the outcome, deciding based on the anticipated costs that affect the government's policy. Hence, I will connect the discussion about the outcome to the costs using Fig. 2.7.

On the one hand, the numeric simulation in Fig. 2.7 produces less surprising results when interpreted in the light of the already discussed hypotheses. The general pattern in Fig. 2.7 shows that with increasing costs for a court from an evasion, there will be fewer outcomes from justified referrals (lower row of Fig. 2.7) but more outcomes from referrals justified with a directive (upper row of Fig. 2.7). This leads to an observable implication (OI) in the third group.

OI3a: With higher costs from an evasion, there are fewer final policies along the curve on which the government responds to a court's decision to re-enact the status quo.

This is an implication regarding hypotheses H1c and H1d. The higher the costs for the court, the more likely are justified referrals with directives and the less likely are only justified referrals. On the other hand, the findings from Fig. 2.7 also yield an additional implication. It has been argued that as the costs from an evasion for the court increase, the density of the funnels that visualize the outcomes increases. This qualifies as an additional observable implication of the JPD game.

OI3b: Higher costs from an evasion lead to more judicial directives, which increases the variation of outcomes over the policy space.

Both implications hold relevance to the literature on judicialization. Judicialization means that policy problems are increasingly redefined in judicial problems (Stone Sweet 2000; Shapiro and Stone Sweet 2002; Hirschl 2008; Hönnige 2011). The implications derived here do not necessarily imply an increase in judicial problems. Figure 2.7 says nothing about the number of referrals that a court has to decide. However, the figure says something about the policies enacted in response to a judicial decision. If the costs of a judicial evasion are high, then the court will present a directive that leads to a substantive policy change. The numeric simulation shows that directives—especially when presented under high costs of an evasion—lead to more policy variation than referrals that are only justified. In other words, courts possess substantive power over policy. If the observation is true that judicial problems are increasingly redefined in judicial problems, then the probability of judicial directives also increases. This will lead to an increase in the substantive influence of a court on policy outputs. This effect is particularly strong when courts face higher costs from an evasion of their decisions.

In order to test the implications, it is necessary to analyze the response by the government to a judicial decision, which is empirically challenging. To my knowledge, data on the response to legal decisions has been used to study the United States Supreme Court (Ignagni and Meernik 1994; Christiansen and Eskridge Jr. 2014) but is not yet available for constitutional courts. Studies assessing compliance explore different institutions such as the interaction between EU member states and the EU Commission (König and Mäder 2014). Looking at constitutional courts, contributions are mostly case study-driven (Gawron and Rogowski 2002, Ch. 11; 2007). Gawron and Rogowski (2007, especially Ch. 5) present a limited descriptive data analysis for the government's response to decisions by the German Federal Constitutional Court over a short period of time. Nevertheless, despite the fact that the German Federal Ministry of Justice has monitored decisions by the Federal Constitutional Court that require a political response (Gawron and Rogowski 2015, 159), no systematic data is available. This is one reason why I will have to leave the observable implications aside.

This section outlines the hypotheses about the court's choice of one judicial activity over another. These hypotheses describe the court's opportunity to exercise direct power by presenting a certain verdict. In other words, the court will show the first face of judicial power. The JPD game enables assessing the dynamics behind an active judiciary. However, as outlined in the introductory chapter, the governing majority could also account for the judicial response and adopt laws anticipating the court's possible interests (Stone 1992; Landfried 1992; Kommers 1994; Stone Sweet 1998, 2000; Vanberg 1998a, b, 2001, 2005; Langer and Brace 2005). This has been defined as "autolimitation" and characterizes the second face of judicial power.

Lemma 3 outlines that the government will only legislate in the initial move if the utility from a response to a judicial directive is worth more than the utility from the existing policy at the status quo. Hence, the game supports the notion of an anticipatory reaction by the government. The government considers the court's action beforehand to avoid an extreme directive. In the next section, I will discuss the government's behavior in the initial move. Through this discussion, I hypothesize about the court's opportunity to show the second face of judicial power.

2.4 Uncertainty in the Government's Initial Choice

The JPD game is built on the assumption of complete and perfect information. This is appropriate for the purpose of a model, which "aims not at replicating the world, but at artificially isolating features in order to study their potential or dynamics" (Chwaszcza 2008, 139). In order to assess the court's choice of one judicial action over another, the assumption of complete knowledge is justified. The court is able to observe the government's action and adopts its own strategy accordingly. This is why the model is appropriate to assess the first face of judicial power and the mechanisms that drive the court's choice.

How will the government choose in the initial move? The government will not always be able to perfectly predict the court's action. When the initial policy at the government's ideal point is at an extreme distance to the court, the court may present an extreme directive. In order to prevent a harsh judicial reaction, the government has two options. First, the government may abstain from legislating as summarized in Lemma 3. It is plausible that this strategy may work to a limited extent only. An inactive government may harm itself by not keeping electoral promises. The government may lose votes, which is linked to the risk of losing office. Consequently, the leading party may lose the majority to promote its own policy agenda (see Strøm 1990). Therefore, not legislating is a feasible strategy, although it may only work over a limited amount of time.

Second, the government may choose to legislate but to prevent a defeat in court the government anticipates the court's interests and designs a bill accordingly. The policy that the government presents will be court-proof while at the same time the government is perceived as an active government implementing an agenda. In sum, assuming that the government is unable to perfectly predict the court's choice, two forms of behavior are plausible in the initial move: on the one hand, the government will either present its own ideal point or abstain from legislating, which is strictly in line with Lemma 3; and on the other hand, the government may try to anticipate the court's interests and presents a policy not at its own ideal point but rather one that it could accept and which prevails in court.

Scholars present justifications for both strategies. Fortunato et al. (2013) find that in bicameral bargaining between two (hostile) chambers a government in the first chamber always presents its ideal policy. This policy will only be modified once a conflict arises. The government can rely on intra-legislative institutions—like a navette system or conciliation committees—to modify bills interacting with the opposition. The intra-legislative institutions help to reduce uncertainty about the interests of the second chamber and allow for targeted modifications (Fortunato et al. 2013, 939). Similar institutions do not exist in legislative–judicial bargaining; instead, the government needs to await a court decision. This is costly as it requires legislating again after losing in court. Such a loss may also cause a public backlash. This is why others conclude that the government presents an initial policy accounting for the court. These scholars discuss the theoretical implications of legislative self-restraint and some use case studies to illustrate the potential existence of self-restraint in legislative–judicial bargaining (Landfried 1992; Kommers 1994; Vanberg 1998a, 2001, 2005; Stone Sweet 2000).

Nevertheless, to my knowledge, no study assesses the empirical nature of the competing views. This is why we are unable to answer the question of what the initial policy by the government will look like. Does the government present an initial policy accounting for the court? Relaxing the assumption of complete and perfect information, this strategy becomes feasible. Hence, to what extent do political actors anticipate judicial power? An answer to this question (1) outlines what the policy at the initial move of the JPD game will look like, (2) highlights whether the court can show a second face of judicial power, and (3) provides for a more complete picture of the dynamics in judicial–political bargaining.

2.5 Autolimitation and Legal Signals

In this section, I only outline the intuition behind autolimitation, which characterizes the second face of judicial power. This is solely to illustrate the logic behind this mechanism. On the one hand, the JPD game yields that the government will not autolimit itself, but rather restrain from legislating when a harsh judicial directive is expected. On the other hand, previous research has provided anecdotal evidence that the government will account for the court's position and legislate. Based on these two contradicting assumptions, I regard the assessment of the second face of judicial power as an empirical challenge rather than a theoretical one. This is why I discuss the major aspects of the second face of judicial power in the empirical chapters.

2.5.1 Judicial Power Through Past Decisions

Autolimitation implies that the government passes a different initial policy (x_{g1}) in the presence of the court than it would in the absence of the court. The reason is that the government fears the court invalidating the policy. This is comparable to the effect of the threat of a presidential veto in respective systems. In order to prevent a veto, legislators may anticipate the presidential power. This is why I adopt the baseline model of Cameron's (2000, 83–99) presidential veto bargaining model and connect the model to the assumptions of the JPD game to outline the intuition behind autolimitation.

Figure 2.9 summarizes the design of the spatial model. The solid horizontal line is the policy space. *C* is the ideal point of the court and *G* is the ideal point of the government. The dashed quadratic functions originating from the actors' ideal points illustrate the utility that the actors can gain or lose when either point on the policy space is chosen and I assume that these individual utility functions are single-peaked and symmetric. Hence, the government and the court each have the most preferred policy at their ideal points. Policies further away from the ideal points are less preferred, whereby the utility of the policy symmetrically decreases from the ideal points (McCarty and Meirowitz 2007, 22).

The government will present an initial policy x_{g1}, knowing that the court will review this policy, as assumed by the JPD game. The court will not accept the new bill x_{g1} being further away from *C* than the policy originally in place at x_{sq}. Simplifying the game and leaving the costs aside in this section, the court could present a judicial directive or justify a referral to

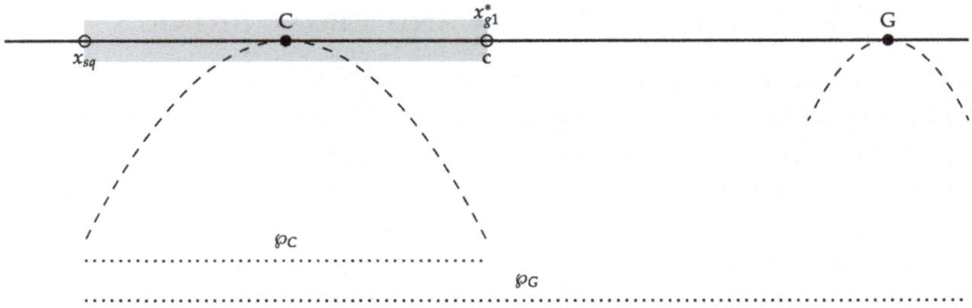

Fig. 2.9 Intuition behind autolimitation in a spatial bargaining model. Note: Adaptation following Cameron's (2000, 91) presidential veto bargaining model. G = Ideal point of the government with the optimal initial policy x^*_{g1} under autolimitation; C = Ideal point of the court with the utility-equivalent point c; x_{sq} = Status quo at the position of the policy in action; $\wp_G$ and $\wp_C$ = Preferred-to-set of the government and the court; Shaded gray area is the winset of $\wp_G \cap \wp_C$

return to the status quo. However, having symmetric utility functions, there is one policy c for every policy that is utility-equivalent to the court. In other words, the court will accept every change to x_{sq} from the left of its ideal point in equivalent distance to the right of its ideal point (Cameron 2000, 89). The dotted line $\wp_C$ illustrates this preferred-to-set of the court in relation to x_{sq}. The bill that is utility-equivalent to the court compared to the status quo is located at the end of the preferred-to-set shown as c. In other words, c becomes the point that the government has to anticipate when presenting an initial policy. To illustrate this, look at the dotted line $\wp_G$. This line highlights the preferred-to-set of the government over the status quo. However, the government cannot freely choose any point on the line, but needs to account for the set $\wp_C$ of the court. Put simply, a bill will prevail where $\wp_G$ and $\wp_C$ overlap (Cameron 2000, 90–91). Hence, the gray shaded area in Fig. 2.9 is the area $\wp_G \cap \wp_C$ known as a winset: "the set of outcomes that can defeat the status quo" (Tsebelis 2002, 21).

Therefore, the major implication of autolimitation is the policy shift of an initial bill proposed by the government in the direction of the shared winset with the court. The closest that the government can move the bill to its own ideal point G is to choose the court's equivalent point c. In sum, optimal autolimitation occurs when the legislative majority presents the optimal bill $x^*_{g1} = c$ if $G < C < x_{sq}$. Hence, if autolimitation occurs, the government will shift the initial policy in the spatial direction of the court. How can the government learn about the position of c to engage in reasonable self-restraint?

The assumption of complete and perfect information has been relaxed at the beginning of this subsection and the position of the court is private information (see McCarty and Meirowitz 2007, 151). The government has to develop beliefs about the court's preferred-to-set. In fact, case studies show that the government is eager to do so. Assessing the development of party finance laws in Germany, Landfried (1994, 117) concludes that "[a]lready during the legislative decision-making process members of Parliament adjust their bills to former decisions of the Court, and anticipate a possible future judicial review." Similar observations have been made in the interaction between the French *Conseil Constitutionnel* and the French *Assemblée Nationale* (Stone Sweet 2000, 80–83), while Marks (2012 [1988]) discusses the influence of the United States Supreme Court's statutory interpretation on Congressional policymaking using *Grove City College vs. Bell* (465 U.S. 555) as an example. In all such cases, former court decisions become legal signals. These decisions reveal information that allow the government to make an educated guess about the shared winset with the judiciary. Autolimitation—characterized by a policy shift in the spatial direction of the court—will become more likely when policymakers debate past court decisions. For example, this will happen in committees where legislators have the time and resources to listen to experts and the ability to substantially modify bills (see Mattson and Strøm 1995; Ismayr 2006, 167). Thus, to assess the initial move by the government in the JPD game, a final hypothesis tested throughout this book is the autolimitation hypothesis:

> *H4* If a legal signal – in the form of citing any prior court decision – is debated in legislative committees, then policy will be shifted in the spatial direction of the court.

In the light of the previous discussion it is worth noting that a measure which includes judicial positions is necessary to assess the hypothesis. However, I outlined above that it is not feasible to use spatial measures based on judicial outcomes to analyze judicial choices. This would lead to an endogeneity problem. Why is this not a problem with regard to hypothesis H4? In order to design a measure to assess the hypothesis, I will have to rely on judicial outcomes to a certain extent. However, the methodological difference to the hypotheses previously derived is that I no longer aim to use this measure to predict judicial choices. Instead, the idea of autolimitation is that a judicial choice is explicitly absent and I only wish to assess legislative behavior. Therefore, I can use the judicial outcomes to design a spatial measure assessing hypothesis H4 without facing the endogeneity problem.

In the next subsection, I will briefly summarize a second form of autolimitation before concluding the chapter.

2.5.2 *Autolimitation and Intra-parliamentary Deals*

While some argue that a government's self-restraint is directly targeted at courts (Landfried 1994; Stone Sweet 1998), others argue that autolimitation will sometimes lead to a policy compromise with the legislative opposition to bypass courts (Vanberg 1998a). When a conflict with courts is costly—for example, in an election year (see Brouard 2009) or when courts exhibit little deference towards the legislature—then the government will compromise with the opposition. Accordingly, the opposition will not refer to courts but appreciate the intra-parliamentary deal (Vanberg 1998a, 313). This second form of autolimitation—aimed at circumventing courts—complements the first form of autolimitation, aimed at accommodating courts.

Nevertheless, in most systems bills still need to be court-proof. The reason is that intra-parliamentary deals will only prevent the opposition from going to court. However, in the next chapter I show that in a cross-country comparison other actors are often empowered to initiate constitutional review. The *European Commission for Democracy through Law* reports that of 35 countries with centralized constitutional review, five allow individuals not directly affected by a public act to refer this act to the constitutional court. In addition, individuals in twelve countries that are directly affected by a public act are granted particular wide-ranging powers to initiate constitutional review. Finally, 31 countries grant lower courts the right to suspend a case to refer a law to the constitutional court for review (Harutyunyan et al. 2011, 61–63). Anticipating all of these plaintiffs to offer them deals to bypass the court is impossible. Hence, while intra-parliamentary deals may reduce referrals by political actors (Vanberg 1998a, 312–313), they do not reduce the universe of plaintiffs. Even if the government compromises with the opposition, bills should meet the position of the court.

2.6 Summary

This chapter has outlined the theoretical considerations to assess the two faces of judicial power. The considerations are embedded in the Judicial-Policy-Dialogue Game following traditional separation of powers models (see e.g., Marks 2012 [1988]; Ferejohn and Weingast 1992; Segal 1997; Vanberg 2001, 2005; Carrubba and Zorn 2010).

The first part of the discussion focused on the court taking a particular action. This characterizes the first face of judicial power. The strong focus on the court differs from the one that existing separation of power models apply. These studies focus on features that drive the political implementation of a judicial decision. The perspective is on the political sphere. For example, Vanberg (2005, 2) questions "[h]ow can courts, and the judges who serve on them, constrain governing majorities in practice?" (similar Vanberg 2001) and Carrubba and Zorn (2010, 812)—who test Vanberg's (2001, 2005) argument in the context of the United States—ask "[w]hy would the U.S. executive obey adverse rulings by the Supreme Court when the Court cannot enforce such a decision?" (comparable Marks 2012 [1988]). Indeed, courts are unable to implement decisions themselves. Previous studies assessed how the judiciary can affect the environment under which political actors may circumvent decisions. The game designed here incorporates the features that define the costs from an evasion for the court and for political actors to react to the court. Moreover, the approach more accurately accounts for the action repertoire available to judges. This repertoire is larger than portrayed by previous studies. For example, they either coded whether "the Supreme Court's final decision on the merits supported the U.S. government's position" (Carrubba and Zorn 2010, 818) or not, or whether the German Federal Constitutional Court upholds a law or not (Vanberg 2001, 355). However, courts take strategic choices either not to justify referrals, to justify referrals, or to present directives. This is why the JPD game outlines judicial decision-making more accurately, focusing on the actual verdict.

Table 2.5 summarizes the hypotheses and parameters that explain judicial choices. The final column highlights that the JPD game is of theoretical importance (Lehnert et al. 2007, 22–25) to a number of debates in judicial politics. Hypothesis H4 addresses the prejudicial process and refers to the second face of judicial power. The game yields that the government anticipates judicial choices but the implications for the position of the initial bill

Table 2.5 Summary of hypotheses and observable implications

	Hypothesis	*Driving variables*	*Choice*	*Theoretical relevance*
H1a	If the costs of the government to legislate in response to a judicial decision are low, then the likelihood that the court will justify a referral and present a directive is higher than when the government's costs to legislate again are high	Costs $\alpha \downarrow$ Costs $\alpha \uparrow$	$jd \uparrow$ $jd \downarrow$	Strategic judicial behavior *First face of power*
H1b	If the costs of the government to legislate in response to a judicial decision are low, then the likelihood that the court will only justify a referral is lower than when the government's costs to legislate again are high	Costs $\alpha \downarrow$ Costs $\alpha \uparrow$	$j \downarrow$ $j \uparrow$	Strategic judicial behavior *First face of power*
H1c	If the costs of a judicial evasion increase, then the likelihood that the court will justify a referral and present a directive also increases	Costs $\gamma \uparrow$ Costs $\gamma \downarrow$	$jd \uparrow$ $jd \downarrow$	Strategic judicial behavior *First face of power*
H1d	If the costs of a judicial evasion increase, then the likelihood that the court will only justify a referral decreases	Costs $\gamma \uparrow$ Costs $\gamma \downarrow$	$j \downarrow$ $j \uparrow$	Strategic judicial behavior *First face of power*
H2a	If the costs of the government are low and the government is positioned between the area in which the court can present a directive and the status quo, then the likelihood that the court does not justify a referral is higher than when the government's costs are high under the same spatial setting	Costs $\alpha \downarrow \cap$ $(x_{sq} > G > x_d \cup$ $x_d > G > x_{sq})$ Costs $\alpha \uparrow \cap$ $(x_{sq} > G > x_d \cup$ $x_d > G > x_{sq})$	$\neg j \uparrow$ $\neg j \downarrow$	Strategic judicial behavior *First face of power*
H2b	If the costs of the government are low and the government is not positioned between the area in which the court can present a directive and the status quo, then the likelihood that the court does not justify a referral is lower than when the government's costs are high under the same spatial setting	Costs $\alpha \downarrow \cap$ $\neg (x_{sq} > G > x_d \cup$ $x_d > G > x_{sq})$ Costs $\alpha \uparrow \cap$ $\neg (x_{sq} > G > x_d \cup$ $x_d > G > x_{sq})$	$\neg j \downarrow$ $\neg j \uparrow$	Strategic judicial behavior *First face of power*
OI3a	With higher costs from an evasion, there are fewer final policies along the curve on which the government responds to a court's decision to re-enact the status quo	Cost $\gamma \uparrow$ $j \downarrow$	Re-enact $x_{sq} \downarrow$	Judicialization *First face of power*
OI3b	Higher costs from an evasion lead to more judicial directives, which increases the variation of outcomes over the policy space	Cost $\gamma \uparrow$ $jd \uparrow$	Variation $x_{g2} \uparrow$	Judicialization *First face of power*
H4	If a legal signal—in the form of citing any prior court decision—is debated in legislative committees, then policy will be shifted in the spatial direction of the court	$x_{g1} \rightarrow C$	*None*	Autolimitation *Second face of power*

$\uparrow$ Parameter increases; $\downarrow$ Parameter decreases; $\neg$ Spatial setting does not occur; $\rightarrow$ Parameter moved in the direction are inconclusive. Scholars have repeatedly hypothesized about autolimitation (Landfried 1992; Kommers 1994; Stone Sweet 1998, 2000; Vanberg 1998a, 2001), but systematic evidence of the inner workings of the mechanism in legislative–judicial bargaining is lacking. This is why autolimitation is mainly addressed in the empirical chapters.

In the next chapter I assess the preconditions of judicial power in Germany and outline that they are representative in a cross-European comparison. This is why Germany is a representative case to analyze the JPD game and a case study presents first insights into the empirical nature of the game.

Notes

1. The citations refer to documents of the German *Bundestag* from the 13th legislative period.
2. C may also reject a referral of x_{g1} on formal grounds. In this case, the referral is inadmissible but this would lead to the same outcome (x_{g1}). To simplify the game, this scenario is not modeled as the general mechanism is included in $\neg j$, making the model parsimonious and more comparable.
3. See Osborn (2004, 166) for a general discussion on the subgame perfect Nash equilibrium.
4. The steps for all calculations are summarized in Appendix B and the numbers of the equations refer to the respective sections in the appendix.
5. If the court only justifies a referral, this is comparable to a directive presented at the status quo. Figure 2.3 illustrates that under these conditions the position of the optimal final policy (x^*_{g2}) is dependent on the size of α but will never be further out than the status quo (see also Appendix B—Step 2.1). Therefore, presenting policy at its own ideal point in the initial move and correcting it in the final move is rational.
6. Drawing C and x_d separately assumes that both parameters are independent from each other. The simulation is used to also explore the assumption that the court uses the directive to present the own ideal point.
7. The uniform distribution has the advantage that it has constant probability and no additional constraining assumptions are necessary (see Jevremović 2011).
8. The high number of draws was chosen for illustrative purposes. A lower number—for example, matching a court's case load—would confirm all following findings but the visualizations would have been less explicit.
9. The 77 scenarios in which the government does not present an initial policy are omitted from Fig. 2.6. In these scenarios, no policy reaches the court.
10. These patterns are also obvious in Fig. 2.8.

References

Amadae, S.M., Bueno de Mesquita, B. (1999). The Rochester School: The Origins of Positive Political Theory. *Annual Review of Political Science*, *2*(1), 269–295.

Anderson IV., R., Tahk, A.M. (2007). Institutions and Equilibrium in the United States Supreme Court. *American Journal of Political Science*, *101*(4), 811–825.

Barnes, R. (2015). Affordable Care Act survives Supreme Court challenge. *The Washington Post, June 25, 2015.* https://www.washingtonpost.com/politics/courts_law/obamacare-survives-supreme-court-challenge/2015/06/25/af87608e-188a-11e5-93b7-5eddc056ad8a_story.html (accessed September 17, 2020).

Brouard, S. (2009). The Politics of Constitutional Veto in France: Constitutional Council, Legislative Majority and Electoral Competition. *West European Politics*, *32*(2), 384–403.

Bueno de Mesquita, B. (2006). *Principles of International Politics. People's Power, Preferences, and Perceptions.* Washington D.C.: CQ Press, 3rd ed.

Cameron, C.M. (1993). New Avenues for Modeling Judicial Politics. *Conference on the Political Economy of Public Law, Rochester* (October 15-16), 1–61.

Cameron, C.M. (2000). *Veto Bargaining: Presidents and the Politics of Negative Power.* Cambridge: Cambridge University Press.

Carey, J.M. (2009). *Legislative Voting and Accountability.* Cambridge: Cambridge University Press.

Carrubba, C.J. (2005). Courts and Compliance in International Regulatory Regimes. *Journal of Politics*, *67*(3), 669–689.

Carrubba, C.J., Zorn, C. (2010). Executive Discretion, Judicial Decision Making, and Separation of Powers in the United States. *Journal of Politics*, *72*(3), 812–824.

Christiansen, M.R., Eskridge Jr., W.N. (2014). Congressional Overrides of Supreme Court Statutory Interpretation Decisions, 1967-2011. *Texas Law Review*, *92*(6), 1317–1515.

Chwaszcza, C. (2008). Game Theory. In D. della Porta, and M. Keating (Eds.) *Approaches and Methodologies in the Social Sciences*, (pp. 139–161). Cambridge: Cambridge University Press.

Clark, T.S. (2011). *The Limits of Judicial Independence.* Cambridge: Cambridge University Press.

Clark, T.S., Lauderdale, B. (2010). Locating Supreme Court Opinions in Doctrine Space. *American Journal of Political Science*, *54*(4), 871–890.

Dahl, R.A. (1957a). Decision-Making in a Democracy: The Supreme Court as a National Policy-Maker. *Journal of Public Law*, *6*, 279–295.

Dahl, R.A. (1957b). The Concept of Power. *Behavioral Science*, *2*(3), 201–215.

De Swaan, A. (1973). *Coalition Theories and Cabinet Formations. A Study of Formal Theories of Coalition Formation Applied to Nine European Parliaments after 1948.* San Francisco: Jossey-Bass Publishers.

Downs, A. (1957). An Economic Theory of Political Action in a Democracy. *Journal of Political Economy, 62*(2), 135–150.
Dyevre, A. (2010). Unifying the Field of Comparative Judicial Politics: Towards a General Theory of Judicial Behaviour. *European Political Science Review, 2*(2), 297–327.
Engst, B.G. (2016). Legal Signals and Policy Change. A text analysis of a causal model reassessing autolimitation. *The First Conference on Empirical Legal Studies in Europe (CELSE), Amsterdam* (June 21-22), 1–24.
Engst, B.G. (2017). Die vierte Gesetzeslesung. Verfassungsgerichte des deutsch-österreichischen Modells als Vetospieler. In V. Frick, O. W. Lembcke, and R. Lhotta (Eds.) *Politik und Recht. Umrisse eines politkwissenschaftlichen Forschungsfeldes*, (pp. 281–301). Baden-Baden: Nomos.
Engst, B.G., Gschwend, T., Schaks, N., Sternberg, S., Wittig, C. (2017). Zum Einfluss der Parteinähe auf das Abstimmungsverhalten der Bundesverfassungsrichter - eine quantitative Untersuchung. *Juristen Zeitung, 72*(17), 816–826.
Epstein, L., Knight, J. (1998). *The Choices Justices Make*. Washington, D.C: CQ Press.
Epstein, L., Knight, J. (2000). Toward a Strategic Revolution in Judicial Politics: A Look Back, A Look Ahead. *Political Research Quarterly, 53*(3), 625–661.
Epstein, L., Knight, J., Shvetsova, O. (2001). The Role of Constitutional Courts in the Establishment and Maintenance of Democratic Systems of Government. *Law and Society Review, 35*(1), 117–164.
Eskridge Jr., W.N. (1991). Reneging on History. Playing the Court/Congress/President Civil Rights Game. *California Law Review, 79*(3), 613–684.
Ferejohn, J.A., Shipan, C. (1990). Congressional Influence on Bureaucracy. *Journal of Law, Economics, and Organization, 6*(Special Issue), 1–20.
Ferejohn, J.A., Weingast, B.R. (1992). A Positive Theory of Statutory Interpretation. *International Review of Law and Economics, 12*(2), 263–279.
Forrest, M., Spriggs, J.R., II., Wahlbeck, P.J. (2000). *Crafting Law on the Supreme Court*. Cambridge: Cambridge University Press.
Fortunato, D., König, T., Proksch, S.-O. (2013). Government Agenda-Setting and Bicameral Conflict Resolution. *Political Research Quarterly, 66*(4), 938–951.
Gawron, T., Rogowski, R. (2002). The Implementation of German Federal Constitutional Court Decisions. Judicial Orders and the Federal Legislature. In R. Rogowski, and T. Gawron (Eds.) *Constitutional Courts in Comparison. The U.S. Supreme Court and the German Federal Constitutional Court* (pp. 239–256). New York: Berghahn Books.
Gawron, T., Rogowski, R. (2007). *Die Wirkung des Bundesverfassungsgerichtes. Rechtssoziologische Analysen*. Baden-Baden: Nomos.

Gawron, T., Rogowski, R. (2015). Die Wirkung des Bundesverfassungsgerichts. In R. C. van Ooyen, and M. H. W. Möllers (Eds.) *Handbuch Bundesverfassungsgericht im politischen System* (pp. 153–168). Wiesbaden: Springer Fachmedien Wiesbaden, 2nd ed.

Gibson, J.L., Caldeira, G.A., Baird, V.A. (1998). On the Legitimacy of National High Courts. *American Political Science Review*, *92*(2), 343–358.

Hale, F.D. (1978). Press Releases vs. Newspaper Coverage of California Supreme Court Decisions. *Journalism and Mass Communication Quarterly*, *55*(4), 696–710.

Hammond, T.H., Bonneau, C.W., Sheehan, R.S. (2005). *Strategic Behavior and Policy Choice on the U.S. Supreme Court.* Stanford: Stanford University Press.

Hanretty, C. (2014). The Bulgarian Constitutional Court as an Additional Legislative Chamber. *East European Politics and Societies*, *28*(3), 540–558.

Harutyunyan, G., Nussberger, A., Paczolay, P. (2011). Study on Individual Access To Constitutional Justice. *Venice Commission [European Commission for Democracy through Law]*, *2009*(538), 1–172.

Helmke, G. (2002). The Logic of Strategic Defection: Court-Executive Relations in Argentina Under Dictatorship and Democracy. *American Political Science Review*, *96*(2), 291–303.

Hirschl, R. (2008). The Judicialization of Politics. In G. A. Caldeira., D. R. Kelemen, and K. E. Whittington (Eds.) *The Oxford Handbook of Law and Politics* (pp. 119–141). Oxford: Oxford University Press.

Hönnige, C. (2007). *Verfassungsgericht, Regierung und Opposition. Die vergleichende Analyse eines Spannungsdreiecks.* Wiesbaden: VS Verlag für Sozialwissenschaften.

Hönnige, C. (2008). Verfassungsgerichte in den EU-Staaten: Wahlverfahren, Kompetenzen und Organisationsprinzipien. *Journal for Comparative Government and European Policy*, *6*(3), 524–553.

Hönnige, C. (2011). Beyond Judicialization: Why We Need More Comparative Research About Constitutional Courts. *European Political Science*, *10*(3), 346–358.

Ignagni, J., Meernik, J. (1994). Explaining Congressional Attempts to Reverse Supreme Court Decisions. *Political Research Quarterly*, *47*(2), 353–371.

Ismayr, W. (2006). *Der Deutsche Bundestag im Politischen System der Bundesrepublik Deutschland.* Wiesbaden: VS Verlag für Sozialwissenschaften, 2nd ed.

Jevremović, V. (2011). Uniform Distribution in Statistics. In M. Lovric (Ed.) *International Encyclopedia of Statistical Science.* (pp. 1621–1623). Heidelberg: Springer.

Kelemen, K. (2013). Dissenting Opinions in Constitutional Courts. *German Law Journal*, *14*(8), 1345–1371.

Koford, K. (1989). Dimensions in Congressional Voting. *American Political Science Review*, *83*(3), 949–962.

Kommers, D.P. (1994). The Federal Constitutional Court in the German Political System. *Comparative Political Studies, 26*(4), 470–491.

König, T., Mäder, L. (2014). The Strategic Nature of Compliance: An Empirical Evaluation of Law Implementation in the Central Monitoring System of the European Union. *American Journal of Political Science, 58*(1), 246–263.

Krehbiel, J.N. (2016). The Politics of Judicial Procedures: The Role of Public Oral Hearings in the German Constitutional Court. *American Journal of Political Science, 60*(4), 990–1005.

Krehbiel, K. (1998). *Pivotal Politics. A Theory of U.S. Lawmaking*. Chicago: University of Chicago Press.

Landfried, C. (1992). Judicial Policy-Making in Germany: The Federal Constitutional Court. *West European Politics, 15*(3), 50–67.

Landfried, C. (1994). The Judicialization of Politics in Germany. *International Political Science Review, 15*(2), 113–124.

Langer, L., Brace, P. (2005). The Preemptive Power of State Supreme Courts: Adoption of Abortion and Death Penalty Legislation. *Policy Studies Journal, 33*(3), 317–340.

Laver, M., Shepsle, K.A. (1996). *Making and Breaking Governments. Cabinets and Legislatures in Parliamentary Democracies*. Cambridge: Cambridge University Press.

Lehnert, M., Miller, B., Wonka, A. (2007). Increasing the Relevance of Research Questions: Considerations on Theoretical and Social Relevance in Political Science. In T. Gschwend, and F. Schimmelfennig (Eds.) *Research Design in Political Science: How to Practice what they Preach* (pp. 21–38). Houndmills: Palgrave MacMillan.

Linos, K., Twist, K. (2016). The Supreme Court, the Media, and Public Opinion: Comparing Experimental and Observational Methods. *Journal of Legal Studies, 45*(2), 223–254.

Marks, B.A. (2012). [1988]. A Model of Judicial Influence on Congressional Policy. Making: Grove City College v. Bell. *Journal of Law, Economics and Organization, 31*(4), 843–875.

Martin, A.D., Quinn, K.M. (2002). Dynamic Ideal Point Estimation via Markov Chain Monte Carlo for the U.S. Supreme Court, 1953-1999. *Political Analysis, 10*(2), 134–153.

Martin, A.D., Quinn, K.M. (2007). Assessing Preference Change on the US Supreme Court. *Journal of Law, Economics, and Organization, 23*(2), 365–385.

Mattson, I., Strøm, K. (1995). Parliamentary Committees. In H. Döring (Ed.) *Parliaments and Majority Rule in Western Europe* (pp. 249–307). Frankfurt: Campus Verlag.

McCarty, N., Meirowitz, A. (2007). *Political Game Theory: An Introduction*. Cambridge: Cambridge University Press.

Morrow, J.D. (1994). *Game Theory for Political Scientists*. Princeton: Princeton University Press.

Müller, W.C., Strøm, K. (1999). *Policy, Office or Votes? How Political Parties in Western Europe Make Hard Decisions*. Cambridge: Cambridge University Press.

Osborn, M.J. (2004). *An Introduction to Game Theory*. Oxford: Oxford University Press.

Parcelle Jr., R.L., Curry, B.W., Marshall, B.W. (2011). *Decision Making by the Modern Supreme Court*. Cambridge: Cambridge University Press.

Poole, K.T., Rosenthal, H. (1991). Patterns of Congressional Voting. *American Journal of Political Science*, *35*(1), 228–278.

Poole, K.T., Rosenthal, H. (2007). *Ideology and Congress: A Political Economic History of Roll Call Voting*. New Brunswick: Transaction Publishers, 2nd ed.

Posner, R.A. (1993). What Do Judges and Justice Maximize? (The Same Thing Everybody Else Does). *Supreme Court Economic Review*, *3*, 1–41.

R Core Team (2018). *R: A Language and Environment for Statistical Computing*. Wien: R Foundation for Statistical Computing.

Raffaelli, R. (2012). *Dissenting Opinions in the Supreme Courts of the Member States*. European Parliament: Directorate General for Internal Policies (PE 462.470). https://www.europarl.europa.eu/document/activities/cont/201304/20130423ATT64963/20130423ATT64963EN.pdf (accessed February 21, 2018).

Rath, C. (2015). Pressearbeit und Diskursmacht des Bundesverfassungsgerichts. In R. C. van Ooyen, and M. H. W. Möllers (Eds.) *Handbuch Bundesverfassungsgericht im politischen System* (pp. 403–412). Wiesbaden: Springer Fachmedien Wiesbaden, 2nd ed.

Riker, W.H. (1962). *The Theory of Political Coalitions*. New Haven: Yale University Press.

Riker, W.H. (1990). Political Science and Rational Choice. In J. E. Alt, and K. A. Shepsle (Eds.) *Perspectives on Positive Political Economy* (pp. 163–180). Cambridge: Cambridge University Press.

Roberts, J.M., Smith, S.S., Haptonstahl, S.R. (2016). The Dimensionality of Congressional Voting Reconsidered. *American Politics Research*, *44*(5), 794–815.

Rogers, J.R. (2001). Information and Judicial Review: A Signaling Game of Legislative-Judicial Interaction. *American Journal of Political Science*, *45*(1), 84–99.

Rogers, J.R., Flemming, R.B., Bond, J.R. (2006). *Institutional Games and the U.S. Supreme Court*. Charlottesville: University of Virginia Press.

Schlink, B. (2007). Abschied von der Dogmatik. Verfassungsrechtsprechung und Verfassungsrechtswissenschaft im Wandel. *Juristen Zeitung*, *62*(4), 157–162.

Schubert, G.A. (1958). The Study of Judicial Decision-Making as an Aspect of Political Behavior. *American Political Science Review*, *52*(4), 1007–1025.

Schubert, G.A. (1965). *The Judicial Mind. Attitudes and Ideologies of Supreme Court Justices, 1946–1963*. Evanston: Northwestern University Press.

Segal, J.A. (1997). Separation-of-Powers Games in the Positive Theory of Congress and Courts. *American Political Science Review*, *91*(1), 28–44.

Segal, J.A., Cover, A.D. (1989). Ideological Values and the Votes of U.S. Supreme Court Justices. *American Political Science Review*, *83*(2), 557–565.

Segal, J.A., Spaeth, H.J. (1993). *The Supreme Court and the Attitudinal Model*. Cambridge: Cambridge University Press.

Segal, J.A., Spaeth, H.J. (2002). *The Supreme Court and the Attitudinal Model Revisited*. Cambridge: Cambridge University Press.

Shapiro, M., Stone Sweet, A. (2002). *On Law, Politics and Judicialization*. Oxford: Oxford University Press.

Shepsle, K.A. (2010). *Analyzing Politics. Rationality, Behavior and Instititutions*. New York: W. W. Norton, 2nd ed.

Sieberer, U. (2006). Strategische Zurückhaltung von Verfassungsgerichten. Gewaltenteilungsvorstellungen und die Grenzen der Justizialisierung. *Zeitschrift für Politikwissenschaft*, *16*(4), 1299–1323.

Slapin, J.B., Proksch, S.-O. (2008). A Scaling Model for Estimating Time-Series Party Positions from Texts. *American Journal of Political Science*, *52*(3), 705–722.

Staton, J.K. (2008). Formal Theory in Comparative Judicial Politics. *Law and Courts Newsletter*, *18*(3), 10–15.

Staton, J.K. (2010). *Judicial Power and Strategic Communication in Mexico*. Cambridge: Cambridge University Press.

Staton, J.K., Vanberg, G. (2008). The Value of Vagueness: Delegation, Defiance, and Judicial Opinions. *American Journal of Political Science*, *52*(3), 504–519.

Sternberg, S., Gschwend, T., Wittig, C., Engst, B.G. (2015). Zum Einfluss der öffentlichen Meinung auf Entscheidungen des Bundesverfassungsgerichts: Eine Analyse von abstrakten Normenkontrollen sowie Bund-Länder-Streitigkeiten 1974 - 2010. *Politische Vierteljahresschrift*, *56*(4), 570–598.

Stone, A. (1992). *The Birth of Judicial Politics in France. The Constitutional Council in Comparative Perspective*. Oxford: Oxford University Press.

Stone Sweet, A. (1998). A Comment on Vanberg: Rules, Dispute Resolution, and Strategic Behavior. *Journal of Theoretical Politics*, *10*(3), 327–338.

Stone Sweet, A. (2000). *Governing with Judges: Constitutional Politics in Europe*. Oxford: Oxford University Press.

Stoutenborough, J.W., Haider-Markel, D.P., Allen, M.D. (2006). Reassessing the Impact of Supreme Court Decisions on Public Opinion: Gay Civil Rights Cases. *Political Research Quarterly*, *59*(3), 419–433.

Strøm, K. (1990). A Behavioral Theory of Competitive Political Parties. *American Journal of Political Science*, *34*(2), 565–598.

Toshkov, D. (2016). *Research Design in Political Science*. London: Palgrave MacMillan.

Tsebelis, G. (2002). *Veto Player: How Political Institutions Work*. New York: Russell Sage Foundation.

Vanberg, G. (1998a). Abstract Judicial Review, Legislative Bargaining, and Policy Compromise. *Journal of Theoretical Politics, 10*(3), 299–326.

Vanberg, G. (1998b). Reply to Stone Sweet. *Journal of Theoretical Politics, 10*(3), 339–346.

Vanberg, G. (2001). Legislative-Judicial Relations: A Game-Theoretic Approach to Constitutional Review. *American Journal of Political Science, 45*(2), 346–361.

Vanberg, G. (2005). *The Politics of Constitutional Review in Germany*. Cambridge: Cambridge University Press.

Wesel, U. (2004). *Der Gang nach Karlsruhe: Das Bundesverfassungsgericht in der Geschichte der Bundesrepublik*. München: Karl Blessing Verlag.

Yanus, A.B. (2009). Full-Court Press: An Examination of Media Coverage of State Supreme Courts. *Justice System Journal, 30*(2), 180–195.

CHAPTER 3

Judicial Power in Germany and the European Union

In this chapter, I introduce the German Federal Constitutional Court (GFCC) as a typical case suitable for assessing the two faces of judicial power. The design of the GFCC and its embeddedness in the separation of powers framework provide for institutionalized and noninstitutionalized features that allow the judiciary to exercise power. After identifying such features, I present a cross-European comparison of the preconditions of judicial power. The comparison shows that the preconditions in Germany are representative of a number of democracies. In a concluding case study, I trace a law referred to the court through the policy process to outline how the GFCC exercises power. This assessment provides a first plausibility check of the hypotheses derived in Chapter 2.

Studying judicial power in the context of the GFCC is reasonable based on the following: first, the GFCC is a theoretically prominent, archetypal constitutional court. The court was established as one of the first constitutional courts and is a direct emulation of the Austrian model of constitutional review proclaimed by Hans Kelsen (2008 [1931]; also, Borowski 2003; Stone Sweet 2000, Ch. 3). Thus, studying the GFCC provides important insights about the system of constitutional review, in contrast to the widely studied system of judicial review used in the United States (Epstein et al. 2001, 120–123; Stone Sweet 2000, Ch. 3). It is important to note that being an archetypal case does not make the GFCC an empirical outlier; instead, second, many constitutional courts in newly established democracies—like those in Central and Eastern Europe (Hönnige 2008, 526)—mirror major institutional features of the GFCC.

B. G. Engst, *The Two Faces of Judicial Power*,
https://doi.org/10.1007/978-3-030-46016-7_3

Studies show that the court clusters with a large number of other constitutional courts when comparing institutional features across countries (Kneip 2008, 648; Engst 2017). Hence, the GFCC is representative of other constitutional courts. Third, easy access to relevant information and reliable data can partially justify a case selection (Leuffen 2007, 153). Assessing constitutional courts, scholars have repeatedly turned to the GFCC (see Landfried 1985; Stone Sweet 2000; Gawron and Rogowski 2002; Vanberg 2005; Dyevre 2011; Kommers and Miller 2012; Krehbiel 2016; Wittig 2016; Brouard and Hönnige 2017), which is why prior knowledge is available. Moreover, I have access to the novel *Constitutional Court Database* (CCDB; Hönnige et al. 2015), which links decisions made by the GFCC to the political environment. The link is essential to this study as (judicial) power is defined in relational terms. Given that power only exists in the—implicit or explicit—interaction between the court and the political branches, it is necessary to understand the link between the two branches. The prior knowledge and the database allow developing such a comprehensive understanding. Fourth, the German parliamentary system is bicameral with incongruent chambers (Lijphart 2012, 199). A decisive feature of the system is that there are two major legislative procedures. On the one hand, the second chamber (the *Bundesrat*) is not explicitly involved when the first chamber (the *Bundestag*) passes a so-called objection bill (*Einspruchsgesetz*) (Fortunato et al. 2013, 940).[1] The second chamber can literally only raise an objection once such a bill is passed. On the other hand, the second chamber has to be explicitly involved when the first chamber passes a so-called consent bill (*Zustimmungsgesetz*).[2] This legislative design makes a study of judicial–legislative interaction in Germany representative of many democracies. When a bill is passed as an objection bill, the government's majority in parliament is less constrained in its legislative behavior. Implicitly, this setup reflects a political system with executive dominance. Nevertheless, when a bill is passed as a consent bill, then the government is more constrained and has to bargain with the second chamber (Fortunato et al. 2013; Manow and Burkhart 2007). Implicitly, this setup represents a congruent, bicameral, parliamentary democracy. Therefore, assessing the interaction between the legislative majority and the court in Germany—accounting for the different legislative procedures—provides for an assessment of judicial–political interactions in systems with different legislative designs.

These four points justify the use of Germany "as *an intensive study of a single unit for the purpose of understanding a larger class of (similar) units*"

(Gerring 2004, 342; emphasis in the original). The court is (1) theoretically important, (2) representative of a larger number of constitutional courts, (3) prior research and a database on the GFCC are available, and (4) the court is embedded in a political system mirroring a variety of legislative procedures. In the next sections, I develop a deeper understanding of the GFCC with a focus on the two faces of judicial power and place the findings in a cross-European perspective.

3.1 The German Federal Constitutional Court

In this section, I provide an institutional overview of the GFCC. I highlight the relevant features to establish the power relations outlined in Chapter 2. In line with the theoretical discussion, judicial power is dependent on the court's ability to (threaten to) make a judicial choice. Thus, it is necessary to understand how the court becomes empowered to make decisions and what type of verdicts are chosen. Finally, the Judicial-Policy-Dialogue Game (JPD game) focuses on the court's ability to exert power vis-à-vis the government with its legislative majority. This is why the (non-)institutionalized features of this interaction are reviewed accordingly.

3.1.1 The Institutional Design of the GFCC

The GFCC is not the court of last resort but rather a specialized judicial entity outside the regular legal hierarchy, empowered to take decisions solely on constitutional matters (Singer 1982, 333; BVerfGE 18, 85 [92–94]; BVerfGE 30, 173 [187–188]).[3] This is typical for a constitutional court and reflects a major difference compared with the Anglo-American supreme court model (Epstein et al. 2001, 120–123; Vanberg 2005, 77–93; Stone Sweet 2000, Ch. 3). The design of the GFCC is based on the writings of the Austrian legal scholar Hans Kelsen.[4] The institutional specifics of the court are outlined in Art. 94 I of the German Basic Law in connection with §1–§12 of the Act on the GFCC.[5] Accordingly, the court comprises two senates, each of which comprises eight judges elected for a nonrenewable term of twelve years. Half of the 16 judges are elected by the second chamber with a two-thirds majority. The remaining eight judges are elected with a two-thirds majority by the first chamber after a legislative–judicial selection committee makes suggestions.[6] Eligible candidates need to fulfill a number of professional requirements, e.g., three judges on each senate must have served on the federal courts prior to joining the constitutional court (§2 III Act on the GFCC).

The role of the individual judge at the GFCC and other highest courts in Europe is discussed elsewhere (see, e.g., Hönnige 2007, 2009; Kranenpohl 2010; Hanretty 2013, 2014; Wittig 2016; Engst et al. 2017, 2020) and set aside here. Instead, I argue that for the study at hand the court can be perceived as a collective actor. It is necessary to account for the fact that the court comprises two senates in later analyses, but these are still collective bodies. By definition, "[e]ach senate *is* the Federal Constitutional Court" (Kommers and Miller 2012, 19, emphasis in the original). Hence, when I refer to the court as a collective actor, this implies that one of the two senates makes a decision. The assumption of a collective actor is valid as the court is approached from an outside perspective here (Staton 2010, 17–18; Dyevre 2010, 304). Moreover, the court's decisions are the tools that allow the court to exercise (the threat of) a judicial veto. The decisions are presented as a product of the court as a whole, especially as individual judicial votes of the court are very rarely published. In fact, the publication of judicial votes rarely occurs in cross-country comparison (Raffaelli 2012, 30; Kelemen 2013, 1345). Individual judges are entitled to write separate opinions (Wittig 2016), but these opinions are not themselves legally binding. Separate opinions seldom occur and are not necessarily in conflict with a decision, but often they reflect a judge's concurring opinion.[7] In sum, it is appropriate to regard the decisions made by the senates as collective outcomes of the court.

The court is chronically overwhelmed by its caseload. This is why in 1986 each senate founded three chambers, comprising three judges each (Kommers and Miller 2012, 20–21; Vanberg 2005, 88). The legal scope of the chambers is limited: they are only empowered to decide on constitutional complaints or requests of concrete judicial review by certain regular courts (§81a and §93b Act on the GFCC). The procedures make up the bulk of the court's work, but the chambers are only allowed to rule on a matter if the key legal question is evident and had been subject to a previous senate decision (Kommers and Miller 2012, 20). Moreover, chambers are not allowed to declare a law unconstitutional (§93c I Act on the GFCC). Instead, the chambers can only take decisions unanimously; otherwise, they need to refer a proceeding to the senate (Wittig 2016, 23–24). This is why chamber decisions only exist in areas where the senates have ruled in the past and exercised power. Moreover, the implications of chamber decisions are limited and given that legal questions are evident, it is plausible that the government considers them beforehand.

Hence, chamber decisions hold minor interest to the power of the court vis-à-vis political actors and are left aside here.

In sum, taking an outside perspective the judicial power rests with the two senates of the GFCC, which make the key decisions over novel or controversial issues. Each senate presents decisions as a collective outcome of the constitutional court. In the next section, I outline how the court makes decisions.

3.1.2 The Key Legal Procedures of the GFCC

The GFCC is the only judicial entity empowered to nullify public acts or declare laws void and incompatible with the constitution (§78 and §95 III Act on the GFCC). The court can nullify a whole law or only certain provisions, whereby the latter has become the norm (Vanberg 2005, 92–93; Stone Sweet 2000, 71). Laws that are nullified and void must no longer be applied with immediate effect, but laws incompatible with the Basic Law can usually be applied until the revised legislation takes effect (Vanberg 2005, 92–93). Moreover, the GFCC can assess the constitutionality of administrative acts and judgments by courts of final appeal. If those acts or respective rulings are based on unconstitutional provisions, the GFCC is empowered to waive them (Schlaich and Korioth 2015, 4–6).[8]

In general, the court applies two steps in making decisions (see, e.g., Schlaich and Korioth 2015, Ch. 5). First, the court assesses whether a referral is admissible, which is a procedural matter. In this step, the court assesses whether a plaintiff can legitimately claim a violation of her constitutional rights and whether she does so fulfilling all required formalities. If this is not the case, the court will reject a referral and the addressed act stands. Second, once the court admits a referral, the judges decide on the merits. They assess whether a law or public act is in accordance with the constitution. If this is the case, the court does not justify a referral and the law or act is constitutional. This is why I consider a decision that a referral is not admissible as equal to the court's choice not to justify a referral. Both decisions lead to the same outcome. However, if the court concludes that constitutional provisions are violated, the judges justify the referral. They can nullify the law or public act. The judicial choices—to justify or not justify—match the theoretical considerations from Chapter 2. Moreover, the court frequently presents directives despite the fact that they are not an institutionalized type of verdict.

The GFCC knows 22 procedures that allow different types of plaintiffs—who fulfill precisely specified preconditions—access to the court. Some of the procedures have never or very rarely been used; such as, the procedure to impeach the Federal President or the forfeiture of fundamental rights.[9] Traditionally, the two senates were in charge of different procedures, but this is no longer enforced and nowadays responsibilities are shared (Kommers and Miller 2012, 18–19). The referral by a plaintiff leads to a proceeding. Different proceedings initiated by different plaintiffs regarding similar legal matters are frequently combined in one judicial decision (Wittig 2016, 27–28). In other words, proceedings are the lowest level to approach the GFCC, but decisions as an outcome of the court can speak to various proceedings. Throughout the later analyses, decisions will become the level of analysis. They are the collective outcome of the court and directives are a function of the decisions. Table 3.1 highlights the proceedings level simply to present insights into how the court's judicial power is activated. The table describes the most common proceedings before the GFCC, the possible plaintiffs who can initiate those proceedings and summarizes the legal implications.[10] In addition, the table lists the number of proceedings and decisions made between December 1990 and September 2009.[11] Moreover, the table mentions the number of proceedings that are part of decisions with directives. The final column outlines the assumed effect of the proceedings on the faces of judicial power.

The most common procedures are 728 constitutional complaints (BvR) considered by the court in 430 decisions. 146 complaints are part of 82 decisions with directives. The complaints can be filed by any person directly affected by a public act or law after all regular legal remedies are exhausted (Kommers and Miller 2012, 11–13). The procedure challenges the government, which is unable to predict the individual behavior of each and every person; instead, the court seriously intervenes in policymaking by presenting a directive in about one in every five decisions following a constitutional complaint. The procedure allows the court to show a strong first face of judicial power. The government should have an incentive to anticipate the court's behavior in response to this very common procedure. This also allows the court to show a strong second face of judicial power.

The 227 concrete judicial reviews (BvL) in 139 decisions between December 1990 to September 2009 are the second most common procedures. They allow regular courts to refer laws for review when they consider laws incompatible with the constitution but decisive to the legal matter at hand (Kommers and Miller 2012, 13). The procedure enlarges the number

Table 3.1 Common legal procedures of the GFCC and the implications of those procedures

Proceeding (*Court's abbr.*)	*Description*	*Possible plaintiffs*	*Legal implications*	*Number of...* proceedings... (in decisions)	*w/ directives (in decisions)*	*Face of power* *First*	*Second*
				[December 1990–September 2009]			
Constitutional complaint (BvR)	Evaluation whether a public act or law is in accordance with constitutional provisions	Any person directly affected by an act or law but possible only after all legal remedies before the regular courts have been exhausted	Public act or law is void or incompatible with the Basic Law. The substantive legal question is referred to the regular courts	728 (430)	146 (82)	Strong	Strong
Concrete judicial review (BvL)	Review of a law's constitutionality initiated by a regular court who considers a law—which is decisive in a particular case—to be unconstitutional	Any regular court	Law is void or incompatible with the Basic Law	227 (139)	98 (50)	Strong	Strong
Abstract judicial review (BvF)	Review of a law's constitutionality independent of a specific legal dispute	Federal government, state government(s), a quarter of the members of the first chamber	Law is void or incompatible with the Basic Law	64 (44)	27 (13)	Strong	Weak

(continued)

Table 3.1 (continued)

Proceeding (*Court's abbr.*)	*Description*	*Possible plaintiffs*	*Legal implications*	*Number of...* proceedings... (in decisions)	*w/ directives (in decisions)*	*Face of power* First	Second
				[December 1990–September 2009]		*First*	*Second*
Dispute btw. high state organs (BvE)	Settlement of a dispute between state organs—or actors equal to those organs—which are in conflict over their constitutional rights or obligations	Federal president, federal government, second chamber, first chamber, federal convention (***Bundesversammlung***), chancellor, federal ministries, individual members of the first chamber	The GFCC finds the contested act as incompatible with the Basic Law. This does ***not*** obligate a specific action but the parties involved are obliged to consider the court's decision	60 (43)	7 (3)	Strong	Weak
Federal—state dispute (BvG)	Evaluation of the competencies the federation or the state(s) have when conflict among them arises	Federal government, state government(s)	The GFCC can recognize a violation of the Basic Law. This does ***not*** obligate a specific action but the parties involved are obliged to consider the court's decision	16 (12)	2 (1)	Weak	Weak
Intrastate constitutional dispute (BvH)	Evaluation of a constitutional-law dispute between states	State governments	The GFCC can recognize a violation of the Basic Law ***and*** the parties involved are obligated to perform or to omit a specific action	12 (12)	0	Weak	Weak

Note: Based on summaries by the German Federal Constitutional Court: http://www.bundesverfassungsgericht.de/EN/Verfahren/Wichtige-Verfahrensarten/wichtige-verfahrensarten_node.html, accessed January 12, 2020. The numbers of proceedings and decisions are computed using information on Senate decisions made by the GFCC between Germany's 12th and 16th legislative periods (December 1990 and September 2010), summarized in the CCDB (Hönnige et al. 2015). During this period the GFCC made a total of 714 Senate decision to address 1199 proceedings of plaintiffs that are located outside the political sphere. The government cannot easily predict the behavior of the regular courts that receive referrals from the public at large. This uncertainty and the large number of referrals contribute to the court's ability to show a strong second face of judicial power. Moreover, about 43% of the proceedings are part of 50 decisions with directives. Thus, the court also shows a strong first face of judicial power using the procedure.

Finally, there are procedures available to political actors only. The most common ones are the abstract judicial review procedure (BvF) and the dispute between high state organs (BvE). The former procedure permits the federal government, state government(s), or a quarter of the members of the first chamber to refer an enacted law to the GFCC for review, independently of a particular legal dispute. In 44 decisions summarizing 64 proceedings between December 1990 to September 2009, the court abstractly reviewed the compatibility of laws with the Basic Law. About 42% of those reviews are part of 13 decisions with directives. While the number of referrals is comparatively low, the few decisions are often used by the GFCC to exercise direct judicial power, thus showing a strong first face of judicial power. The low number of referrals might follow from the fact that only political actors can initiate abstract reviews. For example, Vanberg (1998) argues that the government strikes a bargain with the political opposition to reduce the number of referrals to the court. This is why the procedure weakens the court's ability to show the second face of judicial power.

It is interesting that the GFCC invests resources to present directives in about 12% of the referrals concerning disputes among highest states organs and federal-state disputes (BvG), since the implications of such disputes can be summarized as follows (emphasis added):

> The Federal Constitutional Court *does not* annul acts or declare them to be void, *nor* does it oblige the respondent to perform specific acts. However, the constitutional organs are obliged to *consider* the Federal Constitutional Court's decision and to implement it if necessary. (cf. Art. 20 (3) of the Basic Law)[12]

In other words, political actors have leeway in enacting the decisions, but the court chooses to present directives. Nevertheless, the number of referrals is low compared to the other proceedings. While disputes among high state organs occur as often as abstract reviews, federal-state disputes, and intrastate constitutional disputes (BvH) only occur in about 1% of all proceedings listed in Table 3.1. Moreover, the procedures are only available to political actors. Hence, the federal government can easily engage in bargaining with the actors empowered to refer the proceedings. This is why the court may show a strong first face of judicial power giving directives following federal-state disputes, but in all other instances the GFCC is comparatively weak.

There are two lessons learned from the legal procedures available to the GFCC. First, the court uses decisions to exercise direct power, thus showing the first face of judicial power. Independent of the type of proceeding, the GFCC frequently presents directives. Second, the ability of ordinary people and regular courts to refer to the GFCC strengthens the court's power from a threat of making decisions. In fact, the most frequent procedures are initiated by actors outside the influence of the political sphere. This strengthens the court's ability to show the second face of judicial power. Both findings are fully in line with comparative studies on constitutional courts as veto players. These studies show that the involvement of courts is conditional on plaintiffs, but, once activated, courts are powerful (political) players (Kneip 2007; Engst 2017). The decisions resulting from proceedings initiated by various plaintiffs are the tools that the court has available to exercise power. The next step is to outline the effect of the court using or threatening to use the tools in the interaction with the political branches.

3.1.3 The Political Branches and the GFCC

The political branches in Germany use an elaborated system to assess the constitutionality of bills (so-called *Rechtsförmlichkeitsprüfung*). Figure 3.1 summarizes the institutionalized and noninstitutionalized elements of this system. The figure illustrates how the political branches and the GFCC interact in the separation of powers framework. The focus rests with policy proposals drafted by the federal government. This is the most common procedure. The government drafted about 73% of all successful bills between the 12th and 16th legislative period (December 1990 to September 2009).[13]

The first draft of a policy is prepared by a ministry with expertise on the issue under involvement of this ministry's legal division (Veit 2010, 45). This makes it plausible that constitutional implications are discussed at an early stage, especially as the ministries are required to follow administrative

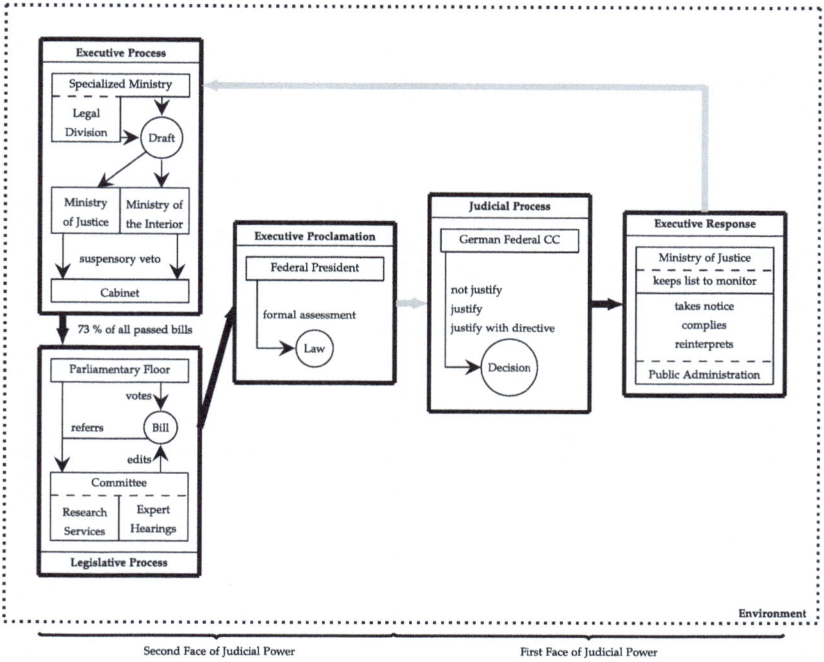

Fig. 3.1 Legal scrutiny of policies in the German separation of powers framework. Note: Own illustration, with information from Brunn (2004), Veit (2010), Gawron (2013), Gawron and Rogowski (2002), and Feldkamp (2011, Ch. 10.1, p. 5); *Gemeinsame Geschäftsordnung der Bundesministerien* and *Geschäftsordnung der Bundesregierung*

provisions published by the Ministry of the Interior and the Ministry of Justice (§42 GGO).[14] Once the specialized ministry settles on the first version of a draft, other ministries are consulted and it is required to involve the Ministry of Justice as well as the Ministry of the Interior. The latter two ministries assess whether a draft meets all legal and constitutional requirements (§45 and §46 GGO; Veit 2010, 273–274). The draft is referred to the Federal Cabinet afterwards. The Ministry of Justice and the Ministry of the Interior are granted the power of a suspensory veto when constitutional issues arise during the cabinet meetings (§26 II GOBReg).[15] Vetoed drafts are reconsidered in the following cabinet meeting and they are only adopted when the majority of the ministers and the chancellor vote in favor of the draft (Veit 2010, 274). All of these steps are institutionalized to rule out constitutional issues, but they are mostly confidential and difficult to observe.

Bills that pass the cabinet are referred to the legislative process (see Fig. 3.1). The legislature has not institutionalized the legal assessment of bills (Brunn 2004), but bills are referred to committees. The committees organize their own hearings, invite experts, are allowed to rewrite bills, and suggest a vote to the floor (Ismayr 2006, 167–194). There is evidence that they assess the legality of bills accounting for the GFCC. Indeed, committees can use the parliament's research services (Brunn 2004, 79). The service provides reports—for example, on the "Constitutionality of a Civic Insurance" (WD 3-3000-486/10; own translation)—structured along legal concepts applied by the GFCC. There is even a report on "[t]he tenseness relationship between the German *Bundestag* and the *Bundesverfassungsgericht*" (WD 3-3000-119/17; own translation).[16] Moreover, committees frequently invite experts for public hearings and between 1990 and 2010 about one-quarter of all bills were part of those hearings (Feldkamp 2011, Ch. 8.7, p. 3). Case studies show that the legislature is eager to develop beliefs about the court in committees (Landfried 1985, 530; 1992, 55; 1994, 117). Some committee reports indicate that the members themselves react to legal matters with statements like that "[s]uch a regulation would not be in accordance with the Basic Law in its current form (see BVerfGE 83, 37 ff.)" (BT Drs. 12/3896, 17; own translation). In sum, the legislature accounts for judicial review by the GFCC.

After the legislative process, the Federal President signs "[l]aws enacted in accordance with the provisions of this Basic Law" (Art. 82 I Basic Law). This requires an assessment of whether bills were passed in compliance with the constitution. The president's right to assess constitutional matters based on a bill's content is debated (see Nettesheim 2003, 1091–1095; Sachs et al. 2018, Art. 82). However, the president holds less interest here. First, the president mostly represents Germany externally and is not a member of the federal government (Art. 55 I Basic Law). Presidents often choose a theme to build a legacy, but they do not have the means to build their own political agenda. This is why they cannot gain or lose from a decision by the GFCC. Second, out of twelve presidents, only six have refused to sign a total of eight bills over 55 years. Hence, the president's legal assessment prior to signing a bill into law becomes a formality (Rütters 2011).

Proclaimed laws can be referred to the court using the proceedings from Table 3.1, but referrals are not necessary, as the gray arrow in Fig. 3.1 highlights. The court presents a verdict in response to a referral, showing the first face of judicial power. Following a decision, political actors can respond, but political scientists rarely study the impact of decisions in the German context (Gawron and Rogowski 2002, 239) and legal scholars focus on critical reviews discussing legal loopholes or strengths of decisions (e.g., Hecker 2006; Palm 2007; Streng 2011). However, there is evidence that the Ministry of Justice monitors decisions that require an executive response. The ministry kept a respective list at least until 1991 (Gawron and Rogowski 2015, 159). Moreover, a department of the ministry traces proceedings with governmental involvement. The gray arrow in Fig. 3.1—from the response back to the executive process—highlights that the government can choose to legislate again but does not have to. If the government chooses to legislate again, then the process starts anew. The public administration is included for completeness but holds less relevance, for several reasons. First, civil servants need to await rulings by regular administrative courts to learn how to apply a decision by the GFCC, since the constitutional court does not decide on substantive matters (Gawron and Rogowski 2015, 229). Case studies show that after authorities take notice of a respective ruling, they either comply with or, more frequently, reinterpret rulings to prevent an overhaul of administrative procedures (see Gawron 2013 for further references). Second, administrative action is legitimized by legislation. If the government chooses to respond to a decision, then the administration implements the new policy. Third, unfavorable decisions do not impose political costs on individual civil servants; instead, political actors are held accountable once legislation fails.

The legislative process in Fig. 3.1 focuses on Germany's first chamber (*Bundestag*), although the second chamber (*Bundesrat*)—comprising the 16 state governments—is also involved in policymaking. There are two legislative procedures that lead to either a symmetric or asymmetric relationships between the chambers (Manow and Burkhart 2007; Fortunato et al. 2013). Consent bills (*Zustimmungsgesetze*) affect the states and require an approval by the second chamber. If there is no consent, either chamber can initiate conciliation via an intra-chamber committee (*Vermittlungsausschuss*). This committee can modify proposals, but the first chamber reconsiders the bills. This is why the legislative process in Fig. 3.1 is partially repeated and the illustration appropriately accounts for consent bills. Objection bills (*Einspruchsgesetze*) do not affect the states and the second chamber can only raise an objection against such bills. While this may lead to the involvement of the conciliation committee, it does not necessarily result in textual changes of bills. The first chamber can reject the objection with a vote by the same majority as the second chamber. This is why the procedure does not alter the legal assessment shown in Fig. 3.1.[17]

Nevertheless, "[t]he way in which a system works will be in part a function of its response to the total social, biological, and physical environment" (Easton 1957, 385). The dotted frame around Fig. 3.1 illustrates that a bill's success is also dependent on the environment. The two procedures to pass legislation alter the environment in which the political branches and the GFCC interact. Conflict between the federal government and the state governments can require extensive (informal) bargaining and legislation may be altered, not due to legal concerns but rather owing to the necessity to seek approval in the second chamber. The government strategically constrains itself interacting with a hostile second chamber (Manow and Burkhart 2007; Fortunato et al. 2013). This is why it is necessary to control for both legislative procedures in later empirical assessments. Moreover, the two procedures make the German case an elegant case to study (König 2001, 418–420). The federal government and its legislative majority can dominate the policy process when passing an objection bill. The role of the second chamber holds minor relevance and there is an executive dominance in the first chamber. Once consent bills are passed, the policy process mirrors a symmetric bicameralism and the government can lose its policy advantage. Controlling for the two different designs, later empirical findings yield implications for a number of democracies realizing either of the two systems.

Finally, the environment is shaped by factors outside of the political sphere. For example, courts are dependent on the public's opinion (Gibson et al. 1998; Epstein and Knight 1998, 157–159; Vanberg 2005; Gibson 2007). Sternberg et al. (2015) found that if the public shares the opposition's opinion on an issue referred to the GFCC by the opposition, then the court is likely to rule in favor of that opinion. In a similar vein, the government faces a dilemma, whereby it has to implement a policy agenda: on the one hand, there are electoral costs if a popular court nullifies the agenda (Vanberg 1998; Brouard 2009); and on the other hand, there are elector costs if the government refrains from implementing the promised agenda. These examples illustrate that the legal interaction between the governing majority and the court also entails external aspects.

In sum, when outlining the power of the GFCC adopting a perspective solely on the court has certain shortcomings; instead, it is necessary to account for the options available to political actors to assess judicial decision-making. Beyond institutionalized executive processes—which are difficult to observe—the legislature has adopted the habit of considering judicial choices. This is why it is appropriate to assess the interaction between the legislature and the GFCC to understand the power of the court over the political process. Moreover, judicial–political interactions take place in an environment that can influence bargaining situations.

3.2 The Power of the GFCC in a European Comparison

The previous sections have outlined features that enable the GFCC to exercise power. First, various plaintiffs can refer to the court using specific proceedings and the GFCC can nullify laws or public acts, frequently presenting directives. Second, legislative committees can listen to experts and modify bills in anticipation of the court. Third, the public's perception influences the interaction between the GFCC and the political branches. In addition, the government has to account for the *Bundesrat*, which can lead to political bargaining in anticipation of a hostile second chamber.

The features of (1) the constitutional court, (2) the legislative committees, and (3) the environment are not specific to Germany. Table 3.2 summarizes the characteristics of these features across countries of the European Union (EU) with constitutional courts.[18] The table is ordered by the occurrence of the features of the constitutional court and afterwards in alphabetic order. Germany and eight other countries from Austria to Spain have all court features and the four countries from Croatia to Slovakia have at least four out of five features. Therefore, the GFCC is a representative court closely matching twelve out of 17 constitutional courts. The table only accounts for repressive review procedures initiated after laws have been proclaimed. The political costs of losing unenforced bills are lower, which does not show particular judicial strength compared to enacted laws.

All legislatures in Table 3.2 can conduct hearings or modify bills. The permitted extent of modifications varies, from low (1)—as in Austria where redrafts are only possible when substantive amendments are necessary (Mattson and Strøm 1995, 287), or in Hungary where a committee on legislation reviews all amendments by regular committees[19]—to high (3), as in Germany, where committees can rewrite bills completely, or in Lithua-

Table 3.2 Institutionalized and noninstitutionalized preconditions of judicial power in EU countries with constitutional courts

	Constitutional Court[a]					*Legislative Committees*[b]		*Environment*	
Country	*Const. complaint*	*Concrete rev.*	*Abstract rev.*	*Nullify laws*	*Directives*	*Influence*	*Hearing*	*Rule of Law*[c]	*2nd Chamber*[d]
Germany	✓	✓	✓	✓	✓	3	✓	**14**	**Suspensory/Absolute**
Austria	✓	✓	✓	✓	✓	1	✓	15	Suspensory
Belgium	✓	✓	✓	✓	✓	3	✓	13	Suspensory
Czech Republic	✓	✓	✓	✓	✓	2	✓	14	Suspensory
Hungary	✓	✓	✓	✓	✓	1	✓	10	Unicameral
Latvia	✓	✓	✓	✓	✓	3	✓	12	Unicameral
Poland	✓	✓	✓	✓	✓	3	✓	12	Suspensory
Slovenia	✓	✓	✓	✓	✓	2	✓	14	Suspensory
Spain	✓	✓	✓	✓	✓	3	✓	15	Suspensory
Croatia	✓	✓	✓	✓		3	✓	11	Unicameral
Italy	✗	✓	✓	✓	✓	3	✓	12	Absolute
Portugal	✗	✓	✓	✓	✓	2	✓	15	Unicameral
Slovakia	✓	✓	✓	✓		3	✓	12	Unicameral
Bulgaria	✗	✓	✓	✓	✗	2	✓	10	Unicameral
France	✗	✗	✓	✓	✓	2	✓	13	Suspensory
Lithuania	✗	✓	✓	✓	✗	3	✓	13	Unicameral
Romania	✗	✓	✗	✓	✓	2	✓	12	Absolute
Luxembourg		✓		✓	✗	2	✓	16	Unicameral

Note: Ordered by the occurrence of the features of the constitutional court and afterwards in alphabetic order. ✓= Measure exists; ✗= Measure does not exist; Some cells are empty when no definitive source was found. [a]Based on Starck and Weber (eds. 2007), Luchterhandt et al. (eds. 2007), and Hönnige (2007, 125); updated with countries' constitutions or acts on constitutional courts. [b]The committees' influence on legislation is based on Mattson and Strøm (1995, 287–291) for Western European countries. Information on Central and Eastern Europe (CEE) taken from countries' constitutions or acts on parliaments; 1 = low to 3 = high influence of committees on the text of bills. Information on the committees' possibilities to perform hearings taken from Russell et al. (2013, 32) and from acts on parliaments or parliamentary websites for the CEE countries. [c]0 = low to 16 = high Rule of Law (adopted from Freedom House 2017). [d]Second chambers have asymmetric influence through suspensory vetoes over bills or symmetric influence through absolute vetoes over bills when parliaments are not unicameral (taken from Drexhage 2015, 23) nia, where committees can initiate legislation (Art. 65 Lithuanian Constitution).[20] Germany's wide-ranging legislative procedures are similar to half of the countries in Table 3.2.

Finally, the index on the countries' rule of law addresses the (legal) environment.[21] While there are measures addressing the *de jure* and *de facto* judicial independence in a country (Rios-Figueroa and Staton 2014; Linzer and Staton 2015; Voigt et al. 2015), an index on the rule of law is used here to measure the legal environment beyond the pure judicial sphere. On the one hand, the rule of law includes the judiciary's independence (Freedom House 2017), which can be limited with political measures. For example, the judicial reform proposed by the Polish Government in 2017 was criticized for limiting the judge's independence. The EU concluded that "some elements of the reform have a striking resemblance with the institutions which existed in the Soviet Union" (Barrett et al. 2017, 19). On the other hand, the index on the rule of law measures equal access to a fair judiciary (Freedom House 2017). Accordingly, the measure accounts for the public's perception of courts, at least to the extent that the public can place trust in the judiciary, with regard to receiving fair treatment. This is why the rule of law is broader than judicial independence measures. The rule of law addresses the general legal efficiency of a political system, accounting for appropriate laws and freedom from oppression and institutions such as the police. For example, if one finds strong courts but unjustified police action, then people might be afraid to involve the police. In turn, this may lead to fewer criminal matters being referred to courts. This also works in the opposite direction: a weak judiciary may be accepted if fair laws are strongly enforced, which ensures a just treatment of the society. Therefore, the measure of the rule of law is used here to reflect the legal environment of a political system at large and not only the judiciary's independence. The measure on the rule of law shown in Table 3.2 theoretically ranges from 0 (low) to 16 (high), although focusing on democracies here, the average score across all countries is about 13 points. Germany is close to average, with a score of 14, which makes the county representative among Eastern and Western European countries.

The last column of Table 3.2 addresses the idea that the environment in which judicial–political bargaining takes place is influenced by a second chamber. In eight unicameral countries, the government is not constrained by a second chamber, in seven countries the second chamber has the ability to block legislation with a suspensory veto—which the first chamber can overrule—and in two countries the second chamber can hinder the passage of a bill with an absolute veto. Hence, in nine countries the government has to account for a possible veto in the second chamber. Germany is representative of these nine countries.

Table 3.2 summarizes features that are preconditions of the two faces of judicial power. The features allow political actors and the judiciary to play the JPD game presented in Chapter 2. How representative is Germany—fulfilling the preconditions of the JPD game—in a cross-European comparison? Some of the variables in the table only address the first face of judicial power; these are (a) proceedings initiated as abstract reviews, and (b) the court's ability to present directives (see Table 3.1). In addition, some of the variables are relevant to the second face of judicial power. These are the abilities of committees to hold hearings and modify bills (see Fig. 3.1). Finally, some measures are beneficial to both faces of judicial power. These are the competences to nullify laws and the right to decide on constitutional complaints and concrete reviews (see Table 3.1). In the following paragraphs I compute two additive indices, one for each face of judicial power. Afterwards, I weight both dimensions by multiplying the indices with the countries' scores on the rule of law scale. Accordingly, I account for the fact that the environment is not part of the two dimensions but affects the dimensions.[22] I do not include the second chamber into the indices, as there are no justifiable ways to do so. Nevertheless, in later analyses, I will control for Germany's legislative procedures and Table 3.2 allows placing the findings in perspective.

Figure 3.2 plots the countries over the two indices with the scores regarding the (non-)institutionalized features relevant to the first face of judicial power on the x-axis and the (non-)institutionalized features relevant to the second face of judicial power on the y-axis. The circles indicate countries where courts use directives, while the triangles indicate countries where courts do not use directives.[23] The higher that a country scores on either index, the more pronounced are the features that empower the country's constitutional court.

The figure shows a strong, positive, linear relationship between the two indices (see the dashed, gray regression line). This is unsurprising given that some factors that allow courts to exercise direct power are necessarily linked to factors that enable courts to threaten judicial review. Put simply, if a court cannot nullify legislative acts, the legislature should not anticipate a decision by the court. Germany (GER) is at the stronger, upper end of the indices. The preconditions that allow the GFCC to exercise judicial power are well developed, although they are typical as the

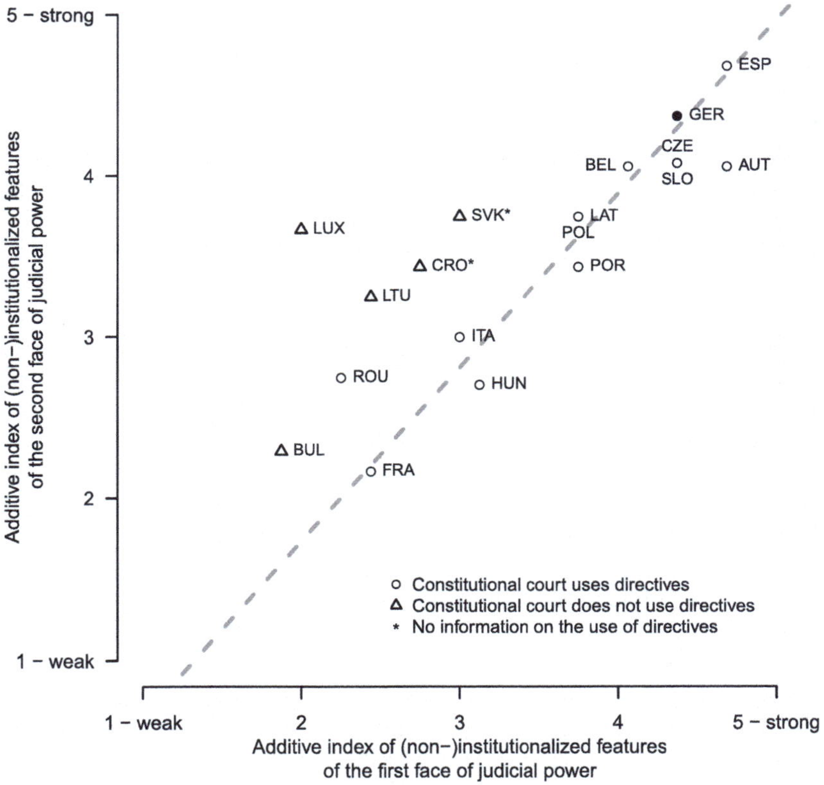

Fig. 3.2 Preconditions of the two faces of judicial power in cross-European comparison

country is placed on the dashed regression line. Austria (AUT), Belgium (BEL), the Czech Republic (CZE), Slovenia (SLO), and Spain (ESP) are positioned in close proximity to Germany. The constitutional courts in the six countries share all institutional features from Table 3.2, whereby the rule of law is well established among the countries and—aside from Austria—legislative committees are well-equipped to modify legislation. It speaks in favor of the indices that Germany and Austria are located next to one another, given that the legal traditions in both countries closely follow the writings of Hans Kelsen (2008 [1931]; Kelsen 1942) and major features of the constitutional courts in both countries are regarded as archetypical. Following the "Third Wave of Democratization" (Huntington 1991) and the regime transitions in Central and Eastern Europe, many countries adopted constitutional courts in line with the Austrian–German model (Hönnige 2007, 28). Indeed, besides the countries already discussed, the Latvian Constitutional Court and the Polish Constitutional Court also share all features with the GFCC. Moreover, the legislative committees in both countries have similar powers to the committees in Germany. The only difference between the three countries is that the established rule of law is lower in Poland and Latvia compared with Germany. Nevertheless, the overall similarities prompt me to assign the two countries to the group of countries similar to Germany. Are the preconditions of judicial power in Germany also similar to the preconditions in Portugal (POR)? Portugal does not allow for constitutional complaints and the influence of committees on bills is smaller than in Germany, but similar to Slovenia. Moreover, Portugal has a strong rule of law—equal to Austria and Spain—which should allow the judiciary to play a vital role. This is why I include Portugal in the group of countries clustering with Germany. Hence, the preconditions of judicial power in Germany are representative of Austria, Belgium, the Czech Republic, Latvia, Poland, Portugal, Slovenia, and Spain, which are half of the countries from Fig. 3.2. The constitutional courts in all of these countries use directives.

The results from a hierarchical cluster analysis shown in Appendix C.1 confirm the preceding grouping. Germany clusters with the eight aforementioned countries, while France (FRA) and Romania (ROU) form a second cluster with Bulgaria (BUL). The constitutional courts in France and Romania are considered among the weakest in the EU (Kneip 2008, 648; Engst 2017, 297). The weakness of the French Constitutional Court prompted Hönnige (2007, 25–26) to argue that Germany and France present a most different system designs. The French reform from 2010—aimed at allowing regular courts to refer cases to the constitutional court—has not significantly changed the institutional strength of the court. Regular courts cannot directly refer to the constitutional court, but only via the highest supreme courts (Art. 61 I French Constitution). Figure 3.2 appropriately reflects the weakness of France. A final cluster comprises countries scoring in the midrange of the indices on the two faces of judicial power (see Appendix C.1). Hungary (HUN)—a country long seen as having one of the strongest European courts (Engst 2017, 297; Scheppele 2003, 222–227)—is part of the midrange cluster. The Hungarian Constitutional Court shares all major features with the GFCC. Why is Hungary weaker compared to other countries in Fig. 3.2?

An advantage of the indices presented here is that they extend beyond the design of the judiciary. They include the legislative procedures that matter to judicial review and countries' general adherence to the rule of law. Figure 3.2 draws a more accurate picture of the power of constitutional courts, which are embedded in a political system and a society. Hungary is a good example of how external changes constrain a court. The country's latest legal reforms are criticized by the EU for shielding "legislation from constitutional control" (Grabenwarter et al. 2013, 19), which undermines the separation of powers. Moreover, with the closing provisions of the new Hungarian Constitution, the case law developed by the constitutional court was repealed in 2012. This limits the judges' ability to constantly develop the constitutional law and leads to legal uncertainty (Grabenwarter et al. 2013, 20–23). In other words, being a strong constitutional court by design, the reform of 2012 negatively affected the Hungarian rule of law (10 in Table 3.2). This constrains the judges' ability to exercise power. Figure 3.2 accounts for this. Overall, the comparison with former studies (Kneip 2008; Engst 2017) and recent developments illustrates that the figure summarizes the preconditions of the power of constitutional courts across the EU appropriately.[24]

In sum, the preconditions of judicial power in Germany are strong and typical, whereby they are representative of the power in half of the countries with constitutional courts in the EU. Moreover, Germany is part of a group of nine out of 13 countries in which constitutional courts use directives. In addition, Germany's constitutional court is—like the Austrian court—an archetypal case. Countries that establish those courts have a civil law tradition, in contrast to the Anglo-American common law tradition (Stone Sweet 2000, 32–34). A comparison across the legal systems of 98 democracies shows that about 55% of the countries follow the civil law tradition.[25] Hence, understanding the use of judicial power in Germany—a civil law country—holds implications for a number of countries. Finally, Table 3.2 highlights an additional advantage of Germany, which uses two competing legislative procedures. This is not included in Fig. 3.2 but controlling for these procedures in later analyses, the findings on Germany are representative of countries where second chambers have either a suspensory veto power or an absolute veto power. For all of these reasons, Germany is an appropriate case to assess the two faces of judicial power and test the considerations from Chapter 2. The reader is encouraged to refer back to Fig. 3.2 to consider later findings from a cross-European perspective. This chapter concludes with a case study to understand how the GFCC commonly exercises power.

3.3 The Power of the GFCC and the Parental Custody Reform

The case study traces the reform of the *Kindschaftsrecht* from 1998 through the policy process. I refer to the reform as the parental custody reform. The assessment of the reform puts the hypotheses from Chapter 2 to a plausibility check as the court had to decide on the law in 2003 (BVerfGE 107, 150).

Scholars often use specific examples to illustrate the interaction between the political branches and the judiciary (see Barreiro 1998; Landfried 1985; Stone Sweet 2000). Landfried (1985, 530–531) used the processes around the German codetermination law and the German law on conscientious objection to illustrate that the legislature anticipates the GFCC. She revisited her argument analyzing the German party finance law and the German law on abortion (Landfried 1992, 53–56; 1994, 116–119; similar Barreiro 1998 for Spain). Stone Sweet (2000, 66–87) assessed judicial law making in cross-European comparison, discussing prominent examples from France, Spain, Germany, and Italy. Moreover, there are studies tracing the development of the United States Supreme Court or the GFCC around the chief judges (Murphy 2014) or prominent decisions (Wesel 2004). However, the focus on highly salient decisions bears the risk of introducing a selection bias in the study of judicial power. Obvious cases can support arguments as examples, although they do not allow generalizing to a population. This is why I draw the decision on the parental custody reform fully at random from among all decisions by the GFCC that address federal laws proclaimed between 1990 to 2010. This makes the decision representative of 20% of all 795 decisions published between 1990 to 2010.[26] Figure 3.3 summarizes a timeline of the parental custody reform. Events from the interaction between the political branches and the GFCC (lower panel) are separated from developments in the environment (upper panel).

The government proposed the reform at the beginning of 1996, pursuing four major aims: first, strengthening the rights of children; second, reducing the influence of the state on families; third, reducing the legal differences between children of married and unmarried couples; and fourth, simplifying the existing parental provisions (BT 13/4899, 29).[27]

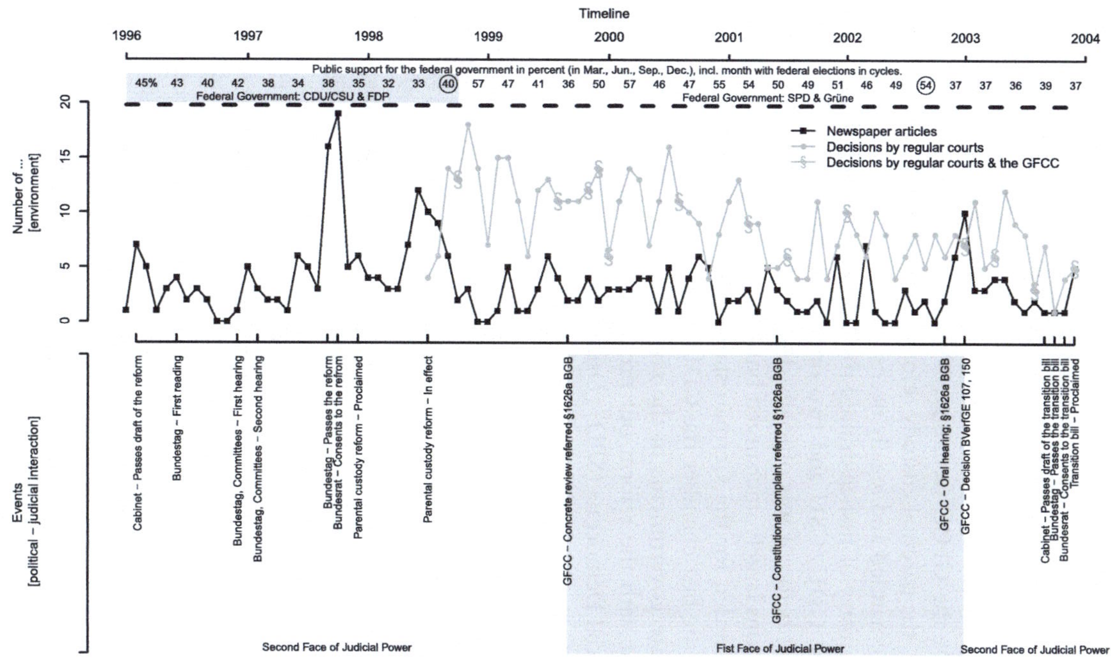

Fig. 3.3 The GFCC exercising power on the parental custody reform. Note: Own illustration, with information from the German legal database *Juris*, the news database *Lexis*, the *F.A.Z.-Bibliotheksportal*, the *Süddeutsche Zeitungs Archiv*, the *Zeit Online Archiv*, the CCDB, the *Politbarometer*, and official documents published by the GFCC and the German *Bundestag* and *Bundesrat*

The reform was important to the governing coalition between the Christian Democrats (CDU/CSU) and the Liberal Democrats (FDP). They explicitly mentioned it in the coalition agreement.[28] In addition, letters published in major newspapers highlighted the public's demand for new regulations.[29] Finally, the GFCC decided in 1991 that existing custody provisions limited the rights of fathers of children born outside of marriage in unconstitutional ways (BVerfGE 84, 168). This was not the only decision by the GFCC (see, e.g., BVerfGE 61, 358; BVerfGE 79, 256). Therefore, the parental custody reform was important to the government, publicly demanded and legally necessary.

The Ministry of Justice drafted the reform, although the legislative faction of the CDU/CSU and two opposition parties criticized provisions of the draft before it was officially discussed (SZ 1995). The ministry left the provisions largely unchanged but added minor revisions to reduce the financial burden for the German states (Dribbusch 1996). As governing parties in the first chamber the CDU/CSU and the FDP had to account for the state governments in the second chamber, which eventually had to consent with the reform but predominantly comprised coalitions led by the Social Democrats (SPD) (Dribbusch 1996). Besides those political considerations, the government argued that the draft addressed the concerns previously raised by the GFCC. The reform proposed a total of 162 changes to 25 laws (BT 13/4899). The Ministry of Justice closely considered the requirements specified by the GFCC. The explanation to the reform cites twelve different decisions by the court and it was often made explicit how the draft addressed the decisions (BT 13/4899, 72–73, 76, 78, 112, 139). The GFCC's past decision-making had a major influence on the executive process and the government accounted for the court's second face of judicial power (compare Hypothesis H4).

It took the *Bundestag* a year to pass the reform. The Judiciary Committee—as the leading committee—and the Committee on Family Affairs held two hearings with lawyers, judges, and youth service organizations (BT 13/8511, 63; SZ 1997). The final report highlights that the committee members introduced changes to the bill considering the GFCC's decision-making (see BT 13/8511, 64–66, 69–72, 80). For example, in response to the court's decision from 1991, the government added §1626a BGB to the bill, which allowed unmarried parents to share parental custody if they jointly agreed. The committee debated whether joint parental custody is advisable under certain conditions, as well as being against the will of a parent. The majority concluded that the respective provision would harm children forced into joint custody, as the parents might constantly be in conflict. Nevertheless, the committee modified the bill to ensure that child protective services would inform unmarried parents about the option of joint custody. Accordingly, parents would not fail to agree to joint parental custody out of ignorance (BT 13/8511, 65–66). This was not the only change that the committee introduced in reference to former decisions by the GFCC (see BT 13/8511, 64, 69–72, 80). Overall, the report repeatedly mentioned five different decisions by the GFCC but explicitly referred to the Basic Law only once. The committee accounted for the court interpreting the constitution, instead of focusing on the constitution per se. The legislators were eager to align the reform with the GFCC's past decision-making (compare Hypothesis H4).

The governing majority also bargained with the SPD—which proposed amendments to the reform (BT 13/1752)—to ensure the bill's passage in the second chamber. The parties reached an agreement (von Münch 1997; Dribbusch 1997) and the bill passed both legislative chambers with votes from the SPD (BT 13/192, 17366; BR 717, 460). While the reform was an important project for the government, the passage did not change the government's decline in public support. The percentages above the dashed line in Fig. 3.3 summarize this support.[30] Throughout the whole process, the government no longer had an electoral majority and after the federal election at the end of 1998 (highlighted by the cycle around the public's support) a new coalition was formed between the SPD and the Green Party.

The parental custody reform became part of the public discourse. The black line in the upper panel of Fig. 3.3 illustrates the aggregated monthly count of German newspaper articles including the term *Kindschaftsrecht*.[31] The reform was mentioned the most in the month when the bill was passed and when the law became proclaimed. With the end of the legislative process, the number of articles decreased, although there are only a few months without any article. The articles help to understand the societal impact of the reform. Published announcements show that communities and parental organizations planned events to inform the public about the reform[32] and other articles reviewed books on parental custody or highlighted expert conferences on the reform.[33] Moreover, the number of children living in conditions that the reform addressed increased: while in 1996 about 17% of newborns were raised by unmarried couples this number had increased to about 23% by 2000 and reached about 28% by 2004.[34] The divorce rate also increased, from about 40% in 1995 to about 46% in 2000, before reaching a tipping point in 2005 at about 52%.[35] These developments illustrate the societal dimension and importance of the reform.

§1626a BGB on the regulation of parental custody among unmarried couples was referred to the GFCC by a regular court in September 1999 (1 BvL 20/99) and by a father whose child was born outside of marriage in 2001 (1 BvR 933/01). Both referrals asked whether it was in accordance with Art. 6 II and V Basic Law that the father of a child born outside of marriage can only exercise custody with the mother if both agreed jointly or married one another (BVerfGE 107, 150 [152]).[36] In the referred cases, the fathers had separated from the mothers who hold custody alone (see §1626a II BGB) although both fathers had established strong ties to their children. The time between the first referral and the judicial decision is the period when the GFCC shows the first face of judicial power (see Fig. 3.3).

The court conducted a hearing that the Ministry of Justice used to emphasize the constitutionality of §1626a BGB. The ministry followed the arguments presented during the legislative process, stating that joint parental custody forced on unmarried parents can lead to conflict among them, which comes as a disadvantage to the child (BVerfGE 107, 150 [162]). The six parental organizations and research institutes that were heard mostly argued in favor of a slight correction of §1626a BGB, to strengthen the rights of fathers, although possible changes could not disadvantage the mothers' initial rights to hold custody alone (BVerfGE 107, 150 [162–167]). The GFCC increased the visibility of its decision-making by conducting a hearing and publishing a press release to invite to this hearing. Moreover, the court emphasized the societal dimension of its decision, holding the hearing on a day when the court was open to the public (GFCC PR 92/2002).

The decision by the GFCC came as a partial success to the government and the fathers. The court argued that a joint agreement to share the custody among unmarried parents is in accordance with the constitution. The right to file for joint custody is one of healthy relationships, where shared custody comes as an advantage to the child and only to a lesser extent a right of couples once they have separated (BVerfGE 107, 150 [177–180]). However, the reform did not account for fathers who separated from their partners before the new law was proclaimed. These fathers were violated in their constitutional right derived from Art. 6 II Basic Law as they had no opportunity to declare joint parental custody while they lived in a healthy relationship (BVerfGE 107, 150 [180]). This is why the court requested that the governing majority designs temporary provisions that would allow those fathers to refer to regular courts, which could then assess on an individual basis whether joint custody is in the interest of their child. The GFCC set a deadline for these changes until the end of 2003 (BVerfGE 107, 150 [185–186]).

Why did the court agree with the reform in general but justified the referrals presenting a directive? The judiciary and the political branches shared a common perspective on the new reform. The GFCC explicitly valued the government's reasoning on joint parental custody among unmarried couples (BVerfGE 107, 150 [173–178]) and the political branches had addressed the court's decision from 1991 (BVerfGE 84, 168). Therefore, the positions of the court and government aligned. This is why it was rational for the court to agree with the reform in general. Nevertheless, the GFCC also saw that a group of fathers was excluded from the reform and justified the respective referrals.

The decision about the reform allowed the GFCC to have an impact on society and the legal community. The media's attention highlighted the societal dimension of the reform. In addition, the *Kindschaftsrecht* (parental custody law) and/or the *Kindschaftsrechtsreform* (parental custody reform) were frequently mentioned by regular courts. The gray line in Fig. 3.3 summarizes the monthly number of decisions by courts that mention either or both of the keywords. There is a slight downward trend in the cases over the years, although sharp monthly variation occurs. The §-Symbol highlights months with at least one decision by the GFCC. The court alone made twelve chamber decisions and five senate decisions since the law's proclamation (including BVerfGE 107, 150). Overall, regular courts made 563 decisions and 275 scholarly contributions (not shown) referenced the reform over the period shown in Fig. 3.3.[37] This is why the GFCC could leave an imprint on the legal community and society in making the decision. From this perspective, an evasion of this decision would have been particularly costly. Therefore, it was rational for the court to draw maximum attention to its decision by presenting a directive (compare Hypothesis H1c). Indeed, in the five senate decisions made between the proclamation of the custody reform and the end of 2004, the court chose to present a directive in three decisions.

The judicial directive did not place the government under strong pressure. The court did not invalidate the major reform but only requested a transition bill to include a defined group of fathers in a rather young reform. Moreover, despite the fact that the government's popularity was only at about 37% around the month when the court made the decision, the electoral consequences of the decision were minimal. The governing parties had just been reelected (see cycle in Fig. 3.3) and agreed on strengthening the welfare of families,[38] which is why the court's decision was an invitation to act in an area of some importance. Finally, the members of the governing parties in the legislature were cohesive in their voting behavior over the years prior to the decision. The average agreement on roll call votes was 0.98 (with 1 being the maximum, implying that all members voted cohesively) among the legislators of the SPD and 0.95 among the legislators of the Green Party between 1998 and 2002 (Bergmann et al. 2016, 32, 40). These open votes are at least a signal that the government could motivate the majority to vote cohesively. In sum, the costs for the government to legislate in response to the court's decision were low. This is why the GFCC's decision to present a directive is convincing, as the court could possibly expect an implementation of the decision (compare Hypothesis H1a).

The government presented a transition bill explicitly referencing the judicial decision in September 2003 and the Judiciary Committee unanimously suggested the adoption of that bill (BT 15/1807). All parties in the *Bundestag* voted in favor of the proposal (BT 15/69, 5931) and the *Bundesrat* consented to the bill (BR 794, 450). The transitional provisions were proclaimed in December 2003, closely matching the directive of the court. Fathers who left an unmarried relationship before July 1998 could request that regular family courts assess whether they are suitable to receive joint parental custody over their children.

This randomly drawn case illustrates a common way in which the GFCC exercises power. The example highlights the importance of external factors such as the legal perception of a topic or the public debate around it. The JPD game from Chapter 2 simplifies the interaction between the political branches and constitutional courts. The case study illustrates the complexity of the interaction and helps to identify variables of interest for the comprehensive analyses conducted in the following chapters.

3.4 Summary

This chapter has introduced the GFCC as a case suitable to analyze the two faces of judicial power. The German example illustrates that the design of the court, its embeddedness in the separation of powers framework and the environment surrounding the interaction between the court and the political branches influence the preconditions of judicial power. This is in line with the strategic model of judicial decision-making. Accordingly, the ability to engage in sincere judicial behavior is constrained or promoted by the developments surrounding courts (Parcelle Jr. et al. 2011, 42–43; Epstein and Knight 1998). The characteristics of the preconditions of judicial power vary in cross-European comparison and the GFCC is situated in a setting strongly empowering the court. However, the GFCC is not an outlier but rather a typical case, representative of a number of constitutional courts. Therefore, the findings of the empirical assessments from the following chapters are also generalizable to other countries.

The events surrounding the decision on the parental custody reform provide a first empirical understanding of the JPD game. Indeed, the political branches and the GFCC engage in a strategic dialogue, despite the fact that each player acts distinctly. Among the three definitions of the term "dialogue" cited by the Webster Dictionary, one states that a dialogue is "an exchange of ideas and opinions."[39] The government presents the custody reform, paying attention to the court's opinions summarized in past decisions. The government's ideas were updated and the bill was passed by the legislative majority, including evaluating judicial implications. The court eventually reviewed the new policy, presenting an additional opinion to the reform. The dialogue concluded with the adaptation of the judicial directive to ensure an appropriate implementation of the policy.

Finally, the course of the dialogue is influenced by a variety of factors that drive the costs of the interaction. The case study has helped to identify such factors and make latent costs—referred to in the hypotheses—measurable. Variables of interest include—for example—the government's electoral support or the societal and legal impact of a decision. The next step is to extend the preliminary test of the JPD game to a larger scale. The insights gained in this chapter provide a foundation for the following empirical analyses of the dynamics in judicial–political bargaining.

Notes

1. The appropriate translation of the *Bundesrat* is debated. I adopt the wording from Fortunato et al. (2013, 940) and the GFCC (BVerfGE 123, 267 [375]) who refer to the *Bundesrat* as a second chamber.
2. Between 1990 and 2010 about 48% of all bills were objection bills (N = 1234). The second chamber only raised an objection in about 4% of those bills. All remaining bills were consent bills passed by both chambers (estimated using Feldkamp 2011, Ch. 10.1, pp. 10–11).

3. Court decisions are cited using the official citation style BVerfGE VOLUME, FIRST PAGE [CITED PAGES].
4. Borowski (2003) and Niclauß (2015) present historical accounts on the development of the GFCC.
5. Laws are cited via the article or paragraph number and the subparagraph as a roman numeral.
6. The procedure has changed in 2015; see *Neuntes Gesetz zur Änderung des Bundesverfassungsgerichtsgesetzes* in Federal Law Gazette 2015 Part I No. 24. In the past, the legislative–judicial selection committee had elected the candidates with a two-thirds majority.
7. Wittig (2016, 111) identifies only 215 separate opinions made between 1972 to 2010, of which one-quarter are concurring opinions.
8. Following the legal citation style the sections cited refer to the book's margin numbers.
9. Official statistics by the GFCC: https://www.bundesverfassungsgericht.de/SharedDocs/Downloads/EN/Statistik/statistics_2018.pdf?__blob=publicationFile\&v=4, accessed January 12, 2020.
10. In order to identify the most common proceedings, the referrals of federal-state disputes (BvG) and intrastate constitutional disputes (BvH) were counted jointly. Both proceedings are similar in nature (see Art. 93 I No. 3 and 4 Basic Law) and the GFCC considers the latter an "exceptional case" of the former, https://www.bundesverfassungsgericht.de/EN/Verfahren/Wichtige-Verfahrensarten/Bund-Laender-Streit/bund-laender-streit_node.html, accessed January 12, 2020.
11. The years cover Germany's 12th to 16th legislative periods. The reasons for focusing on these periods are discussed in Chapter 4.
12. GFCC: https://www.bundesverfassungsgericht.de/EN/Verfahren/Wichtige-Verfahrensarten/Organstreitverfahren/organstreitverfahren_node.html, accessed January 12, 2020.
13. Both legislative chambers are also able to present bills, although they rarely do so. The second chamber presented only 5% of the successful bills between the 12th and 16th legislative period, and the first chamber about 17%. The latter bills were predominantly presented by the parties of the federal government (about 79%). These bills are often written by the government and presented using its own legislative majority to shorten the policy process (Veit 2010, 43). The remaining bills (5%) were joint proposals (own estimations using Feldkamp 2011, Ch. 10.1).
14. The GGO (*Gemeinsame Geschäftsordnung der Bundesministerien*) specifies the procedural rules among ministries: https://www.bmi.bund.de/SharedDocs/downloads/EN/themen/moderne-verwaltung/ggo_en.pdf;jsessionid=498B1C4A0BA83EC68911FD0F2A7FDEC9.1_cid287?__blob=publicationFile&v=1, accessed January 12, 2020.

15. The GOBReg (*Geschäftsordnung der Bundesregierung*) specifies the procedural rules of the cabinet: https://www.bundesregierung.de/Content/DE/StatischeSeiten/Breg/regierung-und-verfassung-geschaeftsordnung-der-bundesregierung.html, accessed January 12, 2020.
16. The documents are available online: https://www.bundestag.de/analysen, accessed January 12, 2020.
17. Conflict between the chambers rarely occurs. The second chamber raised an objection in 4% of all objections bills between the 12th and 16th legislative period and the first chamber rejected 90% of those objections. Moreover, the second chamber did not consent to 6% of all consent bills. The conciliation committee was only involved in about 14% of all 2648 bills considered between the 12th and 16th legislative period and in 87% of such cases the conciliation was successful (estimated using Feldkamp 2011, Ch. 10.1).
18. Malta is excluded, as research with various sources failed to extract the necessary information.
19. Hungarian parliament: http://www.parlament.hu/documents/125505/126210/The+legislative+process++(block+diagram)/695a4da8-0dca-4675-aeee-64cc33fefd99, accessed January 12, 2020.
20. Countries where committee reports have the effect that the "House considers [the] original government bill with amendments added" or where "Committees may present substitute texts which are considered against the original text" (Mattson and Strøm 1995, Table 8.4) are coded as 2.
21. Adopted from Freedom House (2017), comprising expert ratings in the range from 0 to 4 on four statements: "(1) Is there an independent judiciary?; (2) Does due process prevail in civil and criminal matters?; (3) Is there protection from the illegitimate use of physical force and freedom from war and insurgencies?; (4) Do laws, policies, and practices guarantee equal treatment of various segments of the population?"
22. I assign each checkmark a 1 and each cross a 0 in Table 3.2. Empty cells are treated conservatively and are coded 0 as nonexistent. Scores with values beyond 1 (the committees' influence and the rule of law) are rescaled to values between 0 and 1, dividing the respective individual scores by the respective scale's maximum. In sum, the index of the first face of judicial power is calculated as *Rule of Law* × *(Const. complaint* + *Concrete rev.* + *Abstract rev.* + *Nullify laws* + *Directives)* and the index of the second face of judicial power is calculated as *Rule of Law* × *(Const. complaint* + *Concrete rev.* + *Nullify laws* + *Influence* + *Hearing)*.
23. Croatia and Slovakia are marked with an asterisk to indicate that no reliable information on directives is available. They are coded conservatively as countries that do not use directives.
24. Appendix C.2 further confirms the robustness of Fig. 3.2 using alternative measures for the rule of law, which is the most latent concept in Table 3.2.

25. Own estimation based on the legal systems listed in the CIA World Factbook (2017). Countries are counted as democratic if they were assigned this status in two out of the following three studies between the years 2000 and 2010: Freedom House (2017), Polity IV—Marshall et al. (2014), and Dichotomous Coding of Democracy, Version 2.0—Boix et al. (2013).
26. The remaining decisions address state laws, laws proclaimed before 1990, acts by public authorities, rulings by regular courts, and a few special acts, such as electoral reviews.
27. Documents from the legislative process are cited using the official citation style BUNDESTAG or BUNDESRAT LEGISLATIVE PERIOD/DOCUMENT NO., PAGES.
28. Coalition agreement of the 13th legislative period, p. 43: http://www.kas.de/upload/ACDP/CDU/Koalitionsvertraege/Koalitionsvertrag1994.pdf, accessed January 12, 2020.
29. "Plädoyer für beide Eltern." Süddeutsche Zeitung (SZ), January 13, 1995, p. 11. "Kinder als Faustpfand in der Hand der Mütter." SZ, January 14, 1995, p. 907. "Eine Schande für den Rechtsstaat." SZ, January 28, 1995, p. 907. 17 letters addressing a cover story by the magazine *Focus*, February 15, 1995, pp. 240–241. "Väter." Die Tageszeitung (taz), December 22, 1994, p. 14. "Ebenso rührend wie selten." taz, February 29, 1994, p. 14.
30. The support is measured as the monthly average of the weekly electoral choice by the public if a hypothetical federal election were held in a given week (estimated using Politbarometer 2013).
31. The count is based on articles published by major quality press newspapers such as *Die Welt*, *Süddeutsche Zeitung*, *Frankfurter Allgemeine Zeitung*, *Die Tageszeitung*, and *Die Zeit*, tabloids like the *Kölner Express* and magazines like *Bunte* and *Focus*.
32. "Infoabend für werdende Eltern." taz, August 19, 1999, p. 22. "Prenzlauer Berg: Beratung." Berliner Zeitung, January 22, 2000, p. 18. "Die Reform des Kindschaftsrechts." Stuttgarter Zeitung, October 30, 2003, p. 29.
33. "BuchTipps." taz, November 15, 1999, p. 18. "zum lesen empfohlen." taz, March 9, 2002, p. 25. "Als Paar getrennt, als Eltern verantwortlich." General-Anzeiger, June 5, 2003. Even tabloids: "Kindschaftsrecht-Tagung." Kölner Express, September 13, 2000, p. 27.
34. Statistisches Bundesamt. 2018. Anteil der nichtehelich geborenen Kinder an allen Lebendgeborenen in Deutschland von 1970 bis 2015. Statista. https://de.statista.com/statistik/daten/studie/1324/umfrage/uneheliche-kinder-anteil-an-allen-geburten/, accessed January 12, 2020.
35. Statistisches Bundesamt. 2018. Scheidungsquote in Deutschland von 1960 bis 2016. Statista. https://de.statista.com/statistik/daten/studie/76211/umfrage/scheidungsquote-von-1960-bis-2008/, accessed January 12, 2020.
36. *Art. 6 II Basic Law*: "The care and upbringing of children is the natural right of parents and a duty primarily incumbent upon them. The state shall

watch over them in the performance of this duty." *Art. 6 V Basic Law*: "Children born outside of marriage shall be provided by legislation with the same opportunities for physical and mental development and for their position in society as are enjoyed by those born within marriage."

37. All counts are obtained from a search of the judicature and the scholarly references in the German legal database *Juris*: https://www.juris.de, accessed March 11, 2018.
38. Coalition agreement of the 15th legislative period, pp. 29–33: https://www.spd.de/fileadmin/Dokumente/Beschluesse/Bundesparteitag/koalitionsvertrag_bundesparteitag_berlin_2002.pdf, accessed January 12, 2020.
39. Merriam-Webster Dictionary. 2020. "Dialogue": https://www.merriam-webster.com/dictionary/dialogue, accessed January 12, 2020.

References

Barreiro, B. (1998). Judicial Review and Political Empowerment: Abortion in Spain. *West European Politics, 21*(4), 147–162.

Barrett, R., Bazy Malaurie, C., Clayton, R., Dimitrov, P., Grabenwarter, C. (2017). Poland. Opinion on the Draft Act Amending the Act on the National Council of the Judiciary, on the Draft Act Amending the Act on the Supreme Court, Proposed by the President of Poland, and the Act on The Organisation of Ordinary Courts. *Venice Commission [European Commission for Democracy Through Law], 2017*(904), 1–27.

Bergmann, H., Bailer, S., Ohmura, T., Saalfeld, T., Sieberer, U. (2016). Namentliche Abstimmungen im Bundestag 1949 bis 2013: Befunde aus einem neuen Datensatz. *Zeitschrift für Parlamentsfragen, 47*(1), 26–50.

Boix, C., Miller, M.K., Rosato, S. (2013). A Complete Data Set of Political Regimes, 1800–2007. *Comparative Political Studies, 46*(12), 1523–1554.

Borowski, M. (2003). The Beginnings of Germany's Federal Constitutional Court. *Ratio Juris, 16*(2), 155–186.

Brouard, S. (2009). The Politics of Constitutional Veto in France: Constitutional Council, Legislative Majority and Electoral Competition. *West European Politics, 32*(2), 384–403.

Brouard, S., Hönnige, C. (2017). Constitutional Courts as Veto Players: Lessons from the United States, France and Germany. *European Journal of Political Research, 56*(3), 529–552.

Brunn, B. (2004). Möglichkeiten einer Rechtsförmlichkeitsprüfung im parlamentarischen Verfahren. *Zeitschrift für Rechtspolitik, 37*(3), 79–81.

Central Intelligence Agency [CIA]. (2017). *The World Factbook*. Washington, DC: Central Intelligence Agency. https://www.cia.gov/library/publications/the-world-factbook/ (accessed February 21, 2018).

Drexhage, B. (2015). *Bicameral Legislatures. An International Comparison*. The Hague: Ministry of the Interior and Kingdom Relations.
Dribbusch, B. (1996). Gegen Vaters Willen. *taz, die Tageszeitung*, March 8, 1996, 5.
Dribbusch, B. (1997). Heute verabschieded der Bundestag das neue Kindschafzsrecht. *taz, die Tageszeitung*, September 28, 1997, 3.
Dyevre, A. (2010). Unifying the Field of Comparative Judicial Politics: Towards a General Theory of Judicial Behaviour. *European Political Science Review*, *2*(2), 297–327.
Dyevre, A. (2011). The German Federal Constitutional Court and European Judicial Politics. *West European Politics*, *34*(2), 346–361.
Easton, D. (1957). An Approach to the Analysis of Political Systems. *World Politics*, *9*(3), 383–400.
Engst, B.G. (2017). Die vierte Gesetzeslesung. Verfassungsgerichte des deutsch-österreichischen Modells als Vetospieler. In V. Frick, O. W. Lembcke, and R. Lhotta (Eds.) *Politik und Recht. Umrisse eines politkwissenschaftlichen Forschungsfeldes* (pp. 281–301). Baden-Baden: Nomos.
Engst, B.G., Gschwend, T., Schaks, N., Sternberg, S., Wittig, C. (2017). Zum Einfluss der Parteinähe auf das Abstimmungsverhalten der Bundesverfassungsrichter – eine quantitative Untersuchung. *Juristen Zeitung*, *72*(17), 816–826.
Engst, B.G., Gschwend, T., Sternberg, S. (2020). Die Besetzung des Bundesverfassungsgerichts. Ein Spiegelbild gesellschaftlicher Präferenzen? *Politische Vierteljahresschrift*, *61*(1), 39–60.
Epstein, L., Knight, J. (1998). *The Choices Justices Make*. Washington, DC: CQ Press.
Epstein, L., Knight, J., Shvetsova, O. (2001). The Role of Constitutional Courts in the Establishment and Maintenance of Democratic Systems of Government. *Law and Society Review*, *35*(1), 117–164.
Feldkamp, M.F. (2011). *Datenhanbuch zur Geschichte des Deutschen Bundestages 1990 bis 2010. Ergänzungsband*. Baden-Baden: Nomos.
Fortunato, D., König, T., Proksch, S.-O. (2013). Government Agenda-Setting and Bicameral Conflict Resolution. *Political Research Quarterly*, *66*(4), 938–951.
Freedom House. (2017). *Freedom in the World*. https://freedomhouse.org (accessed February 21, 2018).
Gawron, T. (2013). Das ferne Gericht. Wirkungsanalysen zum Verhältnis zwischen Bundersverfassungsgericht und Verwaltungsbehörden. In C. Boulanger, and M. Wrase (Eds.) *Die Politik des Verfassungsrechts. Interdisziplinäre und vergleichende Perspektiven auf die Rolle und Funktion von Verfassungsgerichten* (pp. 217–240). Baden-Baden: Nomos.
Gawron, T., Rogowski, R. (2002). The Implementation of German Federal Constitutional Court Decisions: Judicial Orders and the Federal Legislature. In

R. Rogowski, and T. Gawron (Eds.) *Constitutional Courts in Comparison: The U.S. Supreme Court and the German Federal Constitutional Court* (pp. 239–256). New York: Berghahn Books.

Gawron, T., Rogowski, R. (2015). Die Wirkung des Bundesverfassungsgerichts. In R. C. van Ooyen, and M. H. W. Möllers (Eds.) *Handbuch Bundesverfassungsgericht im politischen System* (pp. 153–168). Wiesbaden: Springer Fachmedien Wiesbaden, 2nd ed.

Gerring, J. (2004). What Is a Case Study and What Is It Good for? *American Political Science Review*, *98*(2), 341–354.

Gibson, J.L. (2007). The Legitimacy of the U.S. Supreme Court in a Polarized Polity. *Journal of Empirical Legal Studies*, *4*(3), 507–538.

Gibson, J.L., Caldeira, G.A., Baird, V.A. (1998). On the Legitimacy of National High Courts. *American Political Science Review*, *92*(2), 343–358.

Grabenwarter, C., Hoffmann-Riem, W., Suchocka, H., Tuori, K., Velares, J. (2013). Opinion on the Fourth Amendment of the Fundamental Law of Hungary. *Venice Commission [European Commission for Democracy through Law]*, *2013*(720), 1–32.

Hanretty, C. (2013). The Decisions and Ideal Points of British Law Lords. *British Journal of Political Science*, *43*(3), 703–716.

Hanretty, C. (2014). The Bulgarian Constitutional Court as an Additional Legislative Chamber. *East European Politics and Societies*, *28*(3), 540–558.

Hecker, W. (2006). Die Entscheidung des Bundesverfassungsgerichts zum Luftsicherheitsgesetz. *Kritische Justiz*, *39*(2), 179–194.

Hönnige, C. (2007). *Verfassungsgericht, Regierung und Opposition. Die vergleichende Analyse eines Spannungsdreiecks.* Wiesbaden: VS Verlag für Sozialwissenschaften.

Hönnige, C. (2008). Verfassungsgerichte in den EU-Staaten: Wahlverfahren, Kompetenzen und Organisationsprinzipien. *Journal for Comparative Government and European Policy*, *6*(3), 524–553.

Hönnige, C. (2009). The Electoral Connection: How the Pivotal Judge Affects Oppositional Success at European Constitutional Courts. *West European Politics*, *32*(5), 963–984.

Hönnige, C., Gschwend, T., Wittig, C., Engst, B.G. (2015). *Constitutional Court Database (CCDB), V17.01 [Mar.].*

Huntington, S.P. (1991). *The Third Wave: Democratization in the Late Twentieth Century.* Norman: Oklahoma UP.

Ismayr, W. (2006). *Der Deutsche Bundestag im Politischen System der Bundesrepublik Deutschland.* Wiesbaden: VS Verlag für Sozialwissenschaften, 2nd ed.

Kelemen, K. (2013). Dissenting Opinions in Constitutional Courts. *German Law Journal*, *14*(8), 1345–1371.

Kelsen, H. (1942). Judicial Review of Legislation: A Comparative Study of the Austrian and the American Constitution. *Journal of Politics*, *4*(2), 183–200.

Kelsen, H. (2008). [1931]. Wer soll der Hüter der Verfassung sein? In R. C. van Ooyen (Ed.) *Wer soll der Hüter der Verfassung sein?Abhandlungen zur Theorie der Verfassungsgerichtsbarkeit in der pluralistischen, parlamentarischen Demokratie* (pp. 58–105). Tübingen: Mohr Siebeck.

Kneip, S. (2007). Starke und schwache Verfassungsgerichte: Gibt es eine optimale Verfassungsgerichtsbarkeit für die Demokratie? In S. Kropp, and H.-J. Lauth (Eds.) *Gewaltenteilung und Demokratie. Konzepte und Probleme der "horizontal accountability" im internationalen Vergleich* (pp. 91–109). Baden-Baden: Nomos.

Kneip, S. (2008). Verfassungsgerichtsbarkeit im Vergleich. In O. W. Gabriel, and S. Kropp (Eds.) *Die EU-Staaten im Vergleich: Strukturen, Prozesse, Politikinhalte* (pp. 631–655). Wiesbaden: VS Verlag für Sozialwissenschaften.

Kommers, D.P., Miller, R.A. (2012). *The Constitutional Jurisprudence of the Federal Republic of Germany*. Durham: Duke University Press, 3rd ed.

König, T. (2001). Bicameralism and Party Politics in Germany: An Empirical Social Choice Analysis. *Political Studies*, *49*(3), 411–437.

Kranenpohl, U. (2010). *Hinter dem Schleier des Beratungsgeheimnisses. Der Willensbildungs- und Entscheidungsprozess des Bundesverfassungsgerichts*. Wiesbaden: VS Verlag für Sozialwissenschaften.

Krehbiel, J.N. (2016). The Politics of Judicial Procedures: The Role of Public Oral Hearings in the German Constitutional Court. *American Journal of Political Science*, *60*(4), 990–1005.

Landfried, C. (1985). The Impact of the German Federal Constitutional Court on Politics and Policy Output. *Government and Opposition*, *20*(4), 522–542.

Landfried, C. (1992). Judicial Policy-Making in Germany: The Federal Constitutional Court. *West European Politics*, *15*(3), 50–67.

Landfried, C. (1994). The Judicialization of Politics in Germany. *International Political Science Review*, *15*(2), 113–124.

Leuffen, D. (2007). Case Selection and Selection Bias in Small-n Research. In T. Gschwend, and F. Schimmelfennig (Eds.) *Research Design in Political Science: How to Practice What They Preach* (pp. 145–160). Houndmills: Palgrave Macmillan.

Lijphart, A. (2012). *Patterns of Democracy: Government Forms and Performance in Thirty-Six Countries*. New Haven and London: Yale University Press, 2nd ed.

Linzer, D.A., Staton, J.K. (2015). A Global Measure of Judicial Independence, 1948–2012. *Journal of Law and Courts*, *3*(2), 223–256.

Luchterhandt, O., Starck, C., Weber, A. (Eds.). (2007). *Verfassungsgerichtsbarkeit in Mittel- und Osteuropa. Teilband I: Berichte*. Baden-Baden: Nomos.

Manow, P., Burkhart, S. (2007). Legislative Self-Restraint Under Divided Government in Germany, 1976–2002. *Legislative Studies Quarterly*, *32*(2), 167–191.

Marshall, M.G., Gurr, T.R., Jaggers, K. (2014). *Polity IV Project: Political Regime Characteristics and Transitions, 1800–2013*. Vienna, VA: Center for Systemic Peace.

Mattson, I., Strøm, K. (1995). Parliamentary Committees. In H. Döring (Ed.) *Parliaments and Majority Rule in Western Europe* (pp. 249–307). Frankfurt: Campus Verlag.

Murphy, W.F. (2014). *Congress and the Court: A Case Study in the American Political Process*. New Orleans: Quid Pro Books.

Nettesheim, M. (2003). III. Der Bundespräsident. In J. Isensee, and P. Kirchhof (Eds.) *Hanbuch des Staatsrechts der Bundesrepublik Deutschland. Band III* (pp. 1005–1113). Heidelberg: C.F. Müller, 3rd ed.

Niclauß, K. (2015). Der Parlamentarische Rat und das Bundesverfassungsgericht. In R. C. van Ooyen, and M. H. W. Möllers (Eds.) *Handbuch Bundesverfassungsgericht im politischen System* (pp. 191–204). Wiesbaden: Springer Fachmedien Wiesbaden, 2nd ed.

Palm, U. (2007). Der wehrlose Staat? Der Einsatz der Streitkräfte im Innern nach der Entscheidung des Bundesverfassungsgerichts zum Luftsicherheitsgesetz. *Archiv des öffentlichen Rechts*, *132*(1), 95–113.

Parcelle Jr., R.L., Curry, B.W., Marshall, B.W. (2011). *Decision Making by the Modern Supreme Court*. Cambridge: Cambridge University Press.

Politbarometer (2013). Partielle Kumulation (1977–2011). *GESIS Datenarchiv, ZA2391* (Version 3.0.0), Köln.

Raffaelli, R. (2012). *Dissenting Opinions in the Supreme Courts of the Member States*. European Parliament: Directorate General for Internal Policies (PE 462.470). https://www.europarl.europa.eu/document/activities/cont/201304/20130423ATT64963/20130423ATT64963EN.pdf (accessed February 21, 2018).

Rios-Figueroa, J., Staton, J.K. (2014). An Evaluation of Cross-National Measures of Judicial Independence. *Journal of Law, Economics, and Organization*, *30*(1), 104–137.

Russell, M., Morris, B., Larkin, P. (2013). *Fitting the Bill: Brining Commons Legislation Committees into Line With Best Practice*. London: University College London—The Constitution Unit.

Rütters, P. (2011). Worüber wir reden, wenn wir über den Bundespräsidenten reden. Oder: ... auf dem Weg zur Präsidentialisierung des Regierungssystems? *Zeitschrift für Parlamentsfragen*, *42*(4), 863–885.

Sachs, M., Nierhaus, M., Mann, T. (2018). Art. 82 [Ausfertigung, Verkündung und Inkrafttreten von Bundesrecht]. In M. Sachs (Ed.) *Grundgesetz. Kommentar* (p. Art. 82). München: C.H. Beck.

Scheppele, K.L. (2003). Constitutional Negotiations: Political Contexts of Judicial Activism in Post-Soviet Europe. *International Sociology*, *18*(1), 219–238.

Schlaich, K., Korioth, S. (2015). *Das Bundesverfassungsgericht. Stellung, Verfahren Entscheidungen*. München: C.H. Beck, 10th ed.
Singer, M. (1982). The Constitutional Court of the German Federal Republic: Jurisdiction over Individual Complaints. *International and Comparative Law Quarterly*, *31*(2), 331–356.
Starck, C., Weber, A. (Eds.). (2007). *Verfassungsgerichtsbarkeit in Westeuropa. Teilband I: Berichte*. Baden-Baden: Nomos, 2 ed.
Staton, J.K. (2010). *Judicial Power and Strategic Communication in Mexico*. Cambridge: Cambridge University Press.
Sternberg, S., Gschwend, T., Wittig, C., Engst, B.G. (2015). Zum Einfluss der öffentlichen Meinung auf Entscheidungen des Bundesverfassungsgerichts: Eine Analyse von abstrakten Normenkontrollen sowie Bund-Länder-Streitigkeiten 1974–2010. *Politische Vierteljahresschrift*, *56*(4), 570–598.
Stone Sweet, A. (2000). *Governing with Judges: Constitutional Politics in Europe*. Oxford: Oxford University Press.
Streng, F. (2011). Die Zukunft der Sicherungsverwahrung nach der Entscheidung des Bundesverfassungsgerichts: Zum Urteil des Zweiten Senats des BVerfG vom 4.5.2011. *Juristen Zeitung*, *17*(9), 827–835.
SZ. (1995). Kindschaftrecht muß warten. Kabinet verschiebt Beratungen / Grüne: Kinderrechte stärken. *Süddeutsche Zeitung*, December 14, 1995, 5.
SZ. (1997). Experten plädieren für gemeinsames Sorgerecht. *Süddeutsche Zeitung*, February 25, 1997, 2.
Vanberg, G. (1998). Abstract Judicial Review, Legislative Bargaining, and Policy Compromise. *Journal of Theoretical Politics*, *10*(3), 299–326.
Vanberg, G. (2005). *The Politics of Constitutional Review in Germany*. Cambridge: Cambridge University Press.
Veit, S. (2010). *Bessere Gesetze durch Folgenabschätzung? Deutschland und Schweden im Vergleich*. Wiesbaden: VS Verlag für Sozialwissenschaften.
Voigt, S., Gutmann, J., Feld, L.P. (2015). Economic Growth and Judicial Independence, a Dozen Years On: Cross-Country Evidence Using an Updated Set of Indicators. *European Journal of Political Economy*, *38*, 197–211.
von Münch, E.M. (1997). Ehelich oder unehelich - In der nächsten Woche wird die Reform des Kindschaftsrechts verabscheidet. *Die Zeit*, September 19, 1997, 1.
Wesel, U. (2004). *Der Gang nach Karlsruhe: Das Bundesverfassungsgericht in der Geschichte der Bundesrepublik*. München: Karl Blessing Verlag.
Wittig, C.E. (2016). *The Occurrence of Separate Opinions at the Federal Constitutional Court: An Analysis with a Novel Database*. Berlin: Logos Verlag Berlin GmbH.

CHAPTER 4

The First Face of Judicial Power

In this chapter, I assess judicial decision-making by the German Federal Constitutional Court (GFCC) to understand when judges make a specific judicial choice. The explicit choice characterizes the first face of judicial power. The theoretical assumption is that changes in the court's costs from an evasion of a decision and the government's costs to legislate influence the variation in judicial choices. The analyses extend studies on the GFCC by explicitly separating directives from the commonly assessed dichotomous judicial choices, namely to justify or not justify referrals (see e.g., Vanberg 2005, 2001; Hönnige 2009; Sternberg et al. 2015). In order to assess judicial choices, I estimate a number of multinomial logistic regressions. Robust findings show that the court uses directives in settings where the costs from an evasion are high but the government's costs of legislating are low. If the government faces high costs of legislating, then the court reduces the use of directives and often chooses not to justify referrals.

The findings suggest that the GFCC acts in a risk-averse manner, presenting decisions that require an implementation—justified referrals or directives—only in settings where the government is capable of legislating. This is evidence in favor of strategic judicial behavior (Epstein and Knight 1998) and judicial self-restraint in anticipation of the implementation of decisions (Hönnige and Gschwend 2010, 519–520). However, once the court faces high costs from an evasion, the use of directives increases. In line with the literature on public opinion, directives may be used to make decisions more easily accessible in an effort to enhance public support and

B. G. Engst, *The Two Faces of Judicial Power*,
https://doi.org/10.1007/978-3-030-46016-7_4

increase the pressure on political branches to implement decisions (see Vanberg 2001, 2005; Staton and Vanberg 2008; Staton 2010).

In the next sections, I first outline the period that the study encompasses. Afterwards, I operationalize the first face of judicial power and outline the strategy used to estimate changes in judicial choices when the government's and court's costs vary. Finally, I test the hypotheses on the first face of judicial power.

4.1 The Context of the Empirical Assessment

In all empirical sections, I focus on judicial–political interactions in Germany from December 2, 1990 (the 12th legislative period) to September 27, 2009 (the end of the 16th legislative period) (Feldkamp 2011, 11). This has a number of advantages.

First, after the fall of the Berlin Wall, the former Eastern German states joined the Federal Republic of Germany in October 1990. Hence, the formal transition following the reunification was completed. Moreover, the GFCC gained supervision of all 16 German states. No institutional changes of comparable size have occurred since 1990.

Second, the focus on 1990 to 2009 ensures alternation in the composition of the government. During the first fifteen years, one of the two major German parties—the Christian Democrats or the Social Democrats—formed coalitions with smaller parties. The Christian Democrats governed with the Liberal Party until 1998 and the Social Democrats formed a coalition with the Green Party until 2005. This implies that one major party was always in the legislative opposition. Therefore, intra-legislative party competition between a major governing party and a major opposition party was present. It is plausible to assume that the dynamics of the intra-legislative competition changed once both major parties formed a grand coalition in 2005 and only parties of a minor size remained in the opposition. Moreover, the two major parties need to reach a consensus to elect judges to serve on the GFCC. The parties informally agreed to take turns in nominating judges (Hönnige 2007, 171; Rudzio 2015, 300–301). This is why judges nominated by the two largest parties are in the majority when there is a grand coalition. If the judges feel loyal to the parties selecting them—as Hönnige's (2007) findings suggest—then the court's behavior may vary in the absence of a grand coalition compared to when such a coalition exists. The period assessed here ensures that the results are not driven by one particular composition of the government.

Third, the judges at the GFCC do not have life tenure, but can serve for one non-renewable term of twelve years, as long as they do not reach the age limit of 68 years (§4 I–III Act on the GFCC). Therefore, assessing a period of about 19 years ensures that there are alternations in the composition of the GFCC.

4.2 Operationalizing the First Face of Judicial Power

The first face of judicial power leads to an explicit judicial choice, whereby judicial decisions and their outcomes become the unit of analysis. In order to predict the probability of a certain judicial choice, it is necessary to link variables from the judicial sphere and the political sphere to decisions. Such a link is achieved using the *Constitutional Court Database* (CCDB; Hönnige et al. 2015).

The database combines multiple pieces of information in four different layers. The 2006 Senate decisions made by the GFCC between 1972 and 2010 are included in a primary layer.[1] Moreover, many legal concepts applied in decisions and collected in the CCDB are converted into variables that are meaningful to political scientists (Wittig 2016, Ch. 2). In addition, aspects from decisions that explicitly relate to political activities are linked to the political environment. In particular, referrals to the GFCC addressing a federal law are linked to the respective legislative process surrounding the passage of the law. Such information is collected in the GESTA dataset on the German federal legislature, originally compiled by Burkhart (2008) and extended by Stecker (2016). The decisions in the CCDB are linked to the dataset on an additional layer. Finally, the CCDB includes a layer with metadata, which has proven useful in judicial politics. The database includes, for example, the monthly rating of the political parties by the public (Politbarometer 2013). In sum, the multiple layers of the relational CCDB allow obtaining preliminary data for the analysis of the first face of judicial power.

Overall, the court's two senates have made 714 senate decisions between the end of 1990 and the end of September 2009. However, not all of these decisions are main decisions (*Hauptentscheidungen*); instead, there are a number of special decisions that can be omitted. The majority of those are 80 provisional orders, which are used to temporarily regulate an issue until a main decision is made (§32 Act on the GFCC). Provisional orders are not the final verdict in cases, and thus I omit those orders. The second largest group are 14 requests to exclude a judge from a case (§19 Act on the GFCC). These are not main decisions and thus they are also omitted. In addition, nine "reminders" are excluded, which the GFCC uses to remind an actor previously defeated in court of her obligations; for example, to pay the costs of a plaintiff. There are more special cases that are omitted; thus 582 main decisions remain.[2] In two cases, it was not possible to code the outcome of decisions, therefore I also exclude them. In sum, the final dataset comprises 580 senate decisions made by the GFCC between January 1991 and September 2009.[3]

4.2.1 Dependent Variable: Judicial Choices

The behavior that I aim to predict is the probability of a judicial choice either not justifying a referral, justifying a referral, or justifying a referral and presenting a directive. The GFCC uses two steps to come to a judicial choice: first, the admissibility of a referral is assessed; and, second, a decision on the merits is made. A referral has to be admissible *and* justified on the merits for the whole decision to be successful from the plaintiff's perspective; otherwise, the decision is not successful from this perspective as the plaintiff's aim is not achieved (see Schlaich and Korioth 2015, Ch. 5, esp. margin number 372).

The GFCC sometimes only partially admits a referral or decides that the merits are partially justified. However, those choices imply that the decision as a whole is successful. It is not possible to violate constitutional rights just a little; instead, once the court sees even a partial violation, the plaintiff's claim is plausible. Following the court's decision, a response is necessary to correct the violation of constitutional rights. Hence, looking at a judicial decision from the outside, a partial admissibility and a partial decision on the merits lead to a decision granting a plaintiff victory.

It is necessary to account for the structure of decisions when coding outcomes. A decision comprises one case, but one case can combine multiple referrals (Wittig 2016, 27–28). While the outcome of a decision exists regarding the case, the GFCC decides on the admissibility and merits of each referral. In other words, if I wish to code the overall outcomes of decisions, it is sometimes necessary to aggregate the judicial choices from multiple referrals to the case levels. This is also necessary because a directive is a feature of the overall outcome and not of referrals. Aggregation is a challenge only in cases where multiple plaintiffs file referrals and the GFCC makes different choices regarding the different referrals. This is the case in only about 11% out of the 580 decisions. In order to aggregate the referrals in those decisions, I follow two steps. First, I assess whether the admissibility is different across the referrals within one decision. If this is not true, then I leave the admissibility unchanged. However, if this is true, then the logical choice is to code all referrals as partially admissible. For example, in a decision with three referrals, where one is partially admissible but the other two referrals are not admissible, I code the whole case as partially admissible. This is feasible as I wish to only code the whole outcome of a decision. From the perspective of a decision, it only matters that the court continues to assess the whole case, even if only one of three referrals is partially admitted. It was necessary to recode the admissibility in 52 decisions. Second, I assess whether the decision on the merits is different across referrals within the same decision. This was true in 33 decisions. Hence, I code all referrals in those cases as partially justified, following the same logic as before. Through this approach, I am able to aggregate the outcomes regarding referrals to the case level.

Finally, based on the admissibility and the choice on the merits, I code the first part of my outcome variable. Hereon, whenever I speak of a *decision as being justified* I imply that the referrals in a decision are (partially) admissible *and* the issues raised in the referrals are (partially) justified; otherwise I speak of a *decision as not being justified.* Plaintiffs successfully raise a constitutional issue when a decision is justified. Plaintiffs do not successfully raise a constitutional issue when a decision is not justified. The next step is to identify whether the GFCC also presents a directive.

A judicial directive is a statement by the judges included in a court's decision, directed at political actors to request their action in response to a constitutional issue. The definition highlights that the court can only pose a request to act, although whether the political branches respond is at their discretion. Directives are a vague concept, which is why four steps are applied to code them. First, a sample of decisions was read carefully to identify statements that meet the given definition. The initial assessment led to four keywords that helped to identify directives.[4] Second, the keywords were used to automatically target paragraphs of interest. The extracted paragraphs were read by an advanced law student specializing in public law and with a background in political science. The student identified whether a paragraph met the definition given above. Third, after applying the semi-automated approach, all decisions were assessed again. The substantial parts of a decision, excluding the parts on the case's facts and the assessments on admissibility, were reviewed to identify possible directives that had previously been missed. Fourth, the student coded a variable indicating his certainty that an identified paragraph is indeed a directive. In 86% of the decisions the coder felt certain, while in about 9% the coder felt somewhat certain, and only in about 5% the coder was uncertain.

Directives were initially separated into three groups according to their level of detail. However, as directives rarely occur, the differentiation leads to a low number of decisions in each group. This is why I group decisions with directives in one category. This reflects the theory, which separates those decisions that include a directive from all other decisions. Moreover, the underlying logic between different directives is always similar: the court presents a position and requests an action. For example, assessing the secret monitoring of computers by state authorities (BVerfGE 120, 274), the GFCC wrote:

> [A] The legislature has to ensure by means of suitable procedural provisions that if data has been collected which relates to the core area of private life, the intensity of the violation of the core area and its impact on the personality and development of the person concerned remain as low as possible. Decisive significance in terms of protection attaches to the viewing of the collected data as to contents which are relevant to the core area, for which suitable procedures are to be provided which sufficiently accommodate the interests of the person concerned. If viewing reveals that data was collected with relevance to the core area, it is to be deleted without delay. (BVerfGE 120, 274 [338–339]; official translation by the GFCC)

In comparison to statement A, the GFCC stated the following when assessing the rights of young apprentices to receive state funding after they successfully completed an apprenticeship but chose to pursue a second academic training (BVerfGE 99, 165):

> [B] [T]he legislature has multiple options to resolve the constitutional violation. It is at the discretion of the legislature to provide state funding based on the concepts given in §11 III S. 1 No. 5 BAföG 1979 to apprentices who begin an additional apprenticeship after their parents have fulfilled their obligatory support. The legislature could also adopt a regulation that allows those apprentices access to funding based on §36 Abs. 1 Satz 1 BAföG. (BVerfGE 99, 165 [184–185]; idiomatic translation)[5]

The GFCC signals its own position in statements A and B. Core personal rights need to be protected by any means (A) and apprentices who seek a second training need to have access to state funding (B). Moreover, in both cases the GFCC requests that the legislature acts to resolve constitutional issues. The legislature has to develop "suitable procedural provisions" (A) or it can choose from two detailed approaches (B). Therefore, both statements qualify as directives, despite the different level of detail. The question is whether implicit statements qualify as directives. An example is given by the GFCC's decision on the import of dangerous dogs (BVerfGE 110, 141). A group of breeders filed a constitutional complaint arguing that the prohibition to import certain breeds violates their rights of occupational freedom (Art. 12 I Basic Law). The GFCC argued that the legislature correctly concluded that the protection of society is more important than the import of dangerous dogs:

> [C] However, the legislature has to monitor the developments. The scientific root causes for aggressive behavior among dogs of different breeds as well as the assumptions made by the legislature are still inconclusive. This is why it is necessary to further monitor the risks from keeping dogs and to assess the biting behavior of dogs mentioned in §2 I S. 1 HundVerbrEinfG; even more than in the past. If these assessments do not confirm the legislature's prognoses about the danger of those dogs, then the legislature will have to adjust the regulations. (BVerfGE 110, 141 [166]; idiomatic translation)[6]

The position of the court is only implicitly included in this statement. The court accepts the current provisions, but if the situation changes, revisions are necessary. This is why the statement has policymaking consequences. The government has to establish procedures to ensure that the constitutional issue does not arise. In this regard, the implicit judicial statement qualifies as a directive. Accordingly, statements like C are included in the main analysis.

Finally, there are cases in which the GFCC does not explicate a directive in a single paragraph, but rather requests an action at the end of a decision. For example, when the court writes that "[t]he legislature has to pass regulations that meet constitutional requirements until December 31, 2005" (BVerfGE 109, 64 [95]; own translation), the sentence explicitly requests an action to resolve a constitutional issue. This is a defining feature of directives. It is not a limitation that the sentence does not include a statement about the court's preferred reaction. This can be inferred from the decision.[7] Therefore, a deadline is a request directed at the government to address a constitutional issue and it qualifies as a directive. If the request

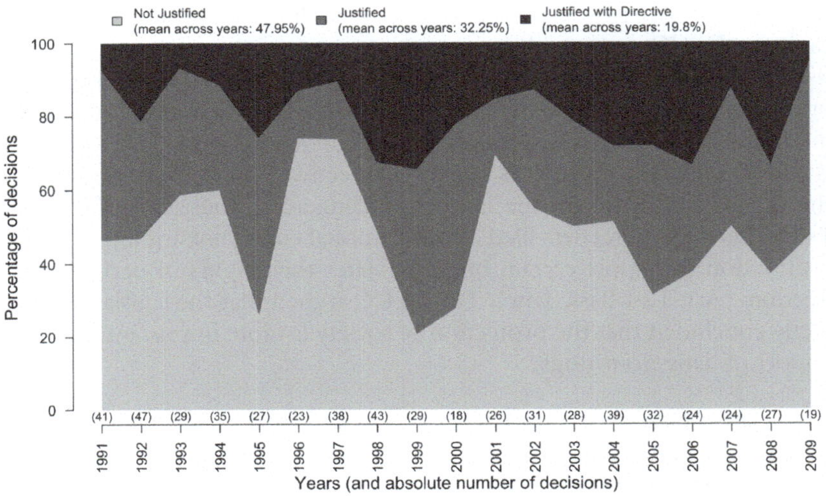

Fig. 4.1 Judicial choices in 580 senate decisions by the GFCC from January 1991 to September 2009

to pass new legislation were not included, then the definition of a directive would not have been met. This latter case occurs when the court presents statements directed at the government but does not justify the decision (compare restrictive interpretation, Brouard 2016). If a decision is not justified, no constitutional issue exists, which implies that the court's request would ask the government to evade a judicial choice (see also Spiller and Tiller 1996). Nevertheless, I acknowledge that in about 8.5% of the decisions not justified and analyzed here statements similar to directives occur. However, the number drops to about 3% when excluding statements similar to vague directives. This low number does not allow for valid inference, which leads me to code the decisions as not justified.

In sum, out of the 580 decisions studied here, 282 decisions are not justified, 182 decisions are only justified, and 116 decisions are justified with a directive. The stacked plot in Fig. 4.1 summarizes the share of outcomes in decisions over time with the absolute number of decisions in a given year in parentheses on the x-axis. The low number of decisions within years prompts me to analyze judicial choices on an aggregated basis. The figure shows that there is variation in the judicial choices, especially in 1998 to 2001 as compared to other years. Nevertheless, not justifying decisions is the common judicial choice. On average, about 48% of decisions in a year are not justified. The second most common judicial choice is to only justify decisions (on average 32% per year). The fact that decisions that are justified with directives are the minority (on average 20% per year) supports the idea that they are self-established by the court. They are not seen as an institutionalized norm, which is why the GFCC cannot "flood" the legal community or political branches with directives. In the next section, I outline the independent variables used to predict different judicial choices.

4.2.2 *Independent Variables: The Government's and the Court's Costs*

In this section, I operationalize the costs to the government for legislating in response to a judicial decision (α) and the costs to the court from an evasion (γ). The assumption is that variation in costs explains variation in judicial choices. The court and the government interact in an environment that can become hostile to both actors. Indeed, research has shown that the judiciary accounts for the public when making decisions (Stephenson 2004; Vanberg 2005; Sternberg et al. 2015). Nevertheless, while a decline in the public's support for the judiciary can lead to a crisis (Limbach 2002, 317; Wesel 2004, 54–75, 308–322), judges on constitutional courts do not depend on a public election (Hönnige 2008, 533–535).[8] The governing majority risks losing public votes in hostile situations. Therefore, I operationalize the factors that drive the government's cost on the outside of the judicial–political interaction separately from the factors that drive those costs on the inside. This separation is not necessary for the factors that drive the court's costs.

4.2.2.1 *External Aspects Driving the Government's Costs*

Government's cohesiveness. The costs to the government for responding to a decision are influenced by the government's opportunity to secure a majority in the legislature.

In general, strong parliamentarianism—which exists in Germany (Bergmann et al. 2016, 26)—seems to favor unified votes among coalition parties (Carey 2009, 159–162). However, constitutional courts make decisions based on constitutional norms. This is why decisions by the courts discuss the core values of a society, which can require legislators to address very controversial issues. A cohesive government can afford to lose a few legislators in a vote. Therefore, a governing coalition that is cohesive is better able to respond to a controversial issue than one that is not. The government's cohesiveness is one measure to operationalize the costs for responding to a judicial decision.

In order to measure the government's cohesiveness, I use data on roll call votes in the German *Bundestag* compiled by Bergmann et al. (2016; see also Sieberer et al. 2020). I follow the authors' suggestion to calculate the cohesiveness among the parties based on an Agreement Index (Hix et al. 2003, 317). This accounts for the fact that abstentions can occur in the *Bundestag* (Bergmann et al. 2016, 38). The agreement among a party i is defined as

$$AI_i = \frac{max\{Y_i, N_i, A_i\} - \frac{1}{2}[(Y_i + N_i + A_i) - max\{Y_i, N_i, A_i\}]}{(Y_i + N_i + A_i)}$$

where Y_i are the "yes" votes of party i on an issue, N_i are the "no" votes, and A_i are the number of abstentions. The index is 1 when the party's voting behavior is unified and 0 when a party is equally divided over all votes (Hix et al. 2003, 317). The agreement of the coalition is the average agreement among the governing parties. Moreover, I average the coalition's agreement score over all roll call votes called over the first or second six months in a year.[9] Finally, I merge the scores to the decisions by year and by whether a decision was taken in the first or second half of a given year.

The measure has limitations. While a vote by the legislature on one proposal is not necessarily comparable to a vote on another proposal (Carrubba et al. 2008; Stecker 2015), by averaging over roll call votes I make this assumption. However, it is difficult to predict which vote on which type of proposal reflects a future response to a possible judicial decision. Moreover, recorded votes only occur on request, which does not happen often in the *Bundestag* (Bergmann et al. 2016, 30–31). Hence, they are most likely systematically different from the majority of the votes in the *Bundestag* (Stecker 2015, 792–793). Hence, the measure has to be used with caution.

The costs of the government to respond to a decision are higher when the coalition's cohesiveness is low, compared with when cohesiveness is high.

Days until the next election. Electoral dynamics require the government to signal policy positions to the electorate. Policies that are attractive to the public ensure electoral support and secure the government's position in office (Müller and Strøm 1999). Therefore, it is costly for the government to lose prestigious projects to reversal by the judiciary shortly before an election (Brouard 2009; Vanberg 1998). Moreover, Brouard (2009, 396–397) identified the dilemma that in competitive elections the government is forced to address extreme positions among the electorate. The respective policies are then more likely to be vetoed by the court. While this argument is compelling for the French presidential run-off elections (Brouard 2009), it is not necessarily true for the German electoral system. Instead, Vanberg (1998) argues that the government aims to prevent conflict with the judiciary during election years by circumventing the court through intra-legislative bargaining. The governing majority seeks a compromise with the opposition to prevent the minority from referring a policy to the court. This perspective highlights that the government is wary of judicial review during election years.

This is why I count the days from a judicial decision to the next federal election. The count is based on the known date of the election. As governing parties, the Social Democrats and the Green Party called for an early election in 2005 (Roberts 2006). To account for this, I use the count of days until the next regular election until the day on which the governing party calls for an early election, at which point I use the days until the early election.[10]

The costs to the government for responding to a judicial decision are higher once an election is close, compared with when such an election is further away.

Public support for the government. The government's electoral support helps to understand how resilient a government is. It is plausible to assume that a government with high levels of support can respond to judicial decisions more easily than one that is already under pressure. Judicial decisions often have negative connotations and the response to such decisions can cause a decline in public support. A government with higher levels of support can take such a decline better than one that already has low levels of support.

In order to measure public support for the governing parties, I use monthly aggregated polling data from the *Politbarometer* (2013). Respondents are asked to identify the parties that they would vote for if an election were held in that month.[11] The sum of the support for the governing parties is the public's support for the governing coalition. Finally, I merged the support for the government in a given month to the decisions based on the month when the decisions were made.

At higher levels of electoral support, it is less costly for the government to respond to a judicial decision than at lower levels of support.

In sum, different levels of (1) the government's cohesiveness, (2) time until the next election, and (3) the public's support for the government are proxies for factors external to the judicial–political interaction that drive the government's costs. In the following section, I discuss factors that define those costs on the inside of the judicial–political interaction.

4.2.2.2 Internal Aspects Driving the Government's Costs

Age of the act referred for review. Electoral considerations require the government to ensure the success of its own policy agenda. Thus, the government should be concerned when the court concludes that a recently passed act is unconstitutional. The majority that passed the policy is directly affected, compared with when the policy addressed by the court is older. This may imply that it is easier to unite legislators to respond to a judicial decision against a recent policy (Ignagni and Meernik 1994, 362). However, this does not take into account the notion that the opposition will use the judicial defeat against the government. Hence, the government faces a dilemma once a recently passed policy is invalidated by the court. The governing majority might be willing to address the decision, although by doing so the majority becomes more vulnerable to the opposition. The opposition can use the parliamentary floor to blame the government for failed policy efforts, which keeps the negative implications of a judicial decision alive. Therefore, the costs of responding to a judicial decision are higher when a recent act is addressed by the court compared with an older act.

Referrals in decisions by the GFCC can address different acts, such as laws, actions by federal agencies, or rulings by regular courts (Wittig 2016, 49–50). It is necessary to aggregate acts addressed in a decision from the level of a referral to that of a decision. Two choices are necessary: first, determining which act is the pressing one; and second, in cases where referrals addressed similar acts from different times, ascertaining which one is the important one. An example clarifies this: imagine a decision from 2009 with three referrals, one of which is directed against a law from 2006, one is directed against a law from 2005, and one is directed against a decision by a regular court from 2004. First, I prioritize among the different types of acts based on assumptions about how the government would prioritize. Referrals addressing a law directly are more important than those addressing a law indirectly, while both of them are more important than referrals addressing an act by a federal agency. All of them are more important than any other act. Hence, from my example only the law from 2005 and the law from 2006 remain. Second, I assume that among one type of act, the government pays attention to the most recent one. Hence, the law from 2006 remains as the issue under consideration. Therefore, the (logged) days between when the decision was made in 2009 and when the law was passed in 2006 define the age of the referred act.

The younger an act addressed in a decision, the higher the costs are for the government to respond to a decision.

Briefs field. Briefs allow an actor to give an opinion in a case before the court makes a decision. The GFCC frequently invites the government to file briefs. Writing briefs is not free, but consumes resources such as time and effort. This is why the government only files briefs in cases that are important to it (Vanberg 2005, 104–105; 2001, 355–356; Krehbiel 2016). Accordingly, briefs are a signal for the government's wish to influence a decision before it is proclaimed. The government invests resources now to reduce the costs of responding to a decision later. Therefore, I include a variable indicating whether a brief was filed by the government or not.

When the government files a brief, the costs of responding to a legal decision are higher compared with when no brief is filed.

Government's topic. Finally, the government's interest in responding to a decision is driven by the substantive topic addressed therein. In this regard, a decision can benefit the government. A decision in an area of interest allows the government to address the issue and set the agenda. It is plausible to assume that encouraging the legislative majority to respond to a topic of interest is easier than when the topic is not of interest. This does not imply that the governing majority legislates in a way desired by the court; rather, it simply assumes that the majority is united behind the topic addressed in a decision. Accordingly, the costs of responding to a judicial decision are lower once the court makes a decision in an area of interest to the government. It is important not to confuse a decision that addresses the government's topic of interest with a decision that addresses a government's policy. The latter is costly to the government, although this is accounted for by the measure addressing the age of an act referred to the court.

The topics addressed in decisions are part of the CCDB. The decisions were classified through double-blind coding with an adopted coding scheme from the *Comparative Agendas Project* (CAP, Bevan 2017). Thus, I code the government's agenda to match this scheme. First, I obtained three documents that outline the government's agenda: (1) the party manifestos of the governing parties (from Volkens et al. 2015), which are directed at the electorate; (2) the coalition agreements between the parties, which are directed at party organizations (self-collected); and (3) the chancellor's state of the union at the beginning of a legislative period (from Busch 2016), which is directed at the legislature and the media. Second, I automatically identify all nouns used at least five times in all documents of a legislative period.[12] Third, the words were reviewed manually for meaningful words that could be classified according to the (adopted) CAP coding scheme. General or abstract words were excluded, e.g., *Zukunft* (future), *Gesellschaft* (society) or *Vertrauen* (trust). The remaining words were classified; for example, *Emessionshandel* (emissions trading) was coded as an issue in the area of the "environment," or *Streitkräfte* (troops) as an issue in the area of "defense."[13] Fourth, I merged the classifications to the noun-frequency matrix from each legislative period and counted the frequency with which nouns from each CAP category occurred. The government's major topic of interest is the CAP category with the highest count, and a variable indicates whether a judicial decision during a certain legislative period addressed this topic or not.

This approach has certain limitations. For instance, there is low variation among the second and third topic of interest between different governments. This suggests that some topics are inflated by common words. Nevertheless, the major topic of a government varies across the legislative periods. The topics are "government operations" for the 12th legislative period, "domestic macro-economic issues" for the 13th legislative period, "labor and employment" for the 14th and 16th legislative periods, and "civil rights, minority issues and civil liberties" for the 15th legislative period. Appendix D.1 provides substantive considerations to validate the topics identified.

The costs to the government of responding to a decision about a topic of interest are lower compared to decisions in an area that is not of interest.

In sum, (1) the age of a referral, (2) the choice whether to file a brief, and (3) the interest in the topic of a decision are proxies for the factors internal to the judicial–political interaction that drive the government's costs. In the following section, I turn to proxies for the costs to the court from an evasion.

4.2.2.3 The Court's Costs from an Evasion

Impact on regular courts and on legal scholars. Courts need to ensure legitimacy and support to enforce their decisions. The audience of the court is not only the well-studied public (see Gibson et al. 1998; Vanberg 2001, 2005; Farganis 2012; Sternberg et al. 2015); instead, regular courts and the scientific legal community also pay close attention to decisions. Regular courts are asked to enforce decisions by constitutional courts in their judgments (§31 I Act on the GFCC) and the legal community frequently assesses the decisions. In order to ensure that legal actors accept the decisions by constitutional courts, it is necessary for the courts to build support among the actors.

A constitutional court needs to build *diffuse support*, which "consists of a reservoir of support that enables a system to weather the many storms when outputs cannot be balanced off against inputs of demands" (Easton 1965, 273). Diffuse support is the support for the institution itself, "independent of the effects of daily outputs" (Easton 1965, 273). Constitutional courts can build diffuse support through *specific support* for their actions. Specific support is "directed to the perceived decisions" (Easton 1975, 437) of the constitutional court. In other words, the recurrent acceptance of individual decisions by the legal community leads to lasting diffuse support for the institution (Easton 1965, 1975). By contrast, if the court frequently is evaded in decisions of relevance to the judicial community, this harms the court's support among the community. Therefore, an evasion of decisions is costly when the legal community pays attention to decisions.

In order to measure the attention that the judicial community pays to a particular decision, I proceeded as follows. First, I identified meaningful keywords for the 580 decisions that reflect on the content of the decisions.[14] Second, I subtracted two years from the date when a referral was submitted to the court. The GFCC has to assess the environment surrounding a referral when preparing to make a decision. I assume that the court will look back two years in time to understand the conditions that led to a referral.[15] Third, the identified keywords were used to search the German legal database *Juris* for the period two years before the earliest referral up to the day when a decision was made. The database provides the number of rulings (*Rechtsprechung*) and bibliographical references (*Literaturnachweise*) that include the keyword during the given period.[16] These counts are used to measure the relevance of a decision to regular courts and the legal community. Fourth, it is necessary to account for the fact that more rulings and bibliographical references exist for referrals that took the GFCC a longer time to make a decision. Thus, I divide the counts from the search by the number of days that were included in the search. This gives two impact scores, one regarding regular courts and another regarding bibliographical references. Fifth, to account for the fact that the total number of primary sources included in databases can vary over years, I calculate the average impact scores for regular courts and bibliographical references across all decisions in a given year. Finally, I compute two variables: one indicates whether the impact score from regular courts in a given decision is above the respective yearly average, while the other variable does the same for bibliographical references. Decisions are important to regular courts and the legal community once the impact scores are above average in a given year. The evasion of a decision with impact is more costly to the GFCC compared to a decision without impact.

Oral hearing. Constitutional courts frequently conduct hearings with experts and political actors. The GFCC conducted a hearing in 142 of the decisions analyzed here. Scholars regard hearings as opportunities to create transparency around a decision, which increases the media's awareness of a case, and in the long run, the public's attention (Vanberg 2005, 103). This way, hearings become strategic tools that allow courts to indirectly place pressure on the government to comply with decisions (Vanberg 2001, 2005; Krehbiel 2016).[17]

Judges highlight in interviews that they use hearings to prepare the parties to the proceeding for the outcome of a decision (see interview no. 16 in Kranenpohl 2010, 101; no. 1 in Kranenpohl 2010, 315). Moreover, hearings are also used to ensure that no important aspects are missed (see interviews no. 12, 22, 30 in Kranenpohl 2010, 101–102). In this regard, a hearing can become the basis for a decision (interview no. 30 in Kranenpohl 2010, 101–102). Therefore, hearings not only increase transparency, but also add decisively to the judges' knowledge. Despite these advantages, hearings are time-intensive and complicated to organize (Kranenpohl 2010, 315). On that account, hearings are used as strategic tools when the consequences from a decision are costly. They allow the judges to inquire whether their perspective is accepted or whether they need to adapt decisions. Hence, hearings are used when the costs from an evasion are high. This is why I code a variable that indicates whether an oral hearing was part of a decision or not.

Importance of a decision to manifest doctrine. Constitutional courts assess referrals based on constitutional provisions. However, the constitution is no longer the only source for developing arguments. Constitutional courts are able to refer to past decisions and develop a line of doctrine (see Clark and Lauderdale 2012), whereby they further develop the constitution. For example, in the decision on the secret monitoring of personal computers by state authorities (BVerfGE 120, 274), the GFCC derived a new fundamental right that protects the individual privacy when using information technology systems (Hoffmann-Riem 2008).

It is plausible to assume that decisions used to develop a certain doctrinal path hold particular importance to constitutional courts. The marginalization of the Hungarian Constitutional Court exemplifies this: despite being one of the strongest constitutional courts in Europe (Scheppele 2003, 222–227; Engst 2017), the court's established case law was invalidated with the reform of the Hungarian Constitution in 2012, which led to a large amount of legal uncertainty (Grabenwarter et al. 2013, 20–23). In Chapter 3, it is outlined that this has profoundly weakened the court's position among European constitutional courts. Therefore, case law holds of relevance to courts in civil law countries (Mattei and Pes 2008, 274), and the evasion of decisions that develop a line of doctrine is costly. This is why I identify decisions that follow a doctrinal path.

In essence, I need to measure the importance of a decision in line with previous decisions. It is not helpful to only identify salient decisions based on how often they are referred to by legal scholars or whether the media considers a decision a landmark decision, given that these types of salience are defined long after a decision has been made. The same applies to retrospective analysis of citation networks (e.g., authority scores in Fowler and Jeon 2008). I wish to measure the importance of decisions when they are made. This is why I count all references in a decision to former decisions. The assumption is that the likelihood that a decision contributes to a certain doctrinal path is higher the more references to former decisions are made. In terms of network analysis, a decision with many citations becomes a "*hub* [...] helping to define which legally relevant decisions are pertinent to a given precedent" (Fowler and Jeon 2008, 20; emphasis in the original). Even if a decision itself does not establish a doctrine, the number of citations of former decisions highlights some level of importance. However, I acknowledge that the number of citations is known only after a decision is announced.

The citations in decisions were extracted with the help of regular expressions.[18] The number of citations is also a function of the age of a decision. In recent decisions, it is possible to cite from a larger pool than in older decisions. To account for this, I estimate the average number of citations over all decisions in a given year. Thus, I code a variable that indicates whether citations occur above or below average in a decision in a given year. Among the decisions that refer to other decisions more than average are decisions that became prominent in the long run, e.g., the decision on privacy while using information technology systems (BVerfGE 120, 274), the decision on abortion (BVerfGE 88, 203), and the decision on "out-of-area" deployments of the German military (BVerfGE 90, 286). Decisions that cite other decisions more than average are important to the court, which makes an evasion costly.

In sum, the evasion of a judicial decision is costly when (1) a decision has an impact on regular courts and the legal community, (2) a hearing is held, and (3) the decision holds importance to a doctrinal path. In what follows, I summarize alternative explanations regarding the occurrence of a certain judicial choice.

4.2.3 *Control Variables: Alternative Explanations for Judicial Choices*

The relevance of public opinion in judicial politics is widely studied (Caldeira 1987; Gibson et al. 1998; Vanberg 2001, 2005; Bartels and Johnston 2013). However, measuring the public's opinion regarding a specific judicial decision is challenging (see Epstein and Martin 2011, Sternberg et al. 2015). Moreover, it is difficult to argue whether the public's opinion increases or reduces the costs from an evasion or the government's costs to respond to a decision. Public opinion can become an ambiguous measure influencing both costs (see Stephenson 2004). In order to acknowledge the role of public opinion in judicial decision-making, I control for the relevance to the media of the topic addressed in a decision. The media communicates the outcome of decisions to society at large (Linos and Twist 2016). This is why I measure the *impact of a topic on the society* using keywords from the decisions on a database with German-speaking newspaper articles.[19] In order to calculate impact scores, I applied the same approach used to calculate the impact of a decision on the legal community. A variable indicates whether a topic addressed in a decision was of above-average importance to the media in a given year.

The GFCC comprises two *senates.* Does the institutional design affect the government's costs of responding to a judicial decision or the court's costs from an evasion? The institutional design alone does not seem able to make a difference. For example, the impact of a decision by the court on the legal community is independent of whether the first or second senate made a decision. Similarly, the public's support for the government is dependent on the issue addressed in a decision and not on the first or second senate making a decision. Finally, the government files a brief regarding the substantive issue in a case and not based on whether a particular senate made a decision. Therefore, the institutional difference alone matters less; rather, the difference that matters is an issue-related difference.

The two senates were originally in charge of different proceedings. The first senate was in charge of decisions directed at the violation of basic, fundamental rights and the second senate was in charge of decisions directed at the organization of the state. This could imply an issue-related difference between the senates. However, the increasing workload led the court to less strictly apply the institutional separation (Wittig 2016, 108; Schlaich and Korioth 2015, 38; Federal Law Gazette 1993 Part I No. 74). Accordingly, the issue-related difference between the senates is reduced nowadays. It follows that controlling for the senates is reasonable, although it is necessary to identify a variable to account for issue-related differences.

Plaintiffs refer a number of different acts to the GFCC; for example, decisions by regular courts, administrative acts, or laws (Wittig 2016, 49–50). An administrative act is directed at a small subgroup of people regulating an issue only for this defined group. A ruling of a regular court addresses a specific issue of relevance to the parties of a legal dispute. A law addresses an issue of importance to a larger population and even the whole society. This is why the scope of the act referred to the GFCC implies issue-related differences. In this regard, I argue that the costs for the government and the court playing the Judicial-Policy-Dialogue Game (JPD game) are most strongly affected by laws, given that their issues have the widest scope. Therefore, in order to account for effects of issue-related differences, I run particular robustness assessments later, separating ***decisions based on referred laws*** from all other decisions.[20]

Table 4.1 summarizes measures of central tendency and dispersion and outlines how the operationalized variables relate to the hypotheses and the concepts from the JPD game. In the next section I turn to the identification strategy to assess the first face of judicial power.

Table 4.1 Independent variables to assess the first face of judicial power

Variable	*Description*	*Costs*	*Range*	*Median*	*Mean*	*SD*
Gov. cohesiveness	The average agreement among the parties of the governing coalition in roll call votes (based on Bergmann et al. 2016)	α	0.83 – 1	0.97	0.95	0.05
Days until election	The (logged) number of days until the next federal election from the day a decision was made	α	1.39 – 7.29	6.71	6.39	0.94
Gov. support	The electoral support for the parties of the governing coalition in the *Bundestag* (based on Politbarometer 2013)	α	0.32 – 0.79	0.44	0.47	0.12
Age of act	The (logged) number of days from the (latest) referral to the GFCC to the day a decision was made	α	0 – 10.37	7.29	7.16	1.23
Brief	Indicates whether the government field a brief to a decision (1) or not (0)	α	0 – 1	0.5	0.5	
Gov. topic	Indicates whether a decision addresses the topics most important to the government (1) or not (0)	α	0 – 1	0	0.12	
Impact on courts*	Indicates whether a topic addressed in a decision is of more than average importance to regular courts (1) or not (0)	γ	0 – 1	0	0.26	
Impact on scholars*	Indicates whether a topic addressed in a decision is of more than average importance to legal scholars (1) or not (0)	γ	0 – 1	0	0.26	
Oral hearing	Indicates whether the court conducted a hearing (1) or not (0)	γ	0 – 1	0	0.24	
Manifest doctrine	Indicates whether a decision cites previous decisions by the GFCC above average (1) or not (0)	γ	0 – 1	0	0.38	

Note: *The two variables correlate highly, which is why only the impact on courts is used in the main analysis. Appendix D.2 elaborates on the table and presents a correlation matrix

4.3 Modeling Judicial Choices to Assess the First Face of Judicial Power

Judges choose one of three judicial actions: (1) not to justify a decision, (2) to justify a decision, or (3) to present a directive. These categories cannot be ordered. A choice not to justify a decision is not worse or better—or lower or higher—than a choice to present a directive; instead, the choices are comparable to judges choosing to join in on a certain type of vote (compare Wahlbeck et al. 1999, 499; Hettinger et al. 2007, 61–62). This is why I model the court's action with a number of multinomial logistic regressions (see Long 1997, Ch. 6). In order to explain the judicial selection (S) from among the three judicial actions (a) with the covariates from Table 4.1, the systematic component of my (complete) model is

$$\boldsymbol{S}_{ia} = \boldsymbol{E}_i\xi_a + \boldsymbol{I}_i\iota_a + \boldsymbol{K}_i\kappa_a + \boldsymbol{X}_i\beta_a + \epsilon_{ia}$$

where $\boldsymbol{E}$ is a vector summarizing the variables from the political environment that define the government's costs of legislating, $\boldsymbol{I}$ summaries variables internal to the judicial-political interaction that define the government's costs, and $\boldsymbol{K}$ summarizes variables that define the court's costs from an evasion. $\boldsymbol{X}$ summarizes the control variables.

The predicted probability of a certain judicial selection from among the three actions ($\neg j = 1, j = 2, jd = 3$) is then defined as (see Long 1997, 152–154)

$$Pr(s_i = a|\boldsymbol{E}_i, \boldsymbol{I}_i, \boldsymbol{K}_i, \boldsymbol{X}_i) = \frac{exp(\boldsymbol{E}_i\xi_a + \boldsymbol{I}_i\iota_a + \boldsymbol{K}_i\kappa_a + \boldsymbol{X}_i\beta_a)}{\sum_{a=1}^{3} exp(\boldsymbol{E}_i\xi_a + \boldsymbol{I}_i\iota_a + \boldsymbol{K}_i\kappa_a + \boldsymbol{X}_i\beta_a)}$$
$$\text{with } \xi_3 \cap \iota_3 \cap \kappa_3 \cap \beta_3 = 0$$

Note that it is necessary to set the coefficients of one judicial action equal to zero for the model to be identified. The models estimated throughout the chapter are computed with directives as the reference category. Overall, I estimate four main models in the next section and afterwards, I test the hypotheses that address the first face of judicial power with quantities of interest (see King et al. 2000).

Table 4.2 Multinomial logistic regressions to assess the first face of judicial power

	Dependent Variable: Judicial Choice							
	Not J. vs. D. [Model 1]	*J. vs D. [Model 1]*	*Not J. vs. D. [Model 2]*	*J. vs D. [Model 2]*	*Not J. vs. D. [Model 3]*	*J. vs D. [Model 3]*	*Not J. vs. D. [Model 4]*	*J. vs D. [Model 4]*
Gov. cohesiveness	−1.370	−2.471					−1.821	−2.959
	(2.467)	(2.586)					(2.698)	(2.872)
Days until election	−0.305**	−0.137					−0.237	−0.050
	(0.140)	(0.152)					(0.155)	(0.169)
Gov. support	−2.224**	−0.175					−2.614**	−0.417
	(0.970)	(0.994)					(1.072)	(1.128)
Age of act			−0.400***	−0.408***			−0.348***	−0.218
			(0.112)	(0.119)			(0.123)	(0.133)
Brief filed (= 1)			−0.717***	−1.086***			−0.495*	−0.803***
			(0.245)	(0.262)			(0.265)	(0.285)
Gov. topic (= 1)			−0.890***	−0.542			−0.847**	−0.505
			(0.327)	(0.347)			(0.369)	(0.384)
Impact on courts (= 1)					−0.903***	−0.856***	−0.805***	−0.705**
					(0.248)	(0.269)	(0.281)	(0.307)
Oral hearing (=1)					−0.854***	−0.322	−1.007***	−0.206
					(0.258)	(0.269)	(0.290)	(0.305)
Manifest doctrine (= 1)					−0.738***	−0.963***	−0.993***	−1.120***
					(0.233)	(0.252)	(0.257)	(0.281)

(continued)

Table 4.2 (continued)

	Dependent Variable: Judicial Choice							
	Not J. vs. D. [Model 1]	*J. vs D. [Model 1]*	*Not J. vs. D. [Model 2]*	*J. vs D. [Model 2]*	*Not J. vs. D. [Model 3]*	*J. vs D. [Model 3]*	*Not J. vs. D. [Model 4]*	*J. vs D. [Model 4]*
Impact on society (= 1)							0.301	0.070
							(0.314)	(0.341)
Senate (= 1)							−0.869***	−0.270
							(0.260)	(0.284)
Referral of law (= 1)							−0.624*	−1.632***
							(0.327)	(0.334)
Constant	5.212**	3.783	4.386***	4.127***	1.710***	1.216***	10.221***	7.888**
	(2.487)	(2.619)	(0.843)	(0.886)	(0.196)	(0.206)	(2.931)	(3.124)
N	580		580		580		580	
logLik	−591.8342		−576.0765		−579.8528		−520.5052	
AIC	1199.668		1168.153		1175.706		1093.01	
PCP	0.48		0.49		0.50		0.56	
McFadden pseudo R^2	0.02		0.04		0.04		0.13	

Note: $^{*}p<0.10$; $^{**}p<0.05$; $^{***}p<0.01$; Not J. = Not justify; J. = Justify; D. = Justify with directive (which is the reference category)

4.4 Empirical Assessment of the First Face of Judicial Power

The Models 1 to 3 in Table 4.2 account for each set of variables used to explain judicial choices separately and Model 4 is the complete model including the control variables. The estimated values are logit coefficients, which are difficult to interpret.[21] This is why the detailed hypothesis tests are conducted with more compelling visualizations.

It was argued that higher levels of cohesiveness reduce the government's costs of responding to a judicial decision. Moreover, lower costs increase the chances that the court presents a directive (see H1a). The negative coefficients for the government's cohesiveness confirm this trend in all models. The chances that the court will not justify a decision or only justify a decision decrease relative to the court's choice to present a directive once the cohesiveness among the governing parties increases. However, the effects are not significant at conventional levels. This may follow from the nature of the measure that was computed from roll call votes in the *Bundestag*. These votes occur very rarely and perhaps are systematically different from other votes on the floor (Stecker 2015).

The estimate for the days until the next election for Not J. vs. D. loses explanatory power at conventional levels of significance from Model 1 to the complete Model 4. The same is true for the estimate measuring the age of an act for J. vs. D. from Model 2 to Model 4. All of the other estimates are stable across models. The level of significance decreases for some coefficients in Model 4, but none vanishes completely.

Multinomial logistic regression assumes the independence of irrelevant alternatives (IIA; Hausman and McFadden 1984; Dow and Endersby 2004). The assumption states that a chooser's preference order "*should* not be affected by the addition or subtraction of other alternatives from the choice set" (Dow and Endersby 2004, 111; emphasis in the original). The Hausman-McFadden test (Hausman and McFadden 1984) yields that the assumption is violated between the choices of only justifying a decision or presenting a directive. Hence, it may be difficult to differentiate between the two choices (Dow and Endersby 2004, 112). Indeed, it is plausible that directives are close to justified decisions. The court is expected not to interfere in policymaking and the examples in the operationalization highlight that the court sometimes shields directives as suggestions. Nevertheless, it is reasonable to differentiate between decisions only justified and directives. Decisions only justified imply that an act is not constitutional, but if the government chooses to present new legislation, justified decisions rarely constrain the policy space.[22] By contrast, suggestions made in directives constrain the action space of the government. Moreover, the response to a directive is easily observable and measurable by outside actors such as the media.[23] Hence, the nuances between decisions only justified and directives have consequences for the way in which policymaking can occur and is monitored. This is why I decide to separate between the judicial choices and "not exaggerate its [IIA] importance in applied settings" (Dow and Endersby 2004, 112). Nevertheless, I address the assumption in two ways. First, I assess that findings from the analyses are subsample stable when excluding vague directives from the estimation. Second, I assess findings using a logistic regression combining justified decisions and directives in one outcome (= 1) compared to not-justified decisions (= 0). If quantities of interest from the logistic regression are comparable to findings from the multinomial logistic regression, then the violation of the IIA assumption seems less of a concern (Dow and Endersby 2004, 112).

The individual models in Table 4.2 are weak in terms of the percentage correctly predicted. About 56% are correctly predicted in the complete model. The judicial choice not to justify a decision—as the most common judicial choice—is often correctly predicted (74%), followed by the court's choice to only justify a decision (42%) and the court's choice to present a directive (34%). While the percentage correctly predicted is fairly low, likelihood-ratio tests comparing the models and accounting for McFadden's pseudo R^2 (= 0.13) suggest that the complete model is an improvement over an empty model.[24] Nevertheless, to account for the lower power of the models, I reestimate all analyses using meaningful subsamples.

In the next section, I assess the complete Model 4 and test the hypotheses on the first face of judicial power with predicted probabilities and first differences as quantities of interest (see King et al. 2000).

4.4.1 Costs as an Explanation for Judicial Choices

The general assumption of the hypotheses is that the judicial choices vary along with the actors' costs. Two quantities are necessary to assess the hypotheses: first, predicted probabilities of different judicial choices when the costs for the government or the court are low and when these costs are high; and second, first differences to understand whether the average probability of a certain judicial choice changes significantly as the actors' costs change.

Table 4.3 Specifications of the variables to simulate quantities of interest

Variable	*Costs*	*Specification*	*Meaning*	*Interpretation (following operationalization)*
Days until election	Low High	Third quartile First quartile	1169 days* 445 days*	A response to a decision is less costly the more days there are to the next election and vice versa
Gov. support	Low High	90th percentile 10th percentile	68% 35%	A response to a decision is less costly the higher the electoral support for the government and vice versa
Age of act	Low High	Third quartile First quartile	2943 days* 643 days*	A response to a decision is less costly as the age of an act reviewed by the court increases
Brief field	Low High	No Yes	0 1	A response to a decision is less costly when no brief was field compared to when a brief was field
Gov. topic	Low High	Yes No	1 0	A response to a decision is less costly when the topic is of interest to the government compared to when it is not
Impact on courts	Low High	No Yes	0 1	An evasion is less costly when a decision does not have an impact on the legal community compared to when it does
Oral hearing	Low High	No Yes	0 1	An evasion is less costly when no oral hearing was held compared to when an oral hearing was held
Manifest doctrine	Low High	No Yes	0 1	An evasion is less costly when the court does not manifest a doctrinal path compared to when it does

Note: *Days are logged in the analyses

The independent variables from Table 4.1 are used to specify the meaning of low and high costs. The specifications are then used to simulate quantities of interest from different scenarios. Table 4.3 summarizes the different specifications for and the meaning of the independent variables. The government's cohesiveness is insignificant and not varied throughout the simulations, but held constant at the mean. The support for the government is an example of a variable that changes. The higher the public support for the government, the less costly it is for the government to respond to a decision compared to when support is low. Support for the government is set to the 90th percentile when costs are low (support for the government at about 68%) and to the 10th percentile when costs are high (about 35%). It was necessary to constrain the analysis and define variable values for the scenarios. The design is flexible, but by choosing percentiles and quartiles, a data-driven approach is used to ensure that the scenarios are sensible.

The lines in Table 4.3 separate the three sets of variables that drive costs: (1) external and (2) internal variables that drive the government's costs and (3) variables that drive the court's costs. The analyses consider the three settings separately, but the variables in one setting jointly.

4.4.2 The Government's Costs and Judicial Choices

In this section, I assess hypotheses H1a and H1b: If the costs of the government to legislate in response to a judicial decision are low, then the likelihood that the court will justify a referral and present a directive is higher than when the government's costs to legislate again are high (H1a). If the costs of the government to legislate in response to a judicial decision are low, then the likelihood that the court will only justify a referral is lower than when the government's costs to legislate again are high (H1b).

External factors defining the government's costs. Figure 4.2 summarizes quantities of interest from the complete Model 4 in Table 4.2.[25] The triangular plot is a ternary plot (King et al. 2000, 358). The tick marks at the sides allow for reading the probabilities of a judicial choice for a simulated decision. For example, the left side of the ternary plot provides the probabilities for the choice not to justify a decision. The probability of that choice would be at 100% in the left vertex of the triangle. The lower side provides the probabilities for the choice to present a directive and the right side presents the probabilities for justifying a decision. The closer that the predicted decisions are to one of the judicial choices at the vertex,

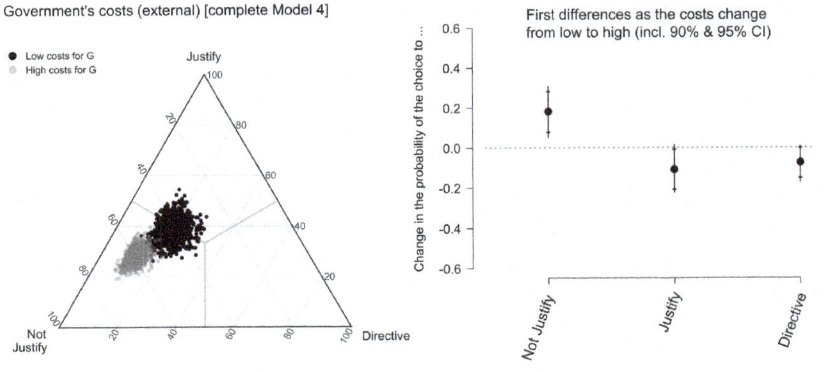

Fig. 4.2 Predicted probabilities and first differences of judicial choices by the government's costs (external). Note: $N = 580$ Senate decisions by the GFCC; 1000 simulations from Model 4 in Table 4.2. Significant variables from the upper rows in Table 4.3 are varied while the other variables are held constant at their means

the higher the probability that the court presents the respective judicial choice. If a simulated decision was located at the centroid of the ternary plot, the probabilities would be equal for every judicial choice. The lines from the centroid to the sides of the triangle partition zones in which a judicial choice wins relative to the other choices.

The ternary plot in Fig. 4.2 summarizes 1000 simulated judicial decisions when the (external) costs to the government for legislating are low (black dots) and when the costs are high (gray dots). According to the findings, the probability of the court not justifying a decision is approximately 41% at low costs and the likelihood of only justifying decisions is on average about 39% at low costs. The likelihood of presenting directives is on average about 20%. The gray dots in the ternary plot illustrate that the probability that the court does not justify decisions increases as the costs increase. This leads to a decrease in the probabilities for the choices to justify decisions or present directives. These findings speak in favor of hypothesis H1a, but not of H1b. How significant are the changes?

The plot to the right of the ternary plot in Fig. 4.2 summarizes the mean first differences across the costs for each judicial choice. The plot shows whether changes in the average probabilities of a judicial choice are significant at conventional levels as the costs change from low to high. The average decrease in the probability of presenting a directive is significant at

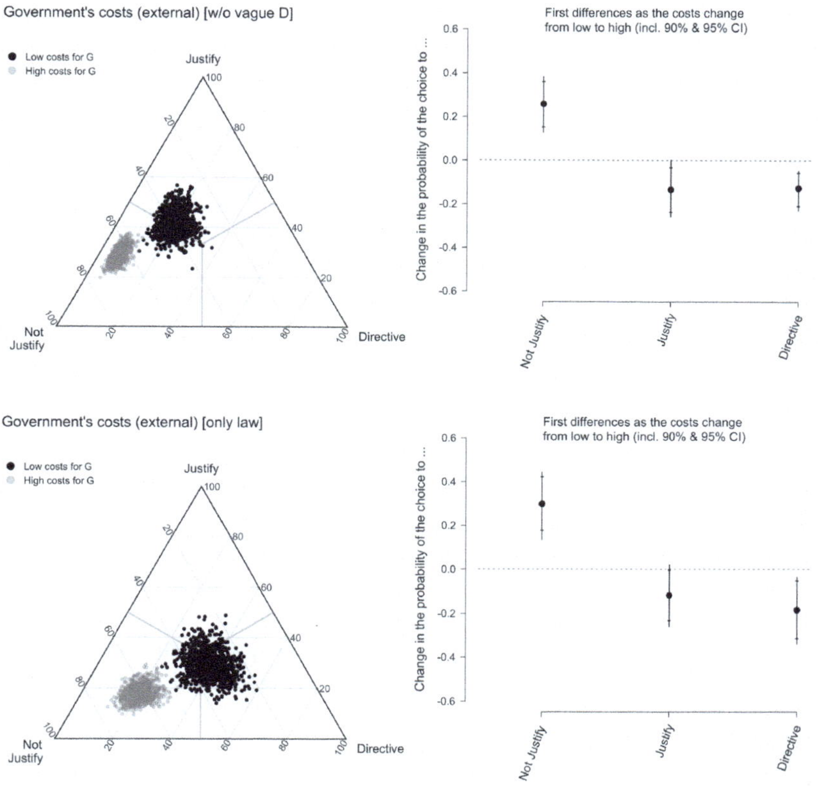

Fig. 4.3 Robustness of judicial choices by the government's costs (external). Note: $N = 549$ Senate decisions [w/o vague D] and $N = 341$ Senate decisions [only law]; 1000 simulations from the respective models in Appendix D.3. Significant variables from the upper rows in Table 4.3 are varied while the other variables are held constant at their means

a 0.10 level of significance, thus confirming H1a. Moreover, the decrease in the probability of only justifying a decision is also significant (at $p<0.10$). However, the direction of the effect does not confirm H1b, but rather the opposite effect. Finally, the relative decrease in the use of directives and justifications is driven by a significant increase in the choice not to justify decisions as the government's costs change from low to high. How robust are these findings?

Figure 4.3 summarizes the results computing the same analyses in two subsamples. Vague directives are excluded from the analysis in the upper panel and only decisions based on referrals that include at least one law are part of the analysis in the lower panel. The ternary plot summarizing the simulations from the sample without vague directives is comparable to the main analysis. There are some minor changes in the choice to present a directive when the government's costs are high, although these are negligible. Moreover, the first differences are in line with the former analysis. Hence, the observations confirm the robustness of the main analysis.

The ternary plot in the lower panel of Fig. 4.3 shows that the initial story is different for proceedings directed against at least one law. The 1000 simulated judicial choices at low costs (black dots) illustrate that the court is less willing to only justify decisions based on referrals that include at least one law. The court behaves similarly to how it behaves in the main analysis when the costs for the government are high, although the average probability that the court justifies a decision remains low at about 18% compared with the main analysis (about 28%). Nevertheless, the first differences confirm the robustness of the main analysis with a slightly larger average effect size for directives. In Appendix D.3, I present simulations from Model 1 (without controls) in Table 4.2, which also confirm the general findings.

In sum, the choice to present a directive is significantly higher when the government's costs—defined by external factors—are low compared to when these costs are high. Accordingly, hypothesis H1a is confirmed. The probability of only justifying decisions is on average lower at high costs compared with at low costs. The effect is not significant and contradicts H1b. Finally, the court's probability of not justifying decisions significantly increases as the costs to the government for legislating change from low to high.

Internal factors defining the government's costs. The ternary plot in Fig. 4.4 summarizes 1000 simulations of judicial decisions from the complete Model 4 in Table 4.2 when the government's costs—driven by factors internal to the judicial–political interaction—are low (black dots) compared with when the costs are high (gray dots).

The plot shows that the average probability of a decision being only justified (about 40%) or not justified (about 37%) is nearly equal at low costs. Directives occur less frequently on average relative to the other choices (about 23%). Moreover, the average probability of directives and justified decisions decreases, while the average probability of decisions not being justified increases as the government's costs increase. These developments

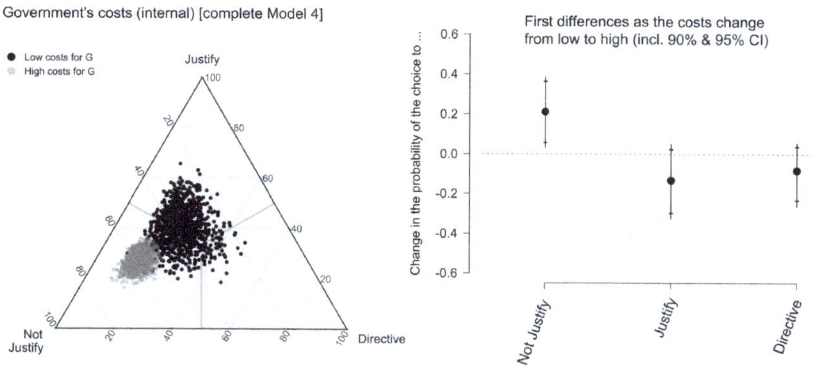

Fig. 4.4 Predicted probabilities and first differences of judicial choices by the government's costs (internal). Note: $N = 580$ Senate decisions by the GFCC; 1000 simulations from Model 4 in Table 4.2. Significant variables from the middle rows in Table 4.3 are varied while the other variables are held constant at their means

speak in favor of H1a but not H1b. However, the first differences to the right of the ternary plot in Fig. 4.4 illustrate that neither the changes in the probabilities for presenting a directive nor the changes in the probabilities of only justifying a decision are significant. While the court's choice to present directives is on average as expected, H1a is not confirmed. Moreover, the change in the choice to only justify decisions is on average different than expected but insignificant, which does not confirm H1b. Are the conclusions the same when assessing subsamples?

The upper panel of Fig. 4.5 summarizes simulations based on the subsample without vague directives. The shown effects are similar to the main findings in Fig. 4.4. The lower panel of Fig. 4.5 summarizes simulations from the subsample based on decisions that include only referrals with at least one law. The ternary plot and the first differences illustrate that the dynamics in the subsample are different from those in the main analysis. First, the average probability of a directive significantly decreases as the costs change from low to high, which confirms H1a. Second, the average probability of the choice to only justify decisions increases as the costs change from low to high. This behavior is hypothesized in H1b, although the first difference is not significant at a conventional level. Third, the average probability of the choice not to justify decisions increases as the costs change, although the increase is not significant. The findings highlight

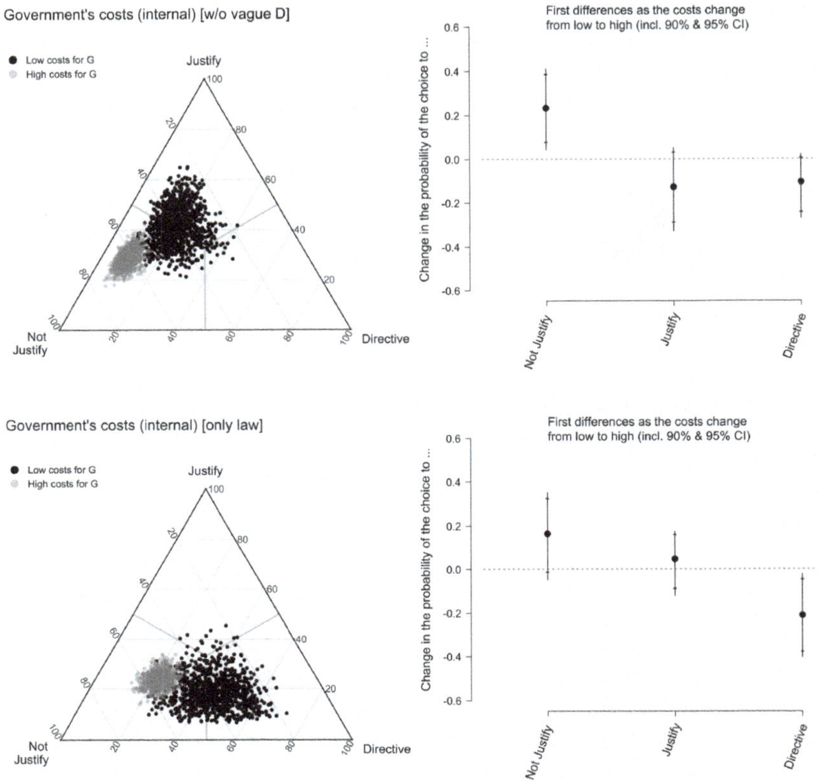

Fig. 4.5 Robustness of judicial choices by the government's costs (internal). Note: $N = 549$ Senate decisions [w/o vague D] and $N = 341$ Senate decisions [only law]; 1000 simulations from the respective models in Appendix D.3. Significant variables from the middle rows in Table 4.3 are varied while the other variables are held constant at their means

again that judicial decision-making is different when analyzing decisions that only include referrals with at least one law.[26]

The variable measuring whether the government filed a brief does not behave as expected in Table 4.2. The argument was that briefs are a sign of high costs. The government would only invest resources in filing briefs when the stakes are high. In line with this reasoning, filing briefs should reduce the likelihood of a judicial directive. However, the coefficient is negative in all models in Table 4.2. This implies that once the government files a brief, the likelihood that the court does not justify a decision or only justifies a decision decreases relative to the choice of presenting a directive. Hence, the likelihood of directives increases. What might explain this effect? It is possible that simply controlling for briefs is insufficient. It could be necessary to account for different types of briefs, namely those in which the government supports the constitutionality of an issue and those in which it does not. However, there is empirical evidence that even when the government argues that a law is constitutional, the court sometimes chooses to rule against the government (Vanberg 2005, 107–108; Krehbiel 2016). Different mechanisms are discussed to explain this outcome (Vanberg 2001, 355–357). One assumption is that briefs are endogenous to the government's expectations about the outcome. The odds that the court presents a decision that is unwanted by the government are already higher once the government files a brief (Vanberg 2001, 355–357). In this regard, briefs are not ideal to measure the government's costs as the government controls the strategic use of briefs.

In sum, explaining judicial choices with the government's costs measured using variables internal to the judicial–political interaction proves less promising. The probability that the court chooses to present directives is on average as expected, but often not significant. The choice to only justify decisions never changes significantly and is in the subsamples not as expected. Hence, H1a and H1b are not confirmed.

After assessing the effect of the government's costs to legislate on judicial choices, I turn to the effect of the court's costs from an evasion on those choices.

4.4.3 *The Court's Costs and Judicial Choices*

In this section, I assess hypotheses H1c and H1d: If the costs of a judicial evasion increase, then the likelihood that the court will justify a referral and present a directive also increases (H1c); if the costs of a judicial evasion increase, then the likelihood that the court will only justify a referral decreases (H1d).

Figure 4.6 summarizes 1000 simulations of decisions using Model 4 in Table 4.2 when the court's costs from an evasion are high (gray dots) and low (black dots). The ternary plot illustrates that the probability of not justifying decisions is the highest relative to other judicial choices at low costs for the court. By contrast, the probability of presenting directives is highest relative to other judicial choices when the court's costs are high. A few simulated decisions spread across the "win lines" (King et al. 2000,

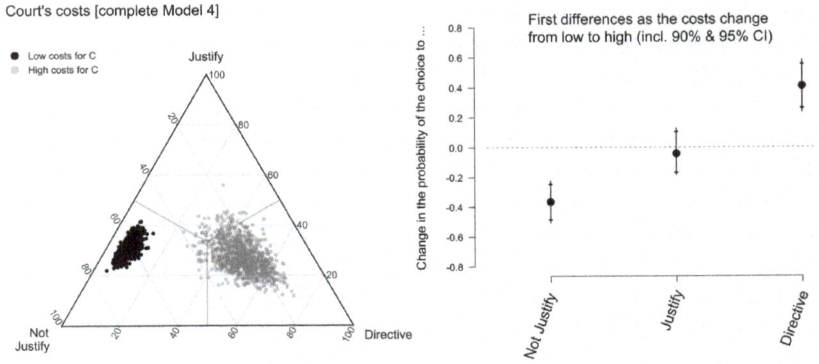

Fig. 4.6 Predicted probabilities and first differences of judicial choices by the court's costs. Note: $N = 580$ Senate decisions by the GFCC; 1000 simulations from Model 4 in Table 4.2. Significant variables from the lower rows in Table 4.3 are varied while the other variables are held constant at their means

358) in the direction of other judicial choices. However, the probability that the court presents directives is on average 48% when the costs are high compared with only about 8% when the costs are low. This is strong evidence in favor of H1c. Moreover, the probability that the court only justifies decisions is on average 31% when the costs are low and 27% when the costs are high. The first difference in Fig. 4.6 significantly decreases for the choice not to justify decisions as the costs increase. Moreover, the probability of the choice to only justify a decision decreases on average, confirming the behavior outlined in H1d, although the change is not significant. Finally, the first difference of the choice to present a directive is significant. This confirms H1c, but H1d is not confirmed. How stable are these findings?

Figure 4.7 summarizes quantities of interest simulating 1000 decisions at low and high costs in the subsample excluding decisions with vague directives (upper panel) and the subsample with decisions based on referrals that include at least one law (lower panel). The findings using the latter subsample confirm the robustness of the main analysis.

The ternary plot in the upper panel of Fig. 4.7 illustrates that there are major differences compared with the main analysis at high costs when excluding vague directives. The average probability of directives is about 32% at high costs in the subsample without vague directives, while the average probability of a directive is about 48% in the main analysis. Accordingly,

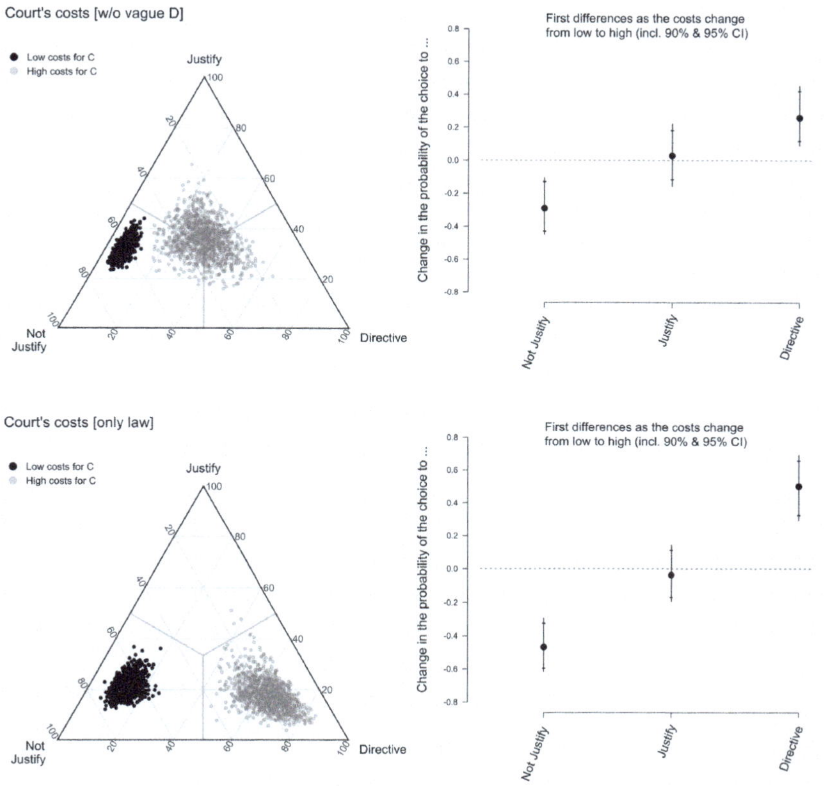

Fig. 4.7 Robustness of judicial choices by the court's costs. Note: $N = 549$ Senate decisions [w/o vague D] and $N = 341$ Senate decisions [only law]; 1000 simulations from the respective models in Appendix D.3. Significant variables from the lower rows in Table 4.3 are varied while the other variables are held constant at their means

the first differences show a smaller effect size compared to the main analysis. However, the first differences are significant for the choice to present directives and the choice not to justify decisions. This is similar to the main analysis and confirms H1c. The difference in the choice to only justify decisions is marginal, but on average positive as the costs change from low to high in the upper panel of Fig. 4.7. This is different from the expected effect, albeit not a significant change. Hence, H1d is not confirmed. Therefore, the outcome of the hypothesis tests in subsamples is the same as in the main analysis. However, the exclusion or inclusion of vague directives matters to the overall judicial choice when the costs are high.

In sum, the probability that the court presents directives is significantly higher when the court's costs from an evasion are high compared with when they are low, which confirms H1c. The findings regarding the choice to only justify decisions do not consistently support H1d. Moreover, the choice not to justify a decision has the highest likelihood relative to the other judicial choices when the court's costs from an evasion are low.[27]

The results of the hypothesis tests are used in the next section to refine judicial behavior.

4.5 Understanding Nuances of the First Face of Judicial Power

Table 4.4 summarizes the hypothesis tests. The ✓ indicates confirmed hypotheses. Hypotheses labeled ○ are not confirmed. The hypothesized behavior occurs on average, but decisive quantities are not significant. The ✗ indicates hypotheses that are not confirmed. Finally, hypotheses are only confirmed "overall" once they are confirmed in all subsamples; otherwise, I coded the weakest level of confirmation (column 2, Table 4.4).

The variables used to approximate the costs for the government with factors that are external to the judicial–political interaction effectively explain significant changes in the relative use of directives (H1a). They do not explain choices to justify decisions as described in H1b; instead, the effects are on average different from those hypothesized. By contrast, the variables used to approximate the government's costs based on factors internal to the judicial–political interaction do not consistently confirm the hypotheses. Finally, changes in the choice to present directives or justify decisions are mainly driven by significant changes in the choice not to justify decisions.

Why do external factors that define costs confirm some expectations and why do internal factors that define costs not confirm the expectations? The nature of the variables in the two groups may provide three explanations. First, significant external factors are not under the government's control; instead, costs are strongly defined by the public's support for the governing parties. Public support is an important explanatory variable for judicial decision-making (Gibson et al. 1998; Vanberg 2001, 2005; Staton 2010; Sternberg et al. 2015). The finding that external vari-

Table 4.4 Summary of the results of the hypothesis tests on the first face of judicial power

					Subsamples	
	Overall	*Hypothesis → addresses*	*Without controls**	*Complete model*	*Without vague directives*	*Against laws*
Government (costs α; external)	✓	H1a → Directive	✓	✓	✓	✓
	✗	H1b → Justify	✗	✗	✗	✗
Government (costs α; internal)	○	H1a → Directive	○	○	○	✓
	✗	H1b → Justify	✗	✗	✗	○
Court (costs γ)	✓	H1c → Directive	✓	✓	✓	✓
	✗	H1d → Justify	✓	○	✗	○
N			580	580	549	341

Note: ✓ confirmed (at least at $p<0.10$) ○ not confirmed, but behavior on average as expected ✗ not confirmed; *see Appendix D.3.

H1a: If the costs of the government to legislate in response to a judicial decision are low, then the likelihood that the court will justify a referral and present a directive is higher than when the government's costs to legislate again are high.

H1b: If the costs of the government to legislate in response to a judicial decision are low, then the likelihood that the court will only justify a referral is lower than when the government's costs to legislate again are high.

H1c: If the costs of a judicial evasion increase, then the likelihood that the court will justify a referral and present a directive also increases.

H1d: If the costs of a judicial evasion increase, then the likelihood that the court will only justify a referral decreases.

ables that define the government's costs effectively explain some judicial choices extends arguments on the relevance of public opinion to judicial decision-making. The findings suggest that the court not only accounts for its own standing; instead, it considers the government's reservoir of electoral support and the next election. If the government's reservoir of support is low, then the court faces a government that is less able to respond to judicial decisions. It is not rational for the court to significantly increase the use of directives in such settings; instead, the court significantly reduces the use of decisions that require a political response. The opposite is true once the government's reservoir of support changes and the general environment becomes more friendly to the government. In brief, the court anticipates the government's situation and adapts its decision-making accordingly. This suggests an anticipatory reaction on the side of the court (see Hönnige and Gschwend 2010, 519–520). Second, the variables that define the government's costs using internal features are partially controlled by the court and the government. The court can delay decision-making, which affects the age of an act or the timing of the government facing a decision in an area of interest. Similarly, the government can file briefs strategically. Thus, the actors are able to alter costs using internal factors. In this regard, the variables can cause endogeneity problems. An actor may use measures strategically when expecting a certain judicial choice (e.g., Vanberg 2001, 356). This is why the variables may not be appropriate to measure costs. Nevertheless, hypothesized trends occur in some subsamples measuring cost with internal variables. Why is H1a consistently confirmed using external factors but only tenuously when using internal factors? The third explanation originates from models of judicial behavior (see Parcelle Jr. et al. 2011, 29–49). Judges may aim to appear as legal technocrats in the judicial arena. In order to achieve this image, they act impartially in the immediate judicial–political interaction, which is why internal factors show no consistent effects. However, judges are strategic actors who carefully observe their surroundings when making choices (Epstein and Knight 1998; Sternberg et al. 2015). In other words, judges are legal experts on the bench, although they are strategic actors when facing society.

The final two rows in Table 4.4 summarize the effect of the court's costs from an evasion on judicial choices. The average probability that the court presents directives is higher at high costs compared with at low costs. This effect is consistently found across models (confirming H1c). However, the choice to only justify decisions is not consistently explained by the court's costs. The direction of effects is on average as expected, but too small to be significant. Instead, the analysis shows that changes in the court's costs significantly affect the probabilities of not justifying decisions or presenting directives. Moreover, relative changes in choices not to justify decisions affect the choices to present directives.

The hypotheses that explain choices to only justify decisions are not confirmed; instead, the effect of the costs on the choice to only justify decisions are often on average the opposite of the hypothesized effect in H1d. Moreover, changes in the choice to only justify decisions are frequently insignificant. In addition, changes often follow along the lines of changes in the choice to present directives. One possible explanation is that it is complicated to differentiate the choice to justify a decision from the choice to present a directive. However, the concluding analysis will show that there are significant differences between the two choices in some settings, which supports the differentiation between the two choices. Nevertheless, choices not to justify decisions or to present directives change more strongly, while the choice to justify decisions only slightly varies on average. This might imply that justified decisions become the option between two extreme choices at low and high costs.[28] In conclusion, the arguments developed here effectively explain significant changes in the choices not to justify decisions or to present directives, but they are less satisfying in explaining significant changes in the choice to justify decisions.

Finally, Table 4.4 illustrates that to include or exclude vague directives matters. Moreover, the table shows that the hypotheses do best in the subsample with decisions based on referrals that include at least one law. These considerations are used for a final analysis varying the court's and the government's costs simultaneously.

4.6 Showing the First Face of Judicial Power

In the concluding analysis, I vary the costs for the court from an evasion and the costs to the government for legislating simultaneously. In order to account for findings from the hypothesis tests, I only vary significant explanatory variables that are exogenous to the court's and the government's interaction. In addition, the analysis is conducted using decisions based on referrals that include at least one law, and I exclude vague directives.

The ternary plot in Fig. 4.8 summarizes 1000 simulated decisions for each possible combination of the costs between the court and the government. The court most likely does not justify decisions relative to the other choices as long as the government's costs are high (black and dark gray dots). The likelihood of directives increases stepwise, although the court chooses to present fewer directives as long as the government's costs are high compared with when these costs are low. This is well in line with the hypothesis tests. Once the costs of both actors are low, the probabilities of the different judicial choices are nearly equal (gray dots at the centroid). Finally, the court most likely chooses to present directives relative to the other choices once the government's costs are low but the court's costs are high (light gray dots).

The right panel in Fig. 4.8 summarizes the first differences between judicial choices by costs for the government and the court including 90% confidence intervals. The plot outlines whether the relative advantage of one judicial choice compared with the other choices in each of the four scenarios is significant. For example, the likelihood of not justifying decisions is the highest relative to the other choices as long as the government's costs are high according to the ternary plot. The first difference between the choices not to justify decisions versus the choice to present directives is significant as long as the government's costs are high (round and diamond shaped estimates). The same is true for the difference between the choices not to justify decisions versus the choice to only justify decisions. This is why the choice not to justify decisions is not only the most likely one relative to all other choices when the government's costs are high; the choice is also significantly higher compared with the other choices. Therefore, the court is risk-averse and is significantly more likely not to justify decisions relative to all other choices once the government's costs are high.

The significant differences between the choice not to justify decisions and the other choices become smaller once the court's costs are high and the government's costs are high, compared with when only the government's costs are high. Moreover, once both actors have low costs, the court is equally likely to choose between all judicial outcomes (triangular estimates). Finally, the difference in the probabilities of not justifying decisions or only justifying decisions significantly decreases relative to the choice to present a directive once the court's costs are high and the government's costs are low (squared estimates). Directives are significantly the most likely choices relative to all other choices when the courts costs are high and the government's costs are low.

Table 4.5 summarizes the order of the judicial choices identified based on the significant first differences between judicial choices and the average probability from among the simulated decisions in Fig. 4.8. Judicial choices

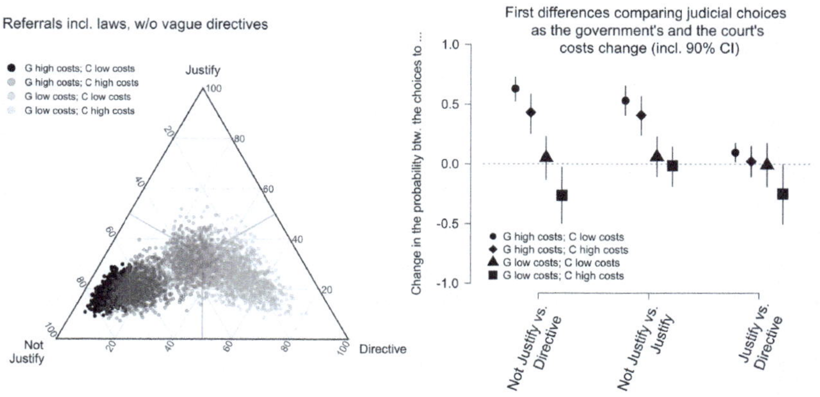

Fig. 4.8 Judicial decisions by costs for the government and the court. Note: $N = 313$ Senate decisions; 1000 simulations from the respective model in Appendix D.4. The variables that measure (1) the government's support, (2) the days until the next election, and (3) the impact on regular courts are varied according to Table 4.3. The other variables are held constant at their means

Table 4.5 Order of judicial choices (referrals incl. laws, w/o vague directives)

Choice level	*G high costs C low costs*	*G high cost C high cost*		*G low cost C low cost*			*G low cost C high cost*	
1st (Average prob.)	Not J. (72.1%)	Not J. (61.4%)		Not J. (37.0%)	D. (31.9%)	J. (31.1%)	D. (50.4%)	
2nd (Average prob.)	J. (18.8%)	J. (20.4%)	D. (18.2%)				J. (25.4%)	Not J. (24.2%)
3rd (Average prob.)	D. (9.1%)							

Note: Not J. = Not Justify; J. = Justify; D. = Directive. Average probabilities without significant first differences between choices are grouped on the same choice level

without significant first differences are assigned to the same choice level. Hence, the last column of the table shows that the probability that the court presents a directive is on average 50.4% when the government's costs of legislating are low and the court's costs from an evasion are high. Directives are the most likely choice and they occur significantly more often relative to the other judicial choices. The average probabilities of choosing to only justify decisions (25.4%) or not to justify decisions (24.2%) are nearly equal and the first difference between the two choices is not significant.

The table allows for some conclusions about the court's decision-making. First, the court chooses not to justify decisions significantly more often compared with the other choices when the government's costs are high. Instead, the court acts in a risk-averse manner. The court knows that the government's ability to implement judicial decisions is limited and refrains from presenting such decisions. Second, there are no significant differences between all of the judicial choices when both actors have low costs; instead, the court is equally likely to choose between the different options. Third, the average probability of the choice to present directives slowly increases throughout the table, while the choice to not justify decisions slowly decreases. Hence, relative changes between judicial choices are driven by these two choices. Fourth, the choice to only justify decisions is often not significantly different from other judicial choices; instead, the probability of this choice is stable, while the probabilities of the other two choices change around that choice.

In Appendix D.4, I repeat the analysis including the vague directives. The average probabilities of the choices vary, although this does not affect the general findings. Moreover, I repeat the analysis coding decisions with vague directives as decisions that are only justified. The results show that directives are still the most likely outcome relative to the other choices when the government's costs are low and the court's costs are high, although the difference compared with decisions that are only justified is no longer significant. This is partially explained by the increase in justified decisions in the data due to the changed coding. However, dealing with vague directives can make a differentiation between directives and justified decisions challenging. Nevertheless, the empirical analyses showed that there are significant differences between justified decisions and directives in some settings. Moreover, it is reasonable to differentiate between the choices on theoretical grounds. However, in order to assess that the separation between the actions does not lead to completely different findings compared with estimations when both actions are regarded as one, I estimate a logistic regression in Appendix D.5. The regression confirms the main findings.[29]

4.7 Summary

When do judges make a specific judicial choice? The analysis of decisions made by the GFCC shows that the government's costs of legislating—

defined by variables outside of the judicial–political interaction—as well as the court's costs from an evasion, influence judicial choices. The court significantly increases the use of directives when the costs from an evasion are high. Moreover, the court anticipates the government's costs of responding to decisions. The court most likely does not justify decisions as long as the government's costs of responding are high. The choice to only justify decisions changes only marginally as the actors' costs change.

The findings hold implications for the literature on public opinion in judicial politics. The court has an interest in the proper implementation of decisions. Public support is important to encourage compliance with judicial decisions and courts use legal tools to address the public (e.g. Vanberg 2001, 2005; Staton 2010; Krehbiel 2016). The analyses have shown that directives are used in settings where evasion is costly for the court; for example, when a decision is essential to the legal community. This may suggest that directives are also tools to increase public awareness. They can at least plausibly promote awareness, to the extent that they are specific (see also Staton and Vanberg 2008, 507; Vanberg 2005, 48). Directives make abstract legal topics tangible and allow the media to report on decisions in detailed ways. Moreover, the response to a directive is measurable, which eases the media's and the public's capabilities to monitor political compliance. Nevertheless, ultimately the governing majority has to take measures to implement decisions. The findings presented here suggest that the court is more likely to present decisions that require an implementation when the government is in a situation where it is capable of responding to a judicial decision. Thus, courts are strategic actors accounting for their environments (see Epstein and Knight 1998) more than they are sincere policy-seekers (see Segal and Spaeth 1993, 2002). The court constraints itself in anticipation of the implementation of a decision, which is evidence in favor of autolimitation on the judicial side (see Hönnige and Gschwend 2010, 519–520). Therefore, when we assess the influence of public opinion on judicial decision-making, we also need to account for the government's capabilities of responding to public and judicial pressure.

The findings contribute to considerations about the use of vagueness in judicial opinions. Staton and Vanberg (2008) argue that when judges expect resistance, they may present vague decisions to cover possible noncompliance. It is plausible to assume that political resistance is more likely when the government's costs of legislating are high compared with when they are low. Moreover, directives are the most specific judgments compared to the other choices outlining legally desired actions. Therefore, if the court presents fewer directives when the government's costs are high compared to when they are low, then this supports the argument concerning the use of vagueness in opinions. Indeed, this is the pattern identified here.[30]

Courts are considered as showing the first face of judicial power. When analyzing judicial decision-making, we need to account for the court's costs from an evasion and the government's capabilities to respond to judicial decisions. Moreover, if we wish to understand judicial decision-making independent of judicial votes, differentiating between the types of choices that judges make is a promising approach. In this regard, directives are defined by the content of a decision. This is why taking the content and opinion clarity more seriously is one area in which to extend the outlined research.

Notes

1. The second layer includes information on the proceedings level of decisions. For example, if one decision comprises multiple referrals, these are coded on the proceedings layer. Judicial directives are a feature of the decisions on the primary layer. Information from the proceedings layer is aggregated to the decision layer when necessary.
2. Excluded are seven reimbursements of expenses, six peremption by other means, six other preliminary decisions, three permissions to withdraw a proceeding, two addendums, two objections, one preliminary judgment by the plenum, one statement by the plenum and one enforcement order.
3. The GFCC did not make any main decisions in December 1990 after the federal election.
4. *Gesetzgeber* (legislature), *Frist* (deadline), *Neuregelung* (revision) and *Zeitraum* (time period).
5. "Eine Nichtigerklärung der verfassungswidrigen Vorschriften scheidet im vorliegenden Fall aus, weil der Gesetzgeber auf verschiedene Weise eine verfassungskonforme Rechtslage herbeiführen kann. Es ist ihm unbenommen, Auszubildende, die eine weitere in sich selbständige Ausbildung beginnen, nachdem ihre Eltern ihnen gegenüber ihre Unterhaltspflicht erfüllt haben, wieder elternunabhängig nach dem Konzept des §11 Abs. 3 Satz 1 Nr. 5 BAföG 1979 zu fördern. Der Gesetzgeber kann aber beispielsweise auch eine Regelung treffen, die diesen Auszubildenden den Zugang zur Förderung nach Maßgabe des §36 Abs. 1 Satz 1 BAföG eröffnet."
6. "Die wissenschaftlichen Erkenntnisse über die Ursachen aggressiven Verhaltens von Hunden der verschiedenen Rassen und über das Zusammenwirken

unterschiedlicher Ursachen sowie die tatsächlichen Annahmen des Gesetzgebers belassen noch erhebliche Unsicherheit. Es ist deshalb notwendig, die Gefährdungslage, die durch das Halten von Hunden entstehen kann, und die Ursachen dafür weiter im Blick zu behalten und insbesondere das Beißverhalten der von §2 Abs. 1 Satz 1 HundVerbrEinfG erfassten Hunde künftig mehr noch als bisher zu überprüfen und zu bewerten. Wird dabei die prognostische Einschätzung der Gefährlichkeit dieser Hunde durch den Gesetzgeber nicht oder nicht in vollem Umfang bestätigt, wird er seine Regelung den neuen Erkenntnissen anpassen müssen."

7. For example, in the given case, the court had to decide whether the required financial support by an employer for an employee who takes maternity leave violates the employer's occupational freedom (Art. 12 Basic Law). The decision took a turn when the court argued that financial support itself is reasonable. However, the GFCC criticized the requirement for being restricted to small businesses, thus excluding large businesses from providing such support (BVerfGE 109, 64 [92–93]). This violates the equality before the law (Art. 3 Basic Law) and had to be changed before the end of 2005 (BVerfGE 109, 64 [95]).
8. Instead, judges sometimes address criticism openly, as an interview with Jutta Limbach—former President of the GFCC—illustrates (see Lamprecht and Lersch 1995).
9. Neither the court nor the government knows exactly how unified the party's voting behavior is. Instead, each actor has to develop a "sense" based on the average behavior of the representatives.
10. I also logged the count. Changes from one day to another are more important shortly before an election compared with when an election is further away.
11. "(v4) Wenn am nächsten Sonntag Bundestagswahl wäre, würden Sie dann zur Wahl gehen? (v5) Und welche Partei würden Sie dann wählen?" Respondents who would not vote were excluded. There were six months for which data was missing. These months are assigned the value from the preceding month.
12. I excluded a number of capitalized stop words from the noun-frequency list.
13. 1159 words were classified with the help of this approach.
14. Keywords were identified using (1) the unofficial name given to a decision, (2) the section of a decision that summarizes the legal question and, (3) an overview from skimming the text.
15. The date of the earliest referral was chosen in 187 decisions that combined multiple referrals. In 17 decisions the date of a referral was imputed. I estimated the average number of days from a referral to the decision across cases with both dates. This was undertaken in subsamples accounting for whether a hearing was held or not. Afterwards, I subtracted the average number of days (accounting for the subsample characteristic) from the decision date in the 17 decisions.
16. https://www.juris.de, accessed March 11, 2018.

17. The logic of this argument is similar to Staton's (2010) argument of strategic media use by a court to increase awareness for decisions, which allows the public to punish noncompliance.
18. I targeted citations of officially-published decisions (e.g. BVerfGE VOLUME, FIRST PAGE).
19. The search was conducted using the database *Nexis*, www.nexis.com, accessed March 11, 2018. The keywords used are the same as identified for calculating impact scores regarding regular courts and bibliographical references. In cases when keywords were too technical, a second keyword was identified.
20. Acts referred to the court are coded in the CCDB. One decision can combine multiple referred acts. To aggregate the acts to the decision level, I separate decisions that include referrals of at least one law from those decisions that only include referrals not directed against laws.
21. The `nnet` package (Venables and Ripley 2002) and the `mlogit` package (Croissant 2018) in R were used to estimate all models. Contents of Tables 4.2, D.3, and D.4 were exported using the `stargazer` package (Hlavac 2018).
22. The policy space is constrained only to the extent that the court regards the former policy as unconstitutional.
23. See media reports like "Bundesverfassungsgericht fordert drittes Geschlecht im Geburtenregister." Süddeutsche Zeitung: http://sz.de/1.3740223, accessed December 30, 2019. Or "Asylbewerber müssen ab sofort mehr Geld bekommen." Der Spiegel: http://spon.de/adHZF, accessed December 30, 2019.
24. Drawbacks of R^2 are discussed, but Veall and Zimmermann (1996) highlight that McFadden's pseudo R^2 can be used in the multinomial context.
25. In order to simulate all quantities the `zeligverse` package (Gandrud 2017) in *R* was used, and to compute the ternary plots the `ggtern` package (Hamilton 2018) was used.
26. In Appendix D.3, I present simulations from Model 2 in Table 4.2 which lead to similar findings as in the main analysis.
27. Simulations from Model 3 in Table 4.2 also confirm the overall findings, albeit showing a negative and significant first difference for the choice to only justify decisions (see Appendix D.3).
28. The reader may argue that this suggests an order of the choices. Not-justified decisions are at the one end and the choice of presenting directives is at the other end, while the choice to only justify decisions is a middle category. I argue that judicial choices are not ordered but rather judges choose from different options (see also Wahlbeck et al. 1999, 499; Hettinger et al. 2007, 61–62). However, it should be noted that even if judicial choices were ordered, the multinomial approach applied here is sufficient, albeit with some efficiency loss. The opposite is not true. Methods for ordinal variables lead

to biased or nonsensical estimates when applied to nominal outcomes (Long 1997, 149). Hence, the chosen approach safely accounts for both arguments.

29. This also addresses the violation of the IIA assumption mentioned at the beginning of this chapter. The violation is of less concern when the results between the estimations are comparable (Dow and Endersby 2004, 112).
30. A brief descriptive assessment yields that if the court presents directives, then the share of vague directives is larger when the government's costs are high compared with when they are low (see Appendix D.6). Therefore, the court's judicial choices favor the idea that opinion clarity decreases as the risk of noncompliance increases (Staton and Vanberg 2008, 513).

References

Bartels, B.L., Johnston, C.D. (2013). On the Ideological Foundations of Supreme Court Legitimacy in the American Public. *American Journal of Political Science*, *57*(1), 184–199.

Bergmann, H., Bailer, S., Ohmura, T., Saalfeld, T., Sieberer, U. (2016). Namentliche Abstimmungen im Bundestag 1949 bis 2013: Befunde aus einem neuen Datensatz. *Zeitschrift für Parlamentsfragen*, *47*(1), 26–50.

Bevan, S. (2017). Gone Fishing: The Creation of the Comparative Agendas Project Master Codebook. *Comparative Agendas Project (CAP)*, *0.9.1*(Beta), August 26, 2017.

Brouard, S. (2009). The Politics of Constitutional Veto in France: Constitutional Council, Legislative Majority and Electoral Competition. *West European Politics*, *32*(2), 384–403.

Brouard, S. (2016). Constitutional Politics: The French Case and Theory-Building. In R. Elgie, E. Grossman, and A. G. Mazur (Eds.) *The Oxford Handbook of French Politics* (pp. 220–242). Oxford: Oxford University Press.

Burkhart, S. (2008). Deutsche Bundesgesetzgebung 1972–2005. *GESIS Datenarchiv*, *ZA4569* (Version 1.0.0), Köln.

Busch, A. (2016). *Korpus Regierungserklärungen. Lehr-Forschungs-Projekt Textanalyse.* Göttingen: Georg-August-Universität.

Caldeira, G.A. (1987). Public Opinion and The U.S. Supreme Court: FDR's Court-Packing Plan. *American Political Science Review*, *81*(4), 1139–1153.

Carey, J.M. (2009). *Legislative Voting and Accountability.* Cambridge: Cambridge University Press.

Carrubba, C., Gabel, M., Hug, S. (2008). Legislative Voting Behavior, Seen and Unseen: A Theory of Roll-Call Vote Selection. *Legislative Studies Quarterly*, *33*(4), 543–572.

Clark, T.S., Lauderdale, B.E. (2012). The Genealogy of Law. *Political Analysis*, *20*(3), 329–350.

Croissant, Y. (2018). mlogit: Multinomial Logit Models. *R Package*, *V.0.3-0.*

Dow, J.K., Endersby, J.W. (2004). Multinomial Probit and Multinomial Logit: A Comparison of Choice Models for Voting Research. *Electoral Studies*, *23*(1), 107–122.
Easton, D. (1965). *A Systems Analysis of Political Life*. New York: Wiley.
Easton, D. (1975). A Re-Assessment of the Concept of Political Support. *British Journal of Political Science*, *5*(4), 435–457.
Engst, B.G. (2017). Die vierte Gesetzeslesung. Verfassungsgerichte des deutsch-österreichischen Modells als Vetospieler. In V. Frick, O. W. Lembcke, and R. Lhotta (Eds.) *Politik und Recht. Umrisse eines politkwissenschaftlichen Forschungsfeldes* (pp. 281–301). Baden-Baden: Nomos.
Epstein, L., Knight, J. (1998). *The Choices Justices Make*. Washington, DC: CQ Press.
Epstein, L., Martin, A.D. (2011). Does Public Opinion Influence the Supreme Court? Probably Yes (But We're Not Sure Why). *University of Pennsylvania Law Review*, *13*(2), 263–281.
Farganis, D. (2012). Do Reasons Matter? The Impact of Opinion Content on Supreme Court Legitimacy. *Political Research Quarterly*, *65*(1), 206–216.
Feldkamp, M.F. (2011). *Datenhanbuch zur Geschichte des Deutschen Bundestages 1990 bis 2010. Ergänzungsband*. Baden-Baden: Nomos.
Fowler, J.H., Jeon, S. (2008). The Authority of Supreme Court Precedent. *Social Networks*, *30*(1), 16–30.
Gandrud, C. (2017). zeligverse: Easily Install and Load Stable Zelig Packages. *R Package*, *V.0.1.1*.
Gibson, J.L., Caldeira, G.A., Baird, V.A. (1998). On the Legitimacy of National High Courts. *American Political Science Review*, *92*(2), 343–358.
Grabenwarter, C., Hoffmann-Riem, W., Suchocka, H., Tuori, K., Velares, J. (2013). Opinion on the Fourth Amendment of the Fundamental Law of Hungary. *Venice Commission [European Commission for Democracy Through Law]*, *2013*(720), 1–32.
Hamilton, N. (2018). ggtern: An Extension to 'ggplot2', for the Creation of Ternary Diagrams. *R Package*, *V.3.0.0*.
Hausman, J., McFadden, D. (1984). Specification Tests for the Multinomial Logit Model. *Econometrica*, *52*(5), 1219–1240.
Hettinger, V.A., Lindquist, S.A., Martinek, W.L. (2007). *Judging on a Collegial Court: Influences on Federal Appellate Decision Making*. Charlottesville: University of Virginia Press.
Hix, S., Kreppel, A., Noury, A. (2003). The Party System in the European Parliament: Collusive or Competitive? *Journal of Common Market Studies*, *41*(2), 309–331.
Hlavac, M. (2018). stargazer: Well-Formatted Regression and Summary Statistics Tables. *R Package*, *V.5.2.1*.

Hoffmann-Riem, W. (2008). Der grundrechtliche Schutz der Vertraulichkeit und Integrität eigengenutzter informationstechnischer Systeme. *Juristen Zeitung, 63*(21), 1009–1022.

Hönnige, C. (2007). *Verfassungsgericht, Regierung und Opposition. Die vergleichende Analyse eines Spannungsdreiecks.* Wiesbaden: VS Verlag für Sozialwissenschaften.

Hönnige, C. (2008). Verfassungsgerichte in den EU-Staaten: Wahlverfahren, Kompetenzen und Organisationsprinzipien. *Journal for Comparative Government and European Policy, 6*(3), 524–553.

Hönnige, C. (2009). The Electoral Connection: How the Pivotal Judge Affects Oppositional Success at European Constitutional Courts. *West European Politics, 32*(5), 963–984.

Hönnige, C., Gschwend, T. (2010). Das Bundesverfassungsgericht im politischen System der BRD – ein unbekanntes Wesen? *Politische Vierteljahresschrift, 51*(3), 507–530.

Hönnige, C., Gschwend, T., Wittig, C., Engst, B.G. (2015). *Constitutional Court Database (CCDB), V17.01 [Mar.].*

Ignagni, J., Meernik, J. (1994). Explaining Congressional Attempts to Reverse Supreme Court Decisions. *Political Research Quarterly, 47*(2), 353–371.

King, G., Tomz, M., Wittenberg, J. (2000). Making the Most of Statistical Analyses: Improving Interpretation and Presentation. *American Journal of Political Science, 44*(2), 347–361.

Kranenpohl, U. (2010). *Hinter dem Schleier des Beratungsgeheimnisses. Der Willensbildungs- und Entscheidungsprozess des Bundesverfassungsgerichts.* Wiesbaden: VS Verlag für Sozialwissenschaften.

Krehbiel, J.N. (2016). The Politics of Judicial Procedures: The Role of Public Oral Hearings in the German Constitutional Court. *American Journal of Political Science, 60*(4), 990–1005.

Lamprecht, R., Lersch, P. (1995). Spiegel Gespräch. 'Die Grenzen sind erreicht.' Jutta Limbach über die Kritik am Kruzifix-Urteil und an den Verfassungsrichtern. *Der Spiegel,* (35), 34–38.

Limbach, J. (2002). Die Integrationskraft des Bundesverfassungsgerichts. In H. Vorländer (Ed.) *Integration durch Verfassung* (pp. 315–327). Wiesbaden: Westdeutscher Verlag.

Linos, K., Twist, K. (2016). The Supreme Court, the Media, and Public Opinion: Comparing Experimental and Observational Methods. *Journal of Legal Studies, 45*(2), 223–254.

Long, J.S. (1997). *Regression Models for Categorical and Limited Dependent Variables.* Thousand Oaks: Sage.

Mattei, U., Pes, L.G. (2008). Civil Law and Common Law: Toward Convergence? In G. A. Caldeira, D. R. Kelemen, and K. E. Whittington (Eds.) *The Oxford Handbook of Law and Politics* (pp. 267–280). Oxford: Oxford University Press.

Müller, W.C., Strøm, K. (1999). *Policy, Office or Votes? How Political Parties in Western Europe Make Hard Decisions*. Cambridge: Cambridge University Press.

Parcelle Jr., R.L., Curry, B.W., Marshall, B.W. (2011). *Decision Making by the Modern Supreme Court*. Cambridge: Cambridge University Press.

Politbarometer. (2013). Partielle Kumulation (1977–2011). *GESIS Datenarchiv, ZA2391* (Version 3.0.0), Köln.

Roberts, G.K. (2006). The German Bundestag Election 2005. *Parliamentary Affairs, 59*(4), 668–681.

Rudzio, W. (2015). *Das politische System der Bundesrepublik Deutschland*. Wiesbaden: VS Verlag für Sozialwissenschaften, 9th ed.

Scheppele, K.L. (2003). Constitutional Negotiations: Political Contexts of Judicial Activism in Post-Soviet Europe. *International Sociology, 18*(1), 219–238.

Schlaich, K., Korioth, S. (2015). *Das Bundesverfassungsgericht. Stellung, Verfahren Entscheidungen*. München: C.H. Beck, 10th ed.

Segal, J.A., Spaeth, H.J. (1993). *The Supreme Court and the Attitudinal Model*. Cambridge: Cambridge University Press.

Segal, J.A., Spaeth, H.J. (2002). *The Supreme Court and the Attitudinal Model Revisited*. Cambridge: Cambridge University Press.

Sieberer, U., Saalfeld, T., Ohmura, T., Bergmann, H., Bailer, S. (2020). Roll-Call Votes in the German Bundestag: A New Dataset, 1949–2013. *British Journal of Political Science 50*(3), 1137–1145.

Spiller, P.T., Tiller, E.H. (1996). Invitations to Override: Congressional Reversals of Supreme Court Decisions. *International Review of Law and Economics, 16*(4), 503–521.

Staton, J.K. (2010). *Judicial Power and Strategic Communication in Mexico*. Cambridge: Cambridge University Press.

Staton, J.K., Vanberg, G. (2008). The Value of Vagueness: Delegation, Defiance, and Judicial Opinions. *American Journal of Political Science, 52*(3), 504–519.

Stecker, C. (2015). How Effects on Party Unity Vary Across Votes. *Party Politics, 21*(5), 791–802.

Stecker, C. (2016). The Effects of Federalism Reform on the Legislative Process in Germany. *Regional and Federal Studies, 26*(5), 603–624.

Stephenson, M.C. (2004). Court of Public Opinion: Government Accountability and Judicial Independence. *Journal of Law, Economics, and Organization, 20*(2), 379–399.

Sternberg, S., Gschwend, T., Wittig, C., Engst, B.G. (2015). Zum Einfluss der öffentlichen Meinung auf Entscheidungen des Bundesverfassungsgerichts: Eine Analyse von abstrakten Normenkontrollen sowie Bund-Länder-Streitigkeiten 1974–2010. *Politische Vierteljahresschrift, 56*(4), 570–598.

Vanberg, G. (1998). Abstract Judicial Review, Legislative Bargaining, and Policy Compromise. *Journal of Theoretical Politics, 10*(3), 299–326.

Vanberg, G. (2001). Legislative-Judicial Relations: A Game-Theoretic Approach to Constitutional Review. *American Journal of Political Science*, *45*(2), 346–361.

Vanberg, G. (2005). *The Politics of Constitutional Review in Germany.* Cambridge: Cambridge University Press.

Veall, M.R., Zimmermann, K.F. (1996). Pseudo-R2 Measures for Some Common Limited Dependent Variable Models. *Journal of Economic Surveys*, *10*(3), 241–259.

Venables, W.N., Ripley, B.D. (2002). *Modern Applied Statistics with S.* New York: Springer New York, 4th ed.

Volkens, A., Lehmann, P., Matthieß, T., Merz, N., Regel, S., Werner, A. (2015). *The Manifesto Data Collection. Manifesto Project (MRG / CMP / MARPOR). Version 2015a.* Berlin: Wissenschaftszentrum Berlin für Sozialforschung.

Wahlbeck, P.J., Spriggs, J.F., II., Maltzman, F. (1999). The Politics of Dissents and Concurrences on the U.S. Supreme Court. *American Politics Quarterly*, *27*(4), 488–514.

Wesel, U. (2004). *Der Gang nach Karlsruhe: Das Bundesverfassungsgericht in der Geschichte der Bundesrepublik.* München: Karl Blessing Verlag.

Wittig, C.E. (2016). *The Occurrence of Separate Opinions at the Federal Constitutional Court: An Analysis with a Novel Database.* Berlin: Logos Verlag Berlin GmbH.

CHAPTER 5

The Second Face of Judicial Power

In this chapter, I assess the empirical nature of the theoretical considerations addressing the second face of judicial power known as autolimitation.[1] Autolimitation embodies the idea that "the legislature censors its own behavior preemptively in anticipation of judicial review" (Vanberg 2001, 352; similar Stone 1992, 122–129; Stone Sweet 2000, 75–80). In order to assess autolimitation, I present a research design to identify the causal effect of the phenomenon in legislative committees. In addition, I use various estimation strategies including a difference-in-differences to analyze autolimitation. Robust findings show that autolimitation has minor effects on committees, but bills exposed to legal signals are drafted accounting for the court compared with bills that are not exposed to signals. Hence, judicial politics scholars need to more strongly account for the pre-legislative process. Moreover, legislative–judicial bargaining functions differently compared with intra-legislative bargain between opposing parties.

The assessment of autolimitation poses an empirical rather than theoretical challenge. Scholars have derived theoretical implications of legislative self-restraint from formal models (Vanberg 1998, 2001; Marks 2012 [1988]) and some have used case studies to illustrate the potential influence of autolimitation (Landfried 1992; Kommers 1994; Stone Sweet 1998, 2000). However, systematic empirical evidence of the existence and inner workings of such a mechanism is lacking. A possible reason is that autolimitation implies a non-decision (see Bachrach and Baratz 1962, 948–945). Accordingly, governments should prioritize one version of a bill over

B. G. Engst, *The Two Faces of Judicial Power*,
https://doi.org/10.1007/978-3-030-46016-7_5

an alternative version under the threat of a judicial review. The alternative version will never be presented. If we wish to fully understand the effect of autolimitation, we would need to compare the spatial location of the presented bill in relation to the position of the court with the location of the bill not presented in relation to the court, which is obviously impossible. Instead, when assessing autolimitation an identification problem exists: of the two versions of the same bill that I need to observe, I am only able to observe one version.

This is why I present a research design that addresses the outlined challenge and I use an identification strategy closely matching the research design to untangle the causal effect of autolimitation.

5.1 The Second Face of Judicial Power in a Causal Inference Framework

Summarizing the theoretical discussion on autolimitation, I hypothesized that if a legal signal—in the form of citing any prior court decision—is debated in legislative committees, then policy will be shifted in the spatial direction of the court (Hypothesis H4). Thus, the research design must allow for assessing policy shifts in the direction of the ideal point of the constitutional court as a result of a bill's exposure to a legal signal in a committee.

A challenge is that autolimitation should already occur when ministerial clerks or deputy staff draft a bill. They can act strategically, having substantial influence on policymaking (Hammond 1986; Montgomery and Nyhan 2017). Nevertheless, assessing the confidential stage when legislation is drafted is difficult, reflecting a limitation of this study. Focusing on legislative committees instead is useful for three reasons. First, according to the definition of autolimitation, the legislative majority restrains itself (see e.g., Landfried 1992; Kommers 1994; Stone Sweet 1998, 2000; Vanberg 1998, 2001). Thus, the herein presented theoretical approach is designed towards the legislature. Second, bills are discussed in committees once presented. Committees can hear experts comparable to ministerial clerks, whereby new issues can arise. Eventually they can request modifications to bills (Mattson and Strøm 1995, 287–291). Third, if self-restraint still occurs in the committee stage, it is an even more conservative measure of autolimitation, assuming that bills should have been screened before.

In an ideal experiment, one would introduce similar bills to committees and randomly assign discussions of former court decisions to half of the committees. In the other half, no court decisions are discussed. Afterwards, one would compare the amendments in final committee reports to assess whether legal signals led to a policy shift towards the ideal point of the constitutional court. Such an experiment is not feasible, which is why I rely on observational data. However, the analysis should mirror the outlined experiment as closely as possible. The research design for such an experiment can be written in potential outcomes notation (Rubin 1974). Accordingly, there is a legal signal (L), which is the treatment that is either present ($L = 1$) or absent ($L = 0$). Furthermore, let Y_i be the potential outcome, which is the position of a bill (i) in relation to the court. Each bill has potential outcomes in the two time periods: once before a legal signal appears (or not) (t), and once after a legal signal has been discussed (or not) ($t + 1$) in a committee. Hence, depending on the presence or absence of a legal signal, there are two outcomes for each bill in the two time periods: either the policy position of the bill prior to the legal signal ($Y_{i;t}^{L=1}$) and the policy position of the bill after the legal signal ($Y_{i;t+1}^{L=1}$), or the policy position of the bill not discussed under the influence of a legal signal at time t ($Y_{i;t}^{L=0}$) and the policy position of the bill not discussed under the influence of a legal signal at time $t + 1$ ($Y_{i;t+1}^{L=0}$). Comparing the strength of the policy shift of a bill i under treatment and control in both time periods reveals the causal effect of legal signals on the policy shift:

$$Y_i = (Y_{i;t+1}^{L=1} - Y_{i;t}^{L=1}) - (Y_{i;t+1}^{L=0} - Y_{i;t}^{L=0})$$

However, in the outlined setting, one faces the fundamental problem of causality, which states that of the four potential outcomes for each bill only two outcomes are actually realized, while the other two outcomes are counterfactual (Imbens and Rubin 2015, 6–7; Holland 1986, 947). One cannot observe the two states of the world ($L = 1$ and $L = 0$) for the same bill. Therefore, it is necessary to compare the change in treated bills ($Y^{L=1}$) with the change in control bills ($Y^{L=0}$). The difference in the strength of the policy shift between the treated and control bills over both time periods is the treatment effect. This possible treatment effect can be estimated as the difference-in-differences (DiD), which is the quantity of interest in accordance with the research design (Card and Krueger 1994).

$$DiD = (Y_{t+1}^{L=1} - Y_t^{L=1}) - (Y_{t+1}^{L=0} - Y_t^{L=0})$$

In sum, I argue that autolimitation is the reaction to a legal signal by a legislative committee. Members of a committee modify a bill regarding a former court decision to account for the position of the court. In what follows, I outline the measurement strategy for a policy shift in committees and the measures for a legal signal as well as alternative explanations of policy shifts. Afterwards, I assess the empirical implications of legal signals on committee bargaining.

5.2 Operationalizing the Second Face of Judicial Power

The autolimitation hypothesis requires me to compare the position of bills in relation to the court that are exposed to a legal signal with that of bills in relation to the court that are not exposed to a signal. Therefore, bills become the level of analysis and are assessed at two points in time of the legislative process.

The preliminary information to compile my data is obtained from the GESTA dataset (Burkhart 2008; Stecker 2016), which summarizes all bills proposed in the German *Bundestag*. I randomly draw 10% of all 2768 bills reaching the committee stage in the legislative periods 12 (December 1990) to 16 (September 2009). The committee stage is the unit where I analyze the bills. Hence, to avoid violating causal assumptions, sampling has to happen at this stage. The final sample comprises $N = 277$ bills. I collected the full text of all drafts of the 277 bills introduced to the *Bundestag* and all 277 versions of the same bills after leaving the leading legislative committee. In addition, I collected the full text of all 81 laws that were referred to the GFCC between 1990 and 2010 but were upheld by the court. All of the 635 documents are used to estimate the policy shift. Moreover, I collected original information from the reports of the primary committees and added a number of variables to control for alternative explanations of policy shift.

In sum, the GESTA dataset (Burkhart 2008; Stecker 2016)—which is linked to the Constitutional Court Database (Hönnige et al. 2015) outlined in Sect. 4.2—can be used to identify a sample of bills for the assessment of the second face of judicial power. The measures to operationalize the constructs for the analysis outlined in the next section are largely self-computed.

5.2.1 Dependent Variable: Policy Shift

The event that I wish to explain is the direction of a policy shift in legislative committees, accounting for the position of the court. Three steps are necessary to measure such a shift: first, one must place the court in a policy space; second, a bill that is sent to a committee (at time t) and the same bill leaving the committee (at time $t+1$) must be placed in the same policy space, whereby the difference between the two positions of the bill is the policy shift; and third, the direction of the shift in relation to the court can be identified estimating the difference between the absolute distance of the court to the bill at time $t+1$ and the absolute distance of the court to the bill at time t.

I apply a text analysis approach to scale (1) the court, (2) the bill at time t, and (3) the bill at time $t+1$. For the purpose of this study, the court and the bill need to be scaled over the same dimension, although it is not necessary to precisely specify the latent dimension; instead, it is only necessary to evaluate shifts on the dimension. To a certain extent, text analysis is applied here only to identify text similarities and the direction of differences. In this regard, it is relevant to pay attention to the comparability of the text type used, the applied language, and the environment producing documents (Slapin and Proksch 2014, 138; Bunea and Ibenskas 2015, 432).

It is plausible to assume that the style and vocabulary in written bills are comparable across bills as they have the same characteristics. This is particularly true for Germany, where the Federal Ministry of Justice and Consumer Protection has published a handbook on how to phrase laws and suggesting the kind of legal language and style that should be used.[2] The handbook itself is no longer updated, although the ministry has established a unit devoted to supporting all federal ministries to verbalize laws consistently. The unit follows laws through the policy process and works with the *Bundestag*, cooperates with the European Union and scientific institutions.[3] This is why it is plausible to assume that the language and style used in bills is consistent. Moreover, the text-producing environment is stable. The institutionalized procedures are established by the administration of ministries and are not dependent on specific political actors. In addition, bureaucrats drafting the actual texts of bills are less frequently changed than political actors (see Ismayr 2006, 250–256). Hence, for the draft of a bill (t) and the version of that bill leaving the committee ($t+1$), I scale the text of that particular bill at each stage of the process.

In order to measure the (mean) position of the court using the same type of text, I can draw on the legal procedures. In particular, I do not wish to predict judicial choices anymore. Instead, I can include judicial outcomes when approximating the position of the court. In every legislative period, the GFCC is asked to review whether bills are in accordance with the German *Basic Law*. Remember that bills are considered in accordance with the constitution once a decision is not justified. Therefore, assuming that bills in accordance with the constitution are supported by the judges, I am able to estimate the court's position using the bills. Hence, I use the same type of text to estimate the court's position as I use to estimate the position of the bills at time t and time $t + 1$. For this purpose, I identified all bills from admissible referrals which were eventually not justified on the merits using information from the CCDB.

Since the style of the collected texts is similar, I use WordFish to estimate scores for each document (see Slapin and Proksch 2008). This method uses unique words and compares texts based on the relative word usage in each text. The advantage of WordFish is that no texts need to be used as anchors, but rather a parametric model based on a Poisson distribution is used to scale texts over one latent dimension (see Proksch and Slapin 2010, 594; Slapin and Proksch 2008, 708–709 for details). The advantages and disadvantages of the method have been discussed, although to a large extent these debates are concerned with the appropriate interpretation of the underlying latent dimension (Slapin and Proksch 2014, 135–138; Klüver 2015; Bunea and Ibenskas 2015). These particular concerns are left aside here as specifying the underlying latent dimension is not of interest here; instead, it is only relevant how texts are changed and moved in one or the other direction of the latent dimension. For this purpose, the comparability of the text type, the conformity in the text style, and similarities in the document-generating process are most important (Slapin and Proksch 2014, 138). As discussed, these prerequisites are given here, which is why using WordFish is appropriate.

Finally, a rigorous approach was used to prepare the documents. The documents were shortened to only include the text of a respective bill and converted to UTF-8 .txt files. Each file was checked manually including a semiautomatic spell check. Special characters and numbers were excluded. There is a debate concerning whether very common words (stop words) should also be excluded and whether words should be reduced to their stem (Lucas et al. 2015, 257–258). I decided to keep all words unchanged for the main analysis as in legal language every word and minor changes may count. Nonetheless, in order to illustrate the robustness of my findings regardless of this choice, I replicate the later analyses with stop words excluded from the documents and words being stemmed.

Ultimately, the position of the court is calculated as the mean of the positions of all laws upheld by the court during a respective legislative period. Using the mean position of the court, it is possible to calculate the direction of a policy shift for each legislative proceeding simply as $p_{shift} = |p_C - p_{t+1}| - |p_C - p_t|$, where p_C is the position of the court and p_t and p_{t+1} are the positions of the bill at t or $t+1$. If p_{shift} is positive, the committee shifted the proposed bill away from the court's position. If p_{shift} is negative, the committee shifted the proposed bill towards the court's position, and if p_{shift} is zero, no change occurred.

In the next section, I outline the operationalization of legal signals in legislative committees as the variable to explain policy shifts in the direction of the court.

5.2.2 *Independent Variable: Legal Signal*

The governing majority facing the threat of judicial review has to develop beliefs about the position of the court in order to enter into meaningful self-restraint. Past decisions by constitutional courts are a plausible tool to consider possible outcomes of judicial review. The decisions reveal information on the court's position on an issue under consideration in the legislature. Indeed, Landfried (1994, 117), observed that as legislative committees discussed the financing of parties in Germany, "[t]he debate centered not so much on where the Basic Law draws the line for the financing of parties but on where the Constitutional Court would draw the line in a judgement." A similar example is given by the Socialists' attempt to pass an antitrust bill in the media sector in France. The legislature extensively changed the newly drafted bill. "Of the original 42 articles, 26 were substantially rewritten; most amendments were made under the explicit threat of referral to the Council [the French Constitutional Court]" (Stone Sweet 2000, 81). The case study in Chapter 3 supports both examples. The legislative committee that assessed the draft on the parental custody reform repeatedly addressed five decisions by the GFCC. The constitution was explicitly mentioned only once. The custody reform was new, although by embedding the reform in past decisions the legislature aimed to address the position of the GFCC to meet future legal concerns. This is why I code legal signals as decisions cited in committee reports.

In order to identify legal signals, committee reports were searched with a number of terms that indicate a decision by the GFCC.[4] A variable indicates whether at least one decision is cited in a committee report or not. For example, decisions by the GFCC were mentioned in sentences like: "[a]t least family members from foreigners with strong ties to Germany cannot be excluded from those benefits. This is also shown by the following quote from the BVerfG (compare BVerfGE 76, S.1 ff.)" (BT 16/2015, 8; idiomatic translation).[5] Another example is the sentence that: "[s]uch a provision would not be in accordance with the constitution in its current form (compare BVerfGE 83, 37 ff.)" (BT 12/3896, 17; idiomatic translation).[6] Moreover, citations are used to highlight that something can only be implemented in ways suggested by the committee to ensure that possible constitutional objections are mitigated. Changing the right to an abortion, the leading committee wrote: "The [medical] counseling must be appropriate to convey all information necessary to a woman to take a responsible decision to either continue or to end an abortion (compare BVerfGE 88, S. 203, 270f.). The necessary regulations are provided for by [the new] §219 StGB in connection with §§5 to 11 SchKG" (BT 13/1850, 20; idiomatic translation).[7] In six committee reports, decisions are cited broadly without a reference number, albeit within a context making clear that particular decisions are meant. For example, "[t]his goal is not in accordance with the GFCC's judicature [...] on informational self-determination" (BT 14/5793, 55; idiomatic translation).[8] These latter statements are also considered as a signal. In later analyses, I account for subsample stability excluding those vague references.

Finally, the coded references in committee reports are the legal signals. Signals occur considering 40 of the 277 bills assessed here. In the next step, I account for alternative explanations that can affect a policy shift.

5.2.3 *Control Variables: Alternative Explanations for a Policy Shift*

Germany has a second chamber—the *Bundesrat*—representing the 16 states through delegates from the state governments (Fortunato et al. 2013, 940). However, not all bills are passed by both chambers. About 47% of the 277 bills studied here are objection bills (*Einspruchsgesetze*) passed by the *Bundestag* only. All other bills are consent bills, requiring the second chamber's approval. This is a challenge when "one party has a majority in parliament while the other controls the second chamber" (Manow and Burkhart 2007, 167). Manow and Burkhart (2007) argue that in such situations the governing majority in the *Bundestag* will anticipate the governing majority in the *Bundesrat* and modify bills. This view has been challenged by Fortunato et al. (2013), who find that the federal government has no incentives to modify bills in early stages of the legislative processes, but rather only once conflict between chambers arises.[9] These mixed findings prompt me to control for the *type of bill*. Observed policy shift is possibly a result of anticipating conflict with the second chamber over a consent bill rather than the court. This is why a variable is coded to indicate consent bills compared to objection bills.

Independent of the type of bill, the strength of the opposition itself might encourage committees to shift a policy. This is especially important because the opposition in the *Bundestag* can dominate the second chamber. If the size of the *opposition in the second chamber* poses a credible threat, the governing majority in the *Bundestag* may account for this opposition. Therefore, I include a variable measuring the vote share of states in the second chamber composed fully of the parties in opposition to the *Bundestag* majority.

Finally, it is plausible that bills designed to address a *legal topic*—like bills to reform the criminal law (e.g., GESTA No. 2112, 3854, 4576)—are discussed and changed with a focus on constitutional rights. These changes may occur independent of the court but as a result of directly interpreting the constitution. Therefore, I include an indicator variable based on the policy field coded in the GESTA dataset. The variable indicates whether a bill is designed to address a legal topic or not.

Table 5.1 summarizes measures of central tendency and dispersion of the variables used to assess the second face of judicial power, separated by treatment status. Notably, there are no significant differences between

Table 5.1 Balance assessment of the control variables used to assess autolimitation

Variable	*No legal signal [control]*				*Legal signal [treatment]*			
	Range	*Median*	*Mean*	*SD*	*Range*	*Median*	*Mean*	*SD*
Consent bill	0 - 1	1	0.54		0 - 1	0	0.48	
Opp. influence	0 - 0.59	0.42	0.36	0.20	0 - 0.59	0.42	0.33	0.22
Legal topic	0 - 1	0	0.12		0 - 1	0	0.13	
12th leg. period	0 - 1	0	0.20		0 - 1	0	0.18	
13th leg. period	0 - 1	0	0.22		0 - 1	0	0.18	
14th leg. period	0 - 1	0	0.21		0 - 1	0	0.23	
15th leg. period	0 - 1	0	0.16		0 - 1	0	0.13	
16th leg. period	0 - 1	0	0.21		0 - 1	0	0.30	

Note: The correlation matrix of the variables is shown in Appendix E.1

treated and control groups regarding any variable. Hence, all characteristics are equally distributed between the two groups. Therefore, the data fulfills the requirements of an ideal randomized experiment, where the treatment assignment mechanism ensures that the covariates are balanced (Hernán and Robins 2019, Ch. 2). Thus, the data is appropriate to use the research design, which mirrors an ideal experiment. The analyses are conducted using the identification strategies outlined in the next section.

5.3 Modeling Choices to Assess Policy Shifts

In order to assess the effect of legal signals on policy shifts, I argued that the DiD is the identification strategy most closely matching the research design. Nevertheless, I use three identification strategies assessing multiple versions of the dependent variable. Accordingly, I increase the complexity of the dependent variable step by step, which allows for a comprehensive analysis of the effect of legal signals on policy shifts.

First, I compute a logistic regression, which is based on the observation that there are bills that are shifted in the direction of the court and bills that are not shifted in the direction of the court. In order to do so, I code a binary outcome variable taking the value of 1 when a policy shift towards the court occurs between t and $t + 1$ and 0 otherwise. The model assumes that a policy shift occurs with a certain probability and does not occur with a certain inverse probability. It is the appropriate model to estimate the probability of a policy shift in direction of the court in general, in response to a legal signal (King 1989; Long 1997).

Second, I compute one outcome variable of the policy shift in the direction of the court over the two time periods t and $t+1$. The variable measures the difference between the absolute distance of a bill from the court at time $t + 1$ and the absolute distance of that bill to the court at time t. With this outcome variable, I estimate the average treatment effect of a legal signal on a policy shift in the direction of the court. This average treatment effect is $E[Y^{L=1} - Y^{L=0}]$, where Y is the outcome among the treated ($Y^{L=1}$) and control units ($Y^{L=0}$) (Hernán and Robins 2019, 3–6). The effect is estimated as the difference between the mean policy shift among bills exposed to a legal signal and the mean policy shift of bills not exposed to a legal signal. As the outcome variable is continuous and all covariates in Table 5.1 are balanced, the average treatment effect is similar to the respective coefficient from an ordinary least square regression (Imbens and Rubin 2015, 172–174). Put simply,

$$Y = L\lambda + X\beta + \epsilon$$

where L is the vector of the legal signal, X is the vector of all covariates from Table 5.1 and λ is the estimated average treatment effect.

Finally, the outcome variable closest to the ideal research design is the absolute distance of a bill from the court's ideal point at each point in time. The difference in the spatial shifts between the treated bills and the control bills over time is the quantity of interest. This quantity (δ) can be estimated using the DiD approach (Card and Krueger 1994, 2000):

$$\delta = (E[Y_{i,t+1}^{L=1}] - E[Y_{i,t}^{L=1}]) - (E[Y_{i,t+1}^{L=0}] - E[Y_{i,t}^{L=0}])$$

where L is the legal signal that is either present (1) or absent (0) and t is the time at which a bill is introduced or voted on by a committee ($t+1$). δ can be estimated as the interaction effect between the legal signal and the time period using a linear parametric model:

$$Y = L\lambda + T\tau + \delta(L \times T) + X\beta + \epsilon$$

where L is the vector of the legal signal, T is the vector of the time and X is the vector of all covariates from Table 5.1. The coefficient δ is the DiD estimator.

In the following section, I apply each identification strategy to analyze the causal effect of a legal signal in legislative committees on a policy shift in the direction of the court.

5.4 Empirical Assessment of the Second Face of Judicial Power

The empirical discussion is undertaken in two steps. First, I assess the effect of legal signals on changes in the WordFish estimates from the whole text of bills. In legal language, every word carries weight; for example, a prime method used by German judges to interpret laws is the *grammatikalische Auslegung* (grammatical interpretation). Accordingly, the analysis of the precise wording of a law is the initial step in any legal interpretation (Boemke and Ulrici 2009, 20–22; Bitter and Rauhut 2009). This is why it is plausible to analyze the effect of legal signals on the whole text of the bills. Nevertheless, from the perspective of the legislator, the topic addressed in a bill matters. Changes to a bill as a result of autolimitation should substantially shape the bill, even after very common words (stop

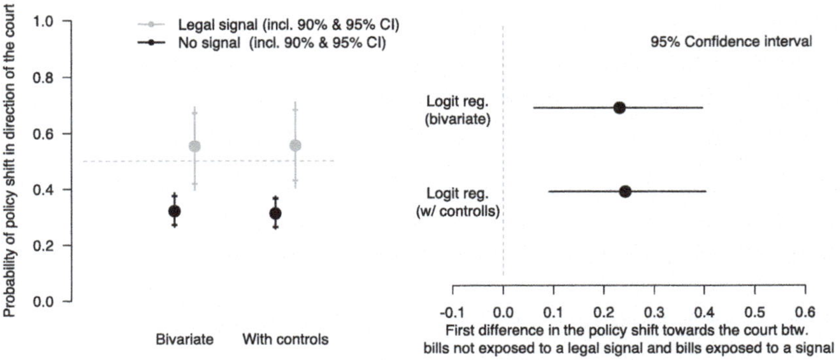

Fig. 5.1 Predicted probabilities and first differences of policy shift in direction of the court. Note: $N = 277$ bills, of which 40 were negotiated under the influence of a legal signal; 1000 simulations from the logistic regression given in Appendix E.2. The treatment variable is set to 0 and to 1, while the other variables are held constant at their means

words) are excluded. This is why in a second step I estimate all findings using WordFish estimates from bills after excluding stop words and stemming the text corpus. This allows assessing the robustness of my findings. With "the *same method*," I should "arrive at the *same results* for the *same phenomenon*" (Miller 2007, 92; emphasis in the original). This should also hold true when I finally use a stricter measure of a legal signal estimating the DiD.

5.4.1 *Findings from the Analyses of the Second Face of Judicial Power*

Figure 5.1 summarizes the general effect of legal signals on policy shifts by computing a logistic regression. The left part of the figure plots the predicted probabilities of a policy shift for bills exposed to a legal signal (gray estimates) and bills not exposed to a legal signal (black estimates). The vertical lines are 95% confidence intervals, with the horizontal marks indicating the span of the 90% confidence intervals. All estimates are simulated from a bivariate logistic regression and a regression including all control variables (see also Appendix E.2).[10]

The left part of Fig. 5.1 illustrates that the average probability of a policy shift in the direction of the court in the absence of a legal signal is about

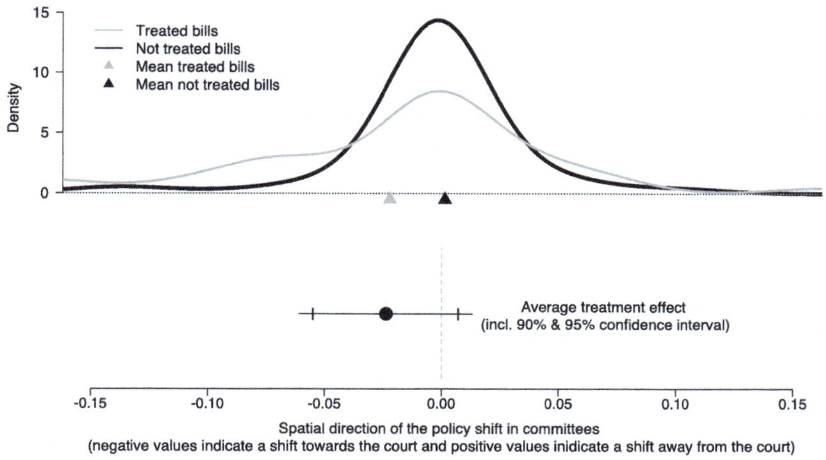

Fig. 5.2 Average treatment effect of a legal signal on policy shift. Note: $N = 277$ bills of which 40 were negotiated under the influence of a legal signal. The upper part of this figure plots the policy shift among treated (colored in gray) and control bills (colored in black) from time t to time $t + 1$. The lower part is the estimated average treatment effect of a legal signal on policy shift. The horizontal line visualizes the 95% confidence interval with the vertical marks indicating the span of the 90% confidence interval

32% in the bivariate model and 31% in the complete model. The probability significantly increases in the presence of a legal signal. Neither of the confidence intervals overlap. The probability of a bill exposed to a legal signal being shifted in direction of the court is on average about 55% in the bivariate model and the complete model. The right part of Fig. 5.1 shows that the first differences in the probability of a policy shift between bills exposed to a legal signal and those not exposed to a legal signal is on average about 23% (bivariate) to 24% (w/controls) and significant in both models. These preliminary findings suggest that policy shifts in the direction of the court might occur in the absence of a legal signal but are significantly more likely when any former decisions by the GFCC are referenced in committee reports. In the next step, it is necessary to understand the strength of the policy shift in the direction of the court in the presence of a legal signal.

For this purpose, Fig. 5.2 summarizes the estimated average treatment effect of a legal signal. The upper part of Fig. 5.2 compares the general policy shift between time t and time $t + 1$ among bills exposed to a legal signal (gray line) and those not exposed to a legal signal (black line). If, on average, no shifts for either bills occurred between the two time periods, the means (indicated by the triangles) would be at zero. If a movement towards the court occurred, the means would be negative and if the bills had moved away from the court, the means would be positive. Indeed, the mean policy shift among bills exposed to a legal signal is directed towards the court but small (gray triangle, $\overline{Y^{L=1}} = -0.022$). However, there is almost no policy shift among bills not exposed to a legal signal: if anything, these bills are moved slightly away from the court (black triangle, $\overline{Y^{L=0}} = 0.001$). Hence, bills exposed to a legal signal are on average moved towards the court. Nevertheless, the lower part of Fig. 5.2 illustrates that the small average treatment effect is not significant, accounting for the full text of the bills. The robustness assessment discussed in the next section and in Appendix E.4 shows that the treatment effect is barely significant (at $p<0.10$ level) once words are stemmed and stop words are excluded. Accounting for the mixed significance and the small, negative effect reveals important insights regarding autolimitation when compared with the logistic regression in Fig. 5.1.

Committees seem to be aware of those bills that are designed under the influence of a legal signal. Figure 5.1 reveals that a movement towards the court is generally more likely among bills exposed to a legal signal. Compared with the findings from Fig. 5.2, it seems plausible that the shifts in committees are only marginal if the bills exposed to a legal signal are already placed closer to the court to begin with, compared with those bills not exposed to a legal signal. This would imply that autolimitation occurs prior to the legislative process when actors sponsoring bills draft these bills. In other words, legal signals are an indicator of autolimitation, highlighting that respective bills were already designed under the influence of self-restraint. If this assumption is true, we should observe significant differences in the spatial placement between treated and control bills in general, albeit not within one group of bills. Hence, the DiD estimation should only highlight a general treatment effect, while the estimator itself will be insignificant.

Figure 5.3 maps the distribution of bills over the spatial distance from the court at time t (black line) and at time $t + 1$ (gray line). The graphs

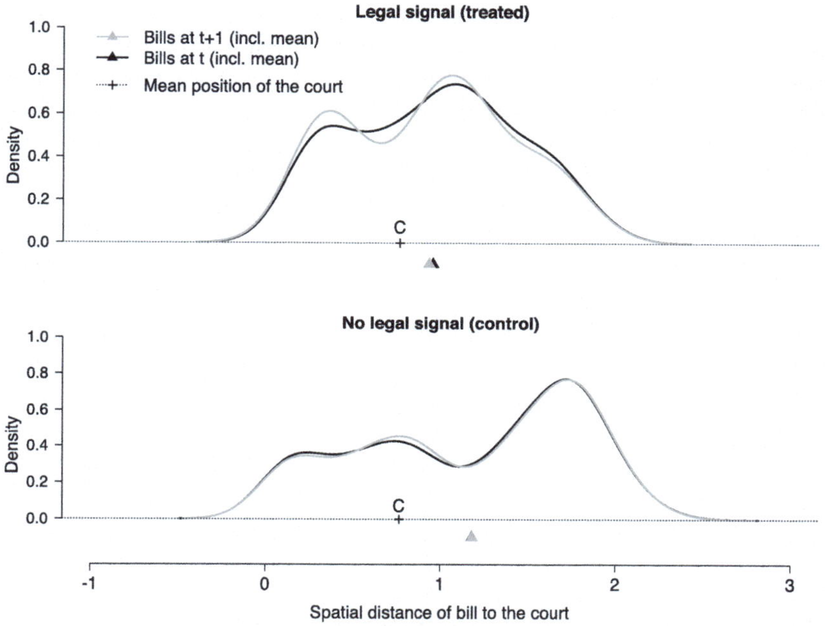

Fig. 5.3 Treated and control bills and their distances from the court over time. Note: $N = 277$ bills, of which 40 were negotiated under the influence of a legal signal

are separated by the (non-) occurrence of legal signals. The black and gray triangles point to the mean position of the respective distributions and the letter *C* indicates the mean position of the court.

The plot supports the intuition that the effect of a legal signal on a policy shift is marginal, but that a first draft of a bill is already designed to account for legal concerns. The mean among the bills exposed to a legal signal moves slightly but insignificantly towards the court in the two time periods ($\overline{Y_t^{L=1}} = 0.957$ to $\overline{Y_{t+1}^{L=1}} = 0.934$). However, among bills not exposed to a legal signal, there is barely any movement, but a neglectable one away from the court ($\overline{Y_t^{L=0}} = 1.182$ to $\overline{Y_{t+1}^{L=0}} = 1.184$). The gray and black triangles in the lower part of Fig. 5.3 overlap. Moreover, t-tests show that the differences between bills exposed to a legal signal and those not exposed to a legal signal are significant within the two time periods. In other words, bills exposed to a legal signal in a committee are placed significantly closer to the court to begin with, compared with bills that are not exposed to a legal signal. This becomes evident when comparing the average position of *C* in Fig. 5.3 with the position of either bills. *C* is always closer to bills exposed to a legal signal. Therefore, bills that committees discuss with reference to former decisions by the GFCC are already referred to the committee, accounting for possible legal challenges. This is strong evidence of autolimitation occurring in general, albeit prior to the legislative process.

Finally, further disentangling Fig. 5.3, Table 5.2 summarizes two models to estimate the DiD. Model 1 is a baseline model without control variables and Model 2 is the complete model including all control variables and dummy variables for the legislative periods (with the 16th legislative period being the reference category).

The estimator for a "Legal Signal" is the difference between treated and control bills at time *t*, prior to the exposure to the committee proceeding. Looking solely at this estimator confirms the conclusions drawn thus far, namely that bills exposed to a legal signal are on average placed significantly

Table 5.2 Ordinary least squares estimates of difference-in-differences

Model	*Baseline*		*With controls*	
DV	*Policy shift*		*Policy shift*	
Independent var.	*b*	*SE*	*b*	*SE*
Legal signal (= 1)	−0.226	0.104**	−0.210	0.104**
Time (after committee vote)	0.001	0.056	0.001	0.056
Legal signal × Time	−0.024	0.147	−0.024	0.146
Consent bill (= 1)			−0.110	0.053**
Opposition influence			−0.408	0.418
Legal topic (= 1)			−0.092	0.080
12th leg. period			0.260	0.151*
13th leg. period			0.360	0.184*
14th leg. period			0.241	0.205
15th leg. period			0.441	0.246*
(Intercept)	1.182	0.040***	1.147	0.068***
R^2	0.02		0.05	
Adjusted R^2	0.01		0.03	

Note: $N = 277$; *$p<0.10$; **$p<0.05$; ***$p<0.01$. 16th legislative period as reference category for the 12th, 13th, 14th, and 15th legislative period

closer to the court at time *t* compared with those bills not exposed to a signal. The estimate is significant and the effect size only slightly decreases from Model 1 to 2.

Based on all prior assessments, it is unsurprising that the estimate of the "Time" is insignificant, tiny, and positive (0.001). Therefore, the time from presenting a bill to a committee to when it leaves the committee alone has no influence on a significant policy shift in the direction of the court. This has implications when interpreting the DiD estimator. This estimator is the interaction term between the "Legal Signal × Time." The estimate has the expected negative direction and is larger than the effect of the time alone, but is also insignificant. Hence, bills exposed to a legal signal are changed in committees over time (−0.024) and this change is larger than the average change to all bills over time (0.001). However, the changes are not significant.

The alternative explanations in the complete model show that bills requiring the second chamber's approval are placed significantly closer to the court compared to bills that require no such approval. There are reasons to believe that this cannot only be explained by the vote share of the opposition in the second chamber. The respective variable is not significant (see "Opposition Influence"). In addition, the general positioning of bills significantly varies in all but the 14th legislative period compared to the 16th legislative period (the reference category). Excluding the 16th legislative period from the sample, the control variables indicating consent bills become insignificant. Moreover, the significant effect size of the legal signal increases (see Appendix E.3). Thus, bills exposed to a legal signal are on average always positioned significantly closer to the court at time *t* compared with bills not exposed to a signal. The effect is even more pronounced when excluding the grand coalition.

In sum, legal signals in committees only lead to minor, insignificant changes towards the court's position over time. In a strict sense, Hypothesis H4 has to be rejected. However, there is strong evidence of autolimitation prior to the legislative process. The finding that bills exposed to legal signals are systematically placed closer to the court compared with bills that are not exposed to legal signals is a strong indicator that bureaucrats in ministries or deputy staff draft bills accounting for judicial influence before presenting a bill to the floor. Hence, bills that draw legal attention in committees are already the product of prior self-censoring. In the next section, I assess the robustness of the findings.

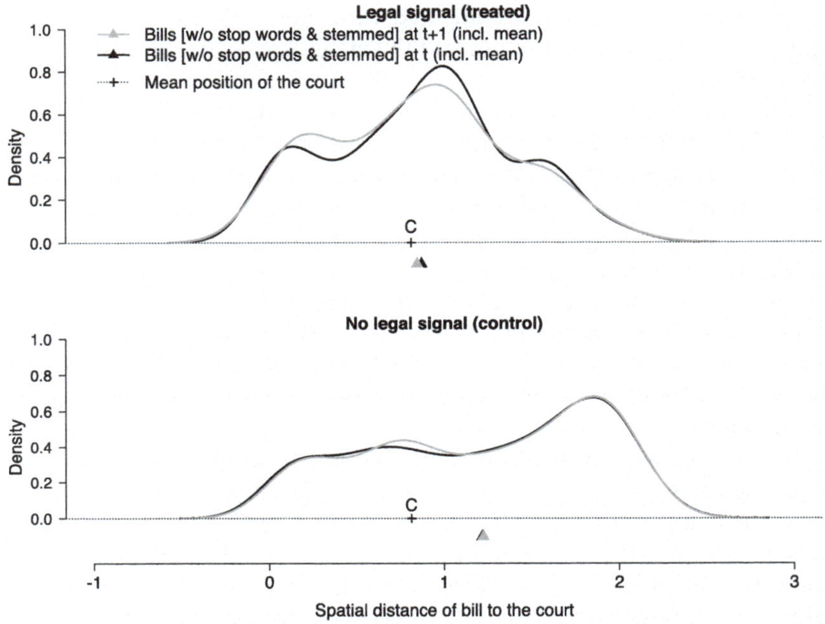

Fig. 5.4 Robustness assessment of the causal effect of a legal signal on policy shift. Note: $N = 277$ bills, of which 40 were negotiated under the influence of a legal signal

5.4.2 Robustness of the Findings on the Second Face of Judicial Power

Figure 5.4 is computed analogous to Fig. 5.3 but using WordFish estimates from bills after stemming words and excluding stop words. The assumption is that after such modifications only the substantive content of a bill remains. Nevertheless, a legal signal should affect those remaining parts in the same way as it affects the complete text. Thus, these bills are suitable to assess the robustness of the findings.

Figure 5.4 directly reflects on the research design and the theoretical considerations. Bills exposed to a legal signal (upper part of Fig. 5.4) are on average always closer to the court than bills not exposed to a legal signal (lower part of Fig. 5.4). *T*-tests reveal that this difference is highly significant. Moreover, in Table E.5 in the appendix I estimate the linear parametric model to assess the robustness of the findings from the DiD in Table 5.2. The effect of the legal signal alone is negative (−0.324) and significant at a 0.01 level of significance in the model including all control variables. This confirms the finding that treated bills are on average always significantly closer to the court than control bills. Finally, Fig. 5.4 shows that over the two time periods (t and $t + 1$) treated bills experience on average only minor, insignificant changes. Bills not exposed to a legal signal are on average not significantly changed (the black and gray triangle overlap in the lower part of the figure). All of these findings confirm the robustness of the previous analysis. Appendix E.4 summarizes further assessments and confirms that the models presented here are robust.[11]

Finally, I estimated the DiD again with the WordFish estimates from the primary analysis, albeit with a stricter measure of legal signals. Hence, I omitted vague references to court decisions in legislative committee reports and only explicit citations of court decisions are included in the measure. Coded in this way, the measure is not conceptually new but rather a stricter version of the original one. The use of this stricter measure of legal signals should have similar effects on the policy shift as produced by the original measure. Therefore, the new, stricter measure provides for a final robustness assessment. The findings in Appendix E.5 are consistent with the ones presented in Table 5.2.

In sum, the empirical assessment of the second face of judicial power—known as autolimitation—reveals that bills exposed to legal signals experience only minor insignificant changes in committees compared with bills not exposed to such signals. However, there is strong evidence in favor of autolimitation throughout the pre-legislative process. Bills exposed to legal signals in committees are already drafted with an eye on the judiciary. The bills are on average significantly closer to the court when presented to a committee compared with bills that are not exposed to a legal signal. While in a strict reading Hypothesis H4 has to be rejected, this study has generated robust empirical evidence in favor of the existence of autolimitation in the pre-legislative process.

5.5 Summary

This chapter has sought to explain the extent to which political actors anticipate judicial power. I argued that legal signals—taking the form of any prior judicial decision of the highest court—prompt legislators to modify bills in committees to account for the position of the court. A causal analysis of the effect of legal signals on committee bargaining in Germany has revealed that bills exposed to legal signals are moved in the direction of the GFCC. These final modifications are only minor insignificant adjustments; instead, bills that are exposed to a legal signal in a committee are already placed closer to the court to begin with compared with bills not exposed to such a signal. This robust finding presents strong evidence of the existence of autolimitation in the pre-legislative process when clerks in ministries or deputy staff draft bills. These results are generalizable to the extent that Germany is a typical case, with the GFCC being representative of many highest courts and the German committee system being similar to many countries (see Chapter 3).

We have learned three major points about the inner workings of autolimitation. First, according to the initial move of the Judicial-Policy-Dialogue Game, the government will anticipate the behavior of the court. If the government fears a harsh judicial reaction, the government could either refrain from legislating or account for the court (see Sect. 2.4). The empirical assessment shows that the government does the latter and accounts for the court's position when presenting an initial policy in a hostile situation.

Second, self-restraint in judicial–legislative bargaining is different from self-restraint in intra-legislative bargaining. Fortunato et al. (2013) find that intra-legislative institutions—like a navette system or conciliation committees—allow governing majorities to reduce uncertainty about the passage of a bill when an opposing second chamber has to vote on a proposal. This is why the governing majority does not engage in a priori self-restraint when facing a hostile second chamber; instead, the intra-legislative institutions help to reduce uncertainty about the interests of the second chamber and allow for targeted modifications. The institutions function as a "safety net" (Fortunato et al. 2013, 939) that does not exist in legislative–judicial bargaining. No institutional setting allows governing majorities to pre-negotiate with the judiciary. Shuttling legislation back and forth between the court and the government is not feasible but very costly. It would entail potential electoral costs, can ruin a political agenda and binds resources when drafting completely new legislation. Therefore, the actor sponsoring a bill tries to design that bill in a court-proof manner from the beginning. In sum, without an institutionalized safety net, legislative-judicial self-restraint follows a different logic compared with intra-legislative self-restraint.

Third, previous studies providing valuable first insights into autolimitation have concentrated on intra-legislative bargaining (see e.g., Vanberg 1998, 2001; Marks 2012 [1988]; Landfried 1994; but Langer and

Brace 2005). Indeed, legislative committees respond to legal signals with a stronger change towards the court than in the absence of such signals. However, these changes systematically affect legislation already drafted with an eye on the court. Therefore, we need to more strongly account for the pre-legislative process when studying political-judicial influence. This is a challenge to the extent that these processes are often confidential. Moreover, it may become necessary to account for a larger institutional variation when bills are drafted. Procedures and strategic behavior differ among parliamentary democracies with coalition governments (see e.g., Martin and Vanberg 2014) and presidential systems where representatives often present legislation (see e.g., Woon 2008) drafted by deputy staff (see e.g., Montgomery and Nyhan 2017). If we are to further understand the silent power of courts, research has to more strongly account for the way in which legislation is drafted.

To conclude, courts are able to show a second face of judicial power. Observing this face, political actors do not interpret it as a bluff but rather as a credible threat to legislation. This encourages policymakers to draft legislation early on, accounting for potential judicial review.

Notes

1. This chapter is adapted from a paper presented by the author at various conferences. The latest version was presented at the First Conference on Empirical Legal Studies in Europe, June 21–22, 2016 (Amsterdam).
2. The so-called *Handbuch der Rechtsförmlichkeiten* is published in its third edition and is available online: http://hdr.bmj.de/page_a.1.html, accessed January 3, 2020.
3. Information from the Federal Ministry of Justice and Consumer Protection: http://www.bmjv.de/DE/Themen/RechtssetzungBuerokratieabbau/Sprachberatung/Sprachberatung_node.html, accessed January 3, 2020.
4. Official reference numbers to court decisions include the character-sensitive abbreviation *Bv*. Published decisions are identified searching for *BVerfG*. An explicit search for *Bundesver* helped to identify references to the *Bundesverfassungsgericht*. Each finding from the search was reviewed.
5. "Zumindest Familienangehörigen von Ausländern mit engen Bindungen an Deutschland wird man daher nicht von den Begünstigungen ausschließen können. Dies belegt auch folgendes Zitat des BVerfG (vgl. BVerfGE 76, S. 1 ff.)."
6. "Eine solche Regelung wäre mit dem Grundgesetz in seiner geltenden Fassung nicht vereinbar (vgl. BVerfGE 83, 37 ff.)."

7. "Dabei muß die Beratung nach Inhalt, Durchführung und Organisation geeignet sein, der Frau die Einsichten und Informationen zu vermitteln, deren sie für eine verantwortliche Entscheidung über die Fortsetzung oder den Abbruch der Schwangerschaft bedarf (vgl. BVerfGE 88, S. 203, 270f.). Die hierfür erforderlichen Regelungen werden durch §219 StGB in Verbindung mit den §§5 bis 11 SchKG getroffen."
8. "Diese Zielsetzung entspricht nicht der Rechtsprechung des BVerfG, [...] auf informationelle Selbstbestimmung."
9. Fortunato et al. (2013) argue that the federal government will respond to a hostile second chamber in a conciliation committee. It is not necessary to control for this committee for three reasons: first, empirically Fortunato et al. (2013) show that there will be no prior anticipation of the committee by the *Bundestag*; second, I only wish to include a measure that reflects on the chances for the second chamber to become involved, whereby controlling for the known type of a bill is a more direct measure than controlling for (rarely occurring) conciliation efforts; and third, the inclusion of the committee would run contrary to the research design. Conciliation will happen after the legislative committee process. Accounting for the conciliation committee would mean including a post-treatment variable.
10. The `zeligverse` package (Gandrud 2017) in `R` was used to estimate the models and to simulate the quantities of interest.
11. All analyzed bills were drawn fully at random and may include bills to enforce international agreements. The DiD was replicated controlling for the committee on foreign affairs which appears plausible to be concerned with those bills. The findings from the analysis do not change the drawn conclusions.

References

Bachrach, P., Baratz, M.S. (1962). Two Faces of Power. *American Political Science Review*, *56*(4), 947–952.

Bitter, G., Rauhut, T. (2009). Grundzüge zivilrechtlicher Methodik. Schlüssel zu einer gelungenen Fallbearbeitung. *Juristische Schulung*, *49*(4), 289–298.

Boemke, B., Ulrici, B. (2009). *BGB Allgemeiner Teil*. Heidelberg: Springer.

Bunea, A., Ibenskas, R. (2015). Quantitative Text Analysis and the Study of EU Lobbying and Interest Groups. *European Union Politics*, *16*(3), 429–455.

Burkhart, S. (2008). Deutsche Bundesgesetzgebung 1972–2005. *GESIS Datenarchiv*, *ZA4569* (Version 1.0.0), Köln.

Card, D., Krueger, A.B. (1994). Minimum Wages and Employment: A Case Study of the Fast-Food Industry in New Jersey and Pennsylvania. *American Economic Review*, *84*(4), 772–793.

Card, D., Krueger, A.B. (2000). Minimum Wages and Employment: A Case Study of the Fast-Food Industry in New Jersey and Pennsylvania. Reply. *American Economic Review*, *90*(5), 1397–1420.

Fortunato, D., König, T., Proksch, S.-O. (2013). Government Agenda-Setting and Bicameral Conflict Resolution. *Political Research Quarterly*, *66*(4), 938–951.

Gandrud, C. (2017). zeligverse: Easily Install and Load Stable Zelig Packages. *R Package, V.0.1.1*.

Hammond, T.H. (1986). Agenda Control, Organizational Structure, and Bureaucratic Politics. *American Journal of Political Science*, *30*(2), 379–420.

Hernán, M.A., Robins, J.M. (2019). *Causal Inference: What If*. Boca Raton: Chapman & Hall and CRC. https://www.hsph.harvard.edu/miguel-hernan/causal-inference-book/.

Holland, P.W. (1986). Statistics and Causal Inference. *Journal of the American Statistical Association*, *81*(396), 945–960.

Hönnige, C., Gschwend, T., Wittig, C., Engst, B.G. (2015). *Constitutional Court Database (CCDB), V17.01 [Mar.]*.

Imbens, G., Rubin, D.B. (2015). *Causal Inference for Statistics, Social, and Biomedical Sciences. An Introduction*. New York: Cambridge University Press.

Ismayr, W. (2006). *Der Deutsche Bundestag im Politischen System der Bundesrepublik Deutschland*. Wiesbaden: VS Verlag für Sozialwissenschaften, 2nd ed.

King, G. (1989). *Unifying Political Methodology: The Likelihood Theory of Statistical Inference*. Cambridge: Cambridge University Press.

Klüver, H. (2015). The Promises of Quantitative Text Analysis in Interest Group Research: A Reply to Bunea and Ibenskas. *European Union Politics*, *16*(3), 456–466.

Kommers, D.P. (1994). The Federal Constitutional Court in the German Political System. *Comparative Political Studies*, *26*(4), 470–491.

Landfried, C. (1992). Judicial Policy-Making in Germany: The Federal Constitutional Court. *West European Politics*, *15*(3), 50–67.

Landfried, C. (1994). The Judicialization of Politics in Germany. *International Political Science Review*, *15*(2), 113–124.

Langer, L., Brace, P. (2005). The Preemptive Power of State Supreme Courts: Adoption of Abortion and Death Penalty Legislation. *Policy Studies Journal*, *33*(3), 317–340.

Long, J.S. (1997). *Regression Models for Categorial and Limited Dependent Variables*. Thousand Oaks: Sage.

Lucas, C., Nielsen, R.A., Roberts, M.E., Stewart, B.M., Storer, A., Tingley, D. (2015). Computer-Assisted Text Analysis for Comparative Politics. *Political Analysis*, *23*(2), 254–277.

Manow, P., Burkhart, S. (2007). Legislative Self-Restraint Under Divided Government in Germany, 1976–2002. *Legislative Studies Quarterly*, *32*(2), 167–191.

Marks, B.A. (2012). [1988]. A Model of Judicial Influence on Congressional Policy Making: Grove City College v. Bell. *Journal of Law, Economics and Organization*, *31*(4), 843–875.
Martin, L.W., Vanberg, G. (2014). Parties and Policymaking in Multiparty Governments: The Legislative Median, Ministerial Autonomy, and the Coalition Compromise. *American Journal of Political Science*, *58*(4), 979–996.
Mattson, I., Strøm, K. (1995). Parliamentary Committees. In H. Döring (Ed.) *Parliaments and Majority Rule in Western Europe*, (pp. 249–307). Frankfurt: Campus Verlag.
Miller, B. (2007). Making Measures Capture Concepts: Tools for Securing Correspondence between Theoretical Ideas and Observations. In T. Gschwend, and F. Schimmelfennig (Eds.) *Research Design in Political Science: How to Practice what they Preach* (pp. 83–102). Houndmills: Palgrave Macmillan.
Montgomery, J.M., Nyhan, B. (2017). The Effects of Congressional Staff Networks in the US House of Representatives. *Journal of Politics*, *79*(3), 745–761.
Proksch, S.-O., Slapin, J.B. (2010). Position Taking in European Parliament Speeches. *British Journal of Political Science*, *40*(3), 587–611.
Rubin, D.B. (1974). Estimating Causal Effects of Treatments in Randomized and Nonrandomized Studies. *Journal of Educational Psychology*, *66*(5), 688–701.
Slapin, J.B., Proksch, S.-O. (2008). A Scaling Model for Estimating Time-Series Party Positions from Texts. *American Journal of Political Science*, *52*(3), 705–722.
Slapin, J.B., Proksch, S.-O. (2014). Words as Data. Content Analysis in Legislative Studies. In S. Martin, T. Saalfeld, and K. W. Strøm (Eds.) *The Oxford Handbook of Legislative Studies*, (pp. 126–144). Oxford: Oxford University Press.
Stecker, C. (2016). The Effects of Federalism Reform on the Legislative Process in Germany. *Regional and Federal Studies*, *26*(5), 603–624.
Stone, A. (1992). *The Birth of Judicial Politics in France. The Constitutional Council in Comparative Perspective*. Oxford: Oxford University Press.
Stone Sweet, A. (1998). A Comment on Vanberg: Rules, Dispute Resolution, and Strategic Behavior. *Journal of Theoretical Politics*, *10*(3), 327–338.
Stone Sweet, A. (2000). *Governing with Judges: Constitutional Politics in Europe*. Oxford: Oxford University Press.
Vanberg, G. (1998). Abstract Judicial Review, Legislative Bargaining, and Policy Compromise. *Journal of Theoretical Politics*, *10*(3), 299–326.
Vanberg, G. (2001). Legislative-Judicial Relations: A Game-Theoretic Approach to Constitutional Review. *American Journal of Political Science*, *45*(2), 346–361.
Woon, J. (2008). Bill Sponsorship in Congress: The Moderating Effect of Agenda Positions on Legislative Proposals. *Journal of Politics*, *70*(1), 201–216.

CHAPTER 6

Conclusion: Implications of Judicial Power

The aim of this study was to understand when and why judges choose one judicial outcome over the other and to what extent political actors anticipate judicial decision-making. In order to answer these questions, I designed a game theoretical model and tested the model in the setting of the German Federal Constitutional Court (GFCC). While the questions were assessed separately they are intricately linked to one another. Judicial decisions are the means courts have available to voice their opinion and to alter political and societal discourses. Courts do not only nullify political decisions but they can also request (political) actions by making directives. In publishing judicial decisions courts are thus able to show the first face of judicial power. Moreover, the mere knowledge that courts can review policies already constrains policymakers. The threat of making decisions allows courts to show the second face of judicial power.

In order to explain relative changes in judicial choices, I examined the variation in the government's costs to legislate and the court's costs from evasion. As expected, an increase in the government's costs to legislate, defined by external factors, was on average associated with a decrease in the use of directives relative to the choice not to justify decisions and vice versa. One possible explanation for this observation is that courts try to appear impartial in the immediate legal interaction, albeit accounting strategically for the government and public when making decisions. In addition, changes in the court's costs associated with an evasion explain relative variation in judicial choices. The GFCC presents directives when an evasion is costly compared with when it is not. This may suggest that directives

B. G. Engst, *The Two Faces of Judicial Power*,
https://doi.org/10.1007/978-3-030-46016-7_6

are a tool to draw the media's and public's attention to decisions when an implementation is essential to the judiciary. Further research is necessary to understand changes in the judicial choice to only justify decisions. Finally, an assessment of overall judicial choices showed that courts act in a risk-averse manner. The choice not to justify decisions is significantly the most likely choice relative to the other judicial choices when the government's costs are high. The costs from an evasion drive the judicial choice in settings when the government's costs to legislate are low. The court is most likely to present directives when the government's costs are low and the court's costs are high. These patterns of judicial behavior are particularly evident in decisions based on referrals that address at least one law.

It is important to note that the risk-averse behavior of courts does not weaken the judiciary per se; instead, the assessment of the second face of judicial power showed that political actors account for past judicial decisions and interpret them as legal signals. Policies drafted under the influence of legal signals were significantly closer to the court's position compared with policies not drafted under such influence. This observation is strong evidence in favor of autolimitation in anticipation of judicial review.

In the following sections I present concluding considerations to link the two faces of judicial power, outline the specific contributions of this book, its implications for the judicialization hypothesis, and present avenues for further research.

6.1 Linking the Two Faces of Judicial Power

Courts possess two faces of judicial power but are only able to show one face at any given point in time. The judiciary either makes a decision or the judiciary is not involved, but political actors anticipate judicial review. Nevertheless, one can link the discussion on both faces. This is why I conclude with an assessment of the laws referred to the GFCC from among those 277 randomly drawn laws which were used to analyze the second face of judicial power. The number of referrals and judicial choices is fairly low. The assessment provides preliminary insights only and conclusions should be drawn with caution.

Table 6.1 separates the 277 laws by their exposure to a legal signal in legislative committees. Legal signals define a courts ability to show the second face of judicial power (similar Landfried 1992; Stone Sweet 1998, 2000). The first two rows of the table illustrate that the number of laws referred to the court is generally low. In total only about 9% of the 277

Table 6.1 Linkages between the two faces of judicial power

		Second face of judicial power (laws passed under the influence of...)	
		legal signals	no legal signals
	Not referred to the GFCC	31 77.5 %	222 93.67 %
	Referred to the GFCC	9 22.5 %	15 6.33 %
	Referrals not justified	13 68.42 %	10 52.63 %
First face of judicial power	Referrals justified	1 5.26 %	1 5.26 %
	Referrals justified with directive	5 26.32 %	8 42.11 %

Note: Based on data used in Chapter 5. Percentages are column percentages on the sum of (non-) referrals (upper rows) or sum of judicial choices (lower rows)

laws are referred for judicial review. Nevertheless, from the few bills that are exposed to legal signals a large share of about 22.5% are referred. The share of laws referred to the GFCC from among the many laws not exposed to a legal signal is comparatively low at 6.33%.

Table 6.1 illustrates that legal signals are an indicator of a possible judicial involvement. Therefore, the government is well advised to engage in legislative self-restraint once legal signals occur. The finding also suggests that the governing majority should not rely only on deals with opposition parties to prevent referral to the GFCC (e.g., Vanberg 1998a). The table does not indicate whether or not the government follows such strategies. However, about a quarter of all bills exposed to legal signals are referred to the GFCC. Hence, legal signals—as possible triggers of autolimitation—do not rule out referrals to courts. Instead, it seems likely that when courts show a strong second face of judicial power they also become directly involved, showing the first face of judicial power.

What happens to laws referred to the GFCC? If legislative self-restraint in anticipation of judicial review is successful then referrals of laws exposed to legal signals are less often justified and are less often accompanied by directives compared with referrals of laws not exposed to legal signals. The three rows below the solid line in Table 6.1 allow to assess this assumption. In those rows the unit of analysis is the judicial choice. Some laws are referred multiple times to the GFCC and the court can make different choices. Reasons are that the circumstances that lead to a referral of a law can change or different sections of a law can be referred. This is why the absolute number of judicial choices in Table 6.1 is higher than the absolute number of referred laws.

Referrals are in general not often justified which is in line with the findings from Chapter 4. In total about 61% of the referrals in Table 6.1 are not justified. The share of referrals not justified which includes laws not exposed to legal signals (53%) is below the total share of referrals not justified. The share of not justified referrals which includes laws passed under the influence of legal signals (68%) is above the total share of referrals which are not justified. This speaks in favor of the idea that legislative self-restraint is successful. Laws developed under the influence of legal signals are more often part of referrals not justified compared with laws not passed under the influence of legal signals. The share of referrals only justified is fairly low in both groups. However, the share of referrals justified with directives is lower among laws originally drafted under the influence of legal signals compared to laws drafted without the influence of legal signals. This supports the idea that political self-restrain is a successful strategy to ensure the survival of laws.

In sum, courts can only show one face of judicial power at any given point in time. However, it seems likely that when courts show a strong second face of judicial power they also become directly involved showing a strong first face of judicial power. Through legislative self-restrain political actor may succeed in accounting for the position of courts.

This book has shown that courts possess two faces of judicial power originating from their ability to (threaten to) make decisions. This power has political and societal implications. Therefore, we need to more strongly account for judicial decisions as the tools available to courts to exercise power. The linkages outlined in this section are based only on a few number of referrals but encourage further research to assess the interplay between the two faces of judicial power in greater detail. In the next section I will conclude outlining further contributions and implications of this study.

6.2 Contributions of This Study

Previous research explaining judicial decision-making by constitutional courts has addressed the dichotomous choice to justify or not justify a law (Vanberg 2001, 2005; Hönnige 2009; Staton 2010; Sternberg et al. 2015). The assumption is that courts use endogenous factors—e.g., oral hearings

(Krehbiel 2016) or strategic media communication (Staton 2010)—to enhance the transparency around their decisions, which increases political compliance with judicial choices (Vanberg 2001, 2005). Thereby, scholars set aside the actual judicial choice and focus on factors that allow for strategic case promotion. This study has accounted for previous research, arguing that courts make choices anticipating the government's capabilities to comply with decisions. Nevertheless, I applied a different perspective focusing on judicial choices. Courts have an enlarged action repertoire available which includes not only the choices to not justify or justify referrals, but also the option to present directives. Extending previous studies assessing the court's costs associated with an evasion—e.g., diminishing influence on the legal community or loosing important case law—showed that the court strategically uses directives once the costs from an evasion are high. This suggests that directives themselves are a tool to promote cases, increase public awareness and pressure policymakers to comply with judicial decisions. Therefore, future research may gain from more nuanced judicial outcome measures.

Recent trends in judicial politics emphasize the need to account more closely for content-specific characteristics when coding outcomes of judicial decisions (e.g., Staton and Vanberg 2008; Clark and Lauderdale 2010, 873–874; Corley and Wedeking 2014; Epstein 2016, 2072). Directives are content-specific to the extent that the constitutional issue is connected to a request directed at political actors. Moreover, it is reasonable to assume that by outlining acceptable political behavior directives are more specific compared to other judicial choices. This is why this study has implications for research on opinion clarity (Baum 1976; Spriggs 1996, 1127–1128; Staton and Vanberg 2008). In particular, the findings generated here suggest that courts significantly increase opinion clarity with decreasing costs for the government to comply with decisions and vice versa. This supports the idea that courts strategically manipulate opinion clarity (Staton and Vanberg 2008). The study could not always disentangle the separation between decisions that were only justified and decisions with directives. Moreover, the empirical assessments demonstrated that in some settings the difference between vague directives and explicit ones matters, while in other settings the difference does not matter. This encourages further research on the clarity of content-specific outcomes of decisions (see Sternberg 2019, Ch. 3).

Finally, this study has generated empirical evidence in favor of autolimitation by political actors in anticipation of judicial review. Previous case studies focused on highly salient political issues strongly affected by legal concerns and judicial decision-making (e.g. Landfried 1985, 1992; Stone 1992; Stone Sweet 2000). These studies did not pay sufficient attention to the fact that in order to isolate legislative self-restraint in anticipation of judicial review it is also necessary to account for less salient issues not exposed to legal threats. The identification strategy used here addressed this issue and the findings suggest that beyond the legislative arena, scholars need to also account for the pre-legislative process and the different drafting stages of bills when assessing autolimitation. Moreover, bills that are not exposed to credible judicial threats are not preemptively altered to account for judicial review. This emphasizes the need for including comparative cases when assessing autolimitation. Nevertheless, the findings suggest that following a legal signal a government will anticipate a court's action, although it is not certain that the court will ever review the respective policy, let alone during the government's time in office. This makes the government's behavior in judicial–political bargaining different compared to its behavior in intra-legislative bargaining between opposing parties across chambers. Political actors are not forced into preemptive self-restraint in intra-legislative bargaining; instead they rely on institutions to alter bills at low costs as the legislative process evolves (Fortunato et al. 2013). However, such institutions do not exist in judicial–political bargaining. Instead, the government takes the indirect power of the court seriously when drafting legislation. Therefore, the dynamics in judicial–political bargaining, when the court shows the second face of judicial power, are different to intra-legislative bargaining.

The findings of this study have wider implications for the judicialization of politics which I outline in the next section.

6.3 Implications for the Judicialization Hypothesis

It has been argued throughout this book that judicial decisions are the means through which courts exercise power. In addressing the political branches through (the threat of) decision-making, constitutional courts contribute to the judicialization of politics, which is an implication of judicial power. The process is characterized by an "expansion of the province of courts and judges in determining public policy outcomes" (Hirschl 2008, 121). Political problems are redefined into judicial problems and courts limit the ability of policymakers to make decisions (Hönnige 2011, 348).

Hirschl (2008) argues that explanations for judicialization can be grouped into three categories: (1) institutional features, (2) judicial behavior, and (3) political determinants. However, there are different views on the process of judicialization. Stone Sweet (1998; 2000) argues that the process leads to a "virtuous circle" (Stone Sweet 2000, 19) and constantly increases while others have outlined that limitations to the process allow for variation (Vanberg 1998a, b, 2015; Santoni and Zucchini 2004; Brouard 2009; Hönnige 2009; Hönnige and Gschwend 2010). This study has generated findings that support Hirschl's (2008) first two explanations of judicialization and the idea that there are limitations to the process.

Institutional features provide the framework that enables the judicialization of politics (Hirschl 2008, 129–132). Indeed, in Chapter 3 I outlined that the institutional design and the embeddedness of courts in the separation of powers affect the preconditions of the two faces of judicial power. It is important to note that when identifying (non-)institutionalized features of importance to the two faces of judicial power, it is not sufficient to focus only on the legal arena; especially the second face of judicial power is shaped by political institutions established to preemptively assess the constitutionality of bills. The institutionalized and noninstitutionalized preconditions of judicial power allow for two forms of variation regarding the judicialization of politics. On the one hand, the strengths of the preconditions may vary across each face of judicial power. On the other hand, the preconditions vary across Europe, with some constitutional courts in weak settings and others in strong ones. However, the preconditions only enable the judicialization of politics, but to understand its scope it is necessary to analyze the actual use of judicial power (Hönnige 2011, 353; Engst 2017, 292).

The judicialization of politics is also shaped by the behavior of courts altering policymaking (Hirschl 2008, 129–132). Judicial behavior in countries with constitutional courts is still understudied (Epstein 2016, 2032–2033; Hönnige 2007, 36–38). A challenge is that in cross-country comparison, countries with constitutional review often do not publish individual judicial votes (Raffaelli 2012, 30; Kelemen 2013, 1345), which is why established procedures to study individual judicial behavior and intra-court bargaining are not readily applicable (e.g., Martin and Quinn 2002; Hanretty 2013, 2014). This book cannot solve the problems associated with studying individual judicial behavior.[1] However, focusing on content-specific judicial outcomes helps us to understand when courts as collective actors present own interests. The dynamics uncovered here suggest that courts act in a risk-averse manner when presenting their own policy positions. Courts anticipate capabilities of the governing majority to respond to judicial requests, which is evidence in favor of strategic judicial self-restraint (see Hönnige and Gschwend 2010, 519–520). Moreover, the patterns found in the variables that were used to approximate the court's costs associated with an evasion indicate that courts do not abuse their power; instead, the use of directives increases in settings when decisions are of higher interest to the legal community and following oral hearings. Interviews with judges suggest that these hearings are also used to prepare recipients for decisions (Kranenpohl 2010, 101, 315). Hence, while courts present their own expectations using directives, the assessment suggests that they do so advisedly. Courts feel constrained by their environment, which is why they alter their behavior strategically (Epstein and Knight 1998, 2000). This leads to variation in the judicialization of politics as courts will not constantly increase their activism. These insights were gained by focusing on content-specific outcomes, which help to open parts of the black box of judicial decision-making.

This study also provided empirical support for a silent form of judicialization as a result of autolimitation in anticipation of judicial review. Courts exert influence on policymaking, although it is not certain that they review a specific policy; instead, political actors constrain themselves based on the agenda courts establish through their decision-making. The degree of silent judicialization is significantly influenced by legal signals. The presence or absence of a signal leads to variation in the scope of judicialization. Future studies may use different signals to further assess the development of the silent judicialization.

The previous paragraphs have outlined the theoretical relevance of the analyses of the two faces of judicial power to the judicialization of politics. In addition, the social relevance of this research is highlighted by the question whether the judicialization of politics is itself acceptable. Directives and political self-restraint in anticipation of judicial review grant courts substantive influence in the political arena. This can shape a political system in the long run, as an increasing influence of courts affects the transition to the consensual form of democracy (Lijphart 2012). However, a political dimension in decision-making is to a certain extent endogenous to a legal system with constitutional review (see Kelsen 2008 [1931], 68), especially as constitutional law also defines a political community (Stone Sweet 2000). In order to sustain a society, constitutional courts need to account for the political dimension of constitutional law. Nevertheless, the findings that courts constrain themselves in anticipation of political power when presenting directives and that the governing majority constrains itself in anticipation of judicial review, suggests that there exists a healthy dialogue in a system of checks and balances, rather than an unintended increasing judicialization. In this regard, the judicialization as a result of the two faces of judicial power may be considered acceptable, although I leave this normative judgment to the reader.

6.4 Avenues for Further Research

This study can be extended in a number of ways already mentioned, although two are particularly evident: first, more comprehensive spatial measures that place all actors in one common dimension would allow for broader assessments of the Judicial-Policy-Dialogue Game; second, the Judicial-Policy-Dialogue Game generates implications regarding the political response to judicial decisions but research on constitutional courts falls short on assessing the compliance with decisions.

As has been emphasized throughout this book computing common spatial measures for constitutional courts that do not publish individual judicial votes is challenging, let alone measures that would allow for placing courts in a common space with other (political) actors. In order to analyze the second face of judicial power I relied on text scores from laws as common texts of relevance to political actors and the judiciary. The positions of political actors were approximated based on randomly drawn bills they had drafted and passed while the court's position was approximated based on laws it upheld. This approach ensured that the same type of text, following the same style and document-generating process, was used to approximate the position of the actors of interest. However, the approach makes use of judicial decisions only implicitly. Some studies have come to use information from decisions explicitly, namely citations, to identify important precedence (Fowler et al. 2007; Fowler and Jeon 2008) and the location of judicial opinions in so-called doctrinal spaces (Clark and Lauderdale 2010, 2012). Combining these approaches with the considerations made here suggests identifying landmark decisions of highest courts with the help of citation analysis and afterwards using additional information from decisions—such as briefs by interest groups—as bridging observations to locate landmark decisions in a space with other actors whose positions are known. Further research may assess the feasibility of such approaches (see e.g. Engst et al. 2019).

In Chapters 2 and 3, I mentioned that hitherto research on (political) compliance with decisions made by constitutional courts is based on a few case studies and anecdotal evidence (e.g. Gawron and Rogowski 2002). The theoretical considerations presented here allow to derive implications for policy outcomes in responses to judicial decisions. Hence, more research on compliance would allow to analyze such implications. In this regard, I wish to argue that the (1) compliance with and the (2) implementation of decisions are two separate things. The former is related to political actors passing acts in response to decisions, while the latter is tied to the public administration enforcing new acts. To a certain extent, the responses to decisions within a political system are similar to the difference between an output and outcome (compare Easton 1965). The governing majority presents an output based on the input judicial decisions provide, although the actual outcome is the result of the interaction of a legislative output with the administrative and societal environment. It is plausible that in such an interaction agency-loss across multiple steps can occur (McCubbins et al. 1987). This further supports the necessity to understand reactions to judicial decisions. Eskridge (1991; also Christiansen and Eskridge Jr. 2014) analyzed efforts by the United States Congress to override statutory interpretation of the Supreme Court. An adaptation of his approach to countries with constitutional review and a replication of the—largely descriptive—study would in itself already make a major contribution.

Highest courts have "no influence over either the sword or the purse" (Hamilton 1788, Federalist No. 78), yet they are granted the power to make decisions. The fact that past decisions lead political actors to constrain themselves in anticipation of judicial review shows that courts are able to exercise power. Moreover, courts have extended their influence by drawing attention to decisions using directives. Nevertheless, they do so strategically, anticipating the capabilities of the governing majority to respond to decisions. It is likely that these dynamics of judicial–political bargaining persist as courts continue to display the two faces of judicial power.

Note

1. For first insights see Wittig (2016) who assesses the motivation of judges at constitutional courts to write separate opinions and Engst et al. (2017) who apply multidimensional scaling to a small number of identifiable votes assessing intra-court networks among a subset of German judges.

References

Baum, L. (1976). Implementation of Judicial Decisions. An Organizational Analysis. *American Politics Quarterly*, *4*(1), 86–114.

Brouard, S. (2009). The Politics of Constitutional Veto in France: Constitutional Council, Legislative Majority and Electoral Competition. *West European Politics*, *32*(2), 384–403.

Christiansen, M.R., Eskridge Jr., W.N. (2014). Congressional Overrides of Supreme Court Statutory Interpretation Decisions, 1967–2011. *Texas Law Review*, *92*(6), 1317–1515.

Clark, T.S., Lauderdale, B. (2010). Locating Supreme Court Opinions in Doctrine Space. *American Journal of Political Science*, *54*(4), 871–890.

Clark, T.S., Lauderdale, B.E. (2012). The Genealogy of Law. *Political Analysis*, *20*(3), 329–350.

Corley, P.C., Wedeking, J. (2014). The (Dis)Advantage of Certainty: The Importance of Certainty in Language. *Law and Society Review*, *48*(1), 35–62.

Easton, D. (1965). *A Systems Analysis of Political Life*. New York: Wiley.

Engst, B.G. (2017). Die vierte Gesetzeslesung. Verfassungsgerichte des deutsch-österreichischen Modells als Vetospieler. In V. Frick, O. W. Lembcke, and R. Lhotta (Eds.) *Politik und Recht. Umrisse eines politkwissenschaftlichen Forschungsfeldes* (pp. 281–301). Baden-Baden: Nomos.

Engst, B.G., Grundmanns, D.M., Gschwend, T. (2019). Judicial Positions on Political Reform. Designing Common Policy Scores From Judicial Text. *13. General Conference of the European Consortium for Political Research*, Wrocław (September 4–7), 1–31.

Engst, B.G., Gschwend, T., Schaks, N., Sternberg, S., Wittig, C. (2017). Zum Einfluss der Parteinähe auf das Abstimmungsverhalten der Bundesverfassungsrichter eine quantitative Untersuchung. *Juristen Zeitung*, *72*(17), 816–826.

Epstein, L. (2016). Some Thoughts on the Study of Judicial Behavior. *William and Mary Law Review*, *57*(6), 2017–2073.

Epstein, L., Knight, J. (1998). *The Choices Justices Make*. Washington, DC: CQ Press.

Epstein, L., Knight, J. (2000). Toward a Strategic Revolution in Judicial Politics: A Look Back, A Look Ahead. *Political Research Quarterly*, *53*(3), 625–661.

Eskridge Jr., W.N. (1991). Reneging on History. Playing the Court/Congress/President Civil Rights Game. *California Law Review*, *79*(3), 613–684.

Fortunato, D., König, T., Proksch, S.-O. (2013). Government Agenda-Setting and Bicameral Conflict Resolution. *Political Research Quarterly*, *66*(4), 938–951.

Fowler, J.H., Jeon, S. (2008). The Authority of Supreme Court Precedent. *Social Networks*, *30*(1), 16–30.

Fowler, J.H., Johnson, T.R., Spriggs, J.F., II., Jeon, S., Wahlbeck, P.J. (2007). Network Analysis and the Law: Measuring the Legal Importance of Precedents at the U.S. Supreme Court. *Political Analysis*, *15*(3), 324–346.

Gawron, T., Rogowski, R. (2002). The Implementation of German Federal Constitutional Court Decisions. Judicial Orders and the Federal Legislature. In R. Rogowski, and T. Gawron (Eds.) *Constitutional Courts in Comparison. The U.S. Supreme Court and the German Federal Constitutional Court* (pp. 239–256). New York: Berghahn Books.

Hanretty, C. (2013). The Decisions and Ideal Points of British Law Lords. *British Journal of Political Science*, *43*(3), 703–716.

Hanretty, C. (2014). The Bulgarian Constitutional Court as an Additional Legislative Chamber. *East European Politics and Societies*, *28*(3), 540–558.

Hirschl, R. (2008). The Judicialization of Politics. In G. A. Caldeira., D. R. Kelemen, and K. E. Whittington (Eds.) *The Oxford Handbook of Law and Politics* (pp. 119–141). Oxford: Oxford University Press.

Hönnige, C. (2007). *Verfassungsgericht, Regierung und Opposition. Die vergleichende Analyse eines Spannungsdreiecks.* Wiesbaden: VS Verlag für Sozialwissenschaften.

Hönnige, C. (2009). The Electoral Connection: How the Pivotal Judge Affects Oppositional Success at European Constitutional Courts. *West European Politics*, *32*(5), 963–984.

Hönnige, C. (2011). Beyond Judicialization: Why We Need More Comparative Research About Constitutional Courts. *European Political Science*, *10*(3), 346–358.

Hönnige, C., Gschwend, T. (2010). Das Bundesverfassungsgericht im politischen System der BRD – ein unbekanntes Wesen? *Politische Vierteljahresschrift*, *51*(3), 507–530.

Kelemen, K. (2013). Dissenting Opinions in Constitutional Courts. *German Law Journal*, *14*(8), 1345–1371.

Kelsen, H. (2008). [1931]. Wer soll der Hüter der Verfassung sein? In R. C. van Ooyen (Ed.) *Wer soll der Hüter der Verfassung sein? Abhandlungen zur Theorie der Verfassungsgerichtsbarkeit in der pluralistischen, parlamentarischen Demokratie*, (pp. 58–105). Tübingen: Mohr Siebeck.

Kranenpohl, U. (2010). *Hinter dem Schleier des Beratungsgeheimnisses. Der Willensbildungs- und Entscheidungsprozess des Bundesverfassungsgerichts.* Wiesbaden: VS Verlag für Sozialwissenschaften.

Krehbiel, J.N. (2016). The Politics of Judicial Procedures: The Role of Public Oral Hearings in the German Constitutional Court. *American Journal of Political Science*, *60*(4), 990–1005.

Landfried, C. (1985). The Impact of the German Federal Constitutional Court on Politics and Policy Output. *Government and Opposition*, *20*(4), 522–542.

Landfried, C. (1992). Judicial Policy-Making in Germany: The Federal Constitutional Court. *West European Politics*, *15*(3), 50–67.

Lijphart, A. (2012). *Patterns of Democracy. Government Forms and Performance in Thirty-Six Countries.* New Haven & London: Yale University Press, 2nd ed.

Martin, A.D., Quinn, K.M. (2002). Dynamic Ideal Point Estimation via Markov Chain Monte Carlo for the U.S. Supreme Court, 1953–1999. *Political Analysis*, *10*(2), 134–153.

McCubbins, M.D., Noll, R.G., Weingast, B.R. (1987). Adminsitrative Procedures as Instruments of Political Control. *Journal of Law, Economics and Organization*, *3*(2), 243–277.

Raffaelli, R. (2012). *Dissenting Opinions in the Supreme Courts of the Member States.* European Parliament: Directorate General for Internal Policies (PE 462.470). https://www.europarl.europa.eu/document/activities/cont/201304/20130423ATT64963/20130423ATT64963EN.pdf (accessed February 21, 2018).

Santoni, M., Zucchini, F. (2004). Does Policy Stability Increases the Constitutional Court's Independence? The Case of Italy During the First Republic (1956–1992). *Public Choice*, *120*(3–4), 439–461.

Spriggs, J.F., II. (1996). The Supreme Court and Federal Administrative Agencies: A Resource-Based Theory and Analysis of Judicial Impact. *American Journal of Political Science*, *40*(4), 1122–1151.

Staton, J.K. (2010). *Judicial Power and Strategic Communication in Mexico.* Cambridge: Cambridge University Press.

Staton, J.K., Vanberg, G. (2008). The Value of Vagueness: Delegation, Defiance, and Judicial Opinions. *American Journal of Political Science*, *52*(3), 504–519.

Sternberg, S. (2019). *No Public, No Power? Analyzing the Importance of Public Support for Constitutional Review with Novel Data and Machine Learning Methods.* Mannheim: University of Mannheim.

Sternberg, S., Gschwend, T., Wittig, C., Engst, B.G. (2015). Zum Einfluss der öffentlichen Meinung auf Entscheidungen des Bundesverfassungsgerichts: Eine Analyse von abstrakten Normenkontrollen sowie Bund-Länder-Streitigkeiten 1974–2010. *Politische Vierteljahresschrift*, *56*(4), 570–598.

Stone, A. (1992). *The Birth of Judicial Politics in France. The Constitutional Council in Comparative Perspective.* Oxford: Oxford University Press.

Stone Sweet, A. (1998). A Comment on Vanberg: Rules, Dispute Resolution, and Strategic Behavior. *Journal of Theoretical Politics*, *10*(3), 327–338.

Stone Sweet, A. (2000). *Governing with Judges: Constitutional Politics in Europe.* Oxford: Oxford University Press.

Vanberg, G. (1998a). Abstract Judicial Review, Legislative Bargaining, and Policy Compromise. *Journal of Theoretical Politics*, *10*(3), 299–326.

Vanberg, G. (1998b). Reply to Stone Sweet. *Journal of Theoretical Politics*, *10*(3), 339–346.

Vanberg, G. (2001). Legislative-Judicial Relations: A Game-Theoretic Approach to Constitutional Review. *American Journal of Political Science*, *45*(2), 346–361.

Vanberg, G. (2005). *The Politics of Constitutional Review in Germany*. Cambridge: Cambridge University Press.

Vanberg, G. (2015). Constitutional Courts in Comparative Perspective: A Theoretical Assessment. *Annual Review of Political Science*, *18*(1), 167–185.

Wittig, C.E. (2016). *The Occurrence of Separate Opinions at the Federal Constitutional Court: An Analysis with a Novel Database*. Berlin: Logos Verlag Berlin GmbH.

Appendix A: Judicial Choices in Comparison

Table A.1 summarizes the sources of information shown in Table 1.1. In addition, Table A.2 summarizes information on EU countries with supreme courts which are not included in the main analysis. The Greek Court is a special case, being neither clearly a constitutional nor a supreme court (Hufen et al. eds. 2008, 31). Art. 100 IV S. 2 Greek Constitution would allow deadlines. However, the highest court is rarely involved and exercises review powers cautiously. The court does not often declare laws void (see Hufen et al. eds. 2008, 33–35). Denmark (Hufen et al. eds. 2008, 18–19), Finland (Hufen et al. eds. 2008, 24), and Sweden (Hufen et al. eds. 2008, 76–78) have relatively inactive highest courts, while the British Supreme Court is fairly young. This is why clear traditions of judicial review are not (yet) established in those countries.

B. G. Engst, *The Two Faces of Judicial Power*,
https://doi.org/10.1007/978-3-030-46016-7

Table A.1 Summary of sources pertaining to Table 1.1

Country	*Directive*	*Deadline*
Austria	Hufen et al. (2008, 63)	Art. 140 V S. 3–4 Constitution; no longer than 18 months
Belgium	*obiter dictum*, Hufen et al. (2008, 14)	Art. 8 III Act on Const. Court; Hufen et al. (2008, 11)
Bulgaria	According to Luchterhandt et al. (2007, 55) and similar Hufen et al. (2008, 16) interpretation of Art. 22 IV Act on Const. Court	Hufen et al. (2008, 17); Art. 151 II S. 3 Constitution
Croatia		Art. 55 II Act on Const. Court
Czech Republic	Decisions Pl. US 8/07 [74, 97]; Pl. US-st 27/09 [23]; Pl. US 24/10 [54]; Pl. US 1/12 [73]; Pl. US 16/12 [51–53]	§70 I Act on Const. Court
France	Hufen et al. (2008, 28); example Stone (1992, 162)	Art. 62 S. 2 Constitution
Germany	Directives and deadlines are identified as part of the analyses.	
Hungary	Luchterhandt et al. (2007, 270, Fn. 81) and legislative omission, Sec. 46 I Act on Const. Court (similar Sec. 40 II Act on Const. Court)	Hufen et al. (2008, 95–96)
Italy	Hufen et al. (2008, 46, 48)	Ludewig (2012, 34)
Latvia	The court provides guidelines if a law is unconstitutional. These guidelines are to apply until new legislation is passed (see Hufen et al. 2008, 52–53).	Sec. 32 III Act on Const. Court
Lithuania	The final repeal of an act is duty of the legislature (see Hufen et al. 2008, 55)	Hufen et al. (2008, 55)
Luxembourg	The court limits the judgments to interpretation and explicitly rejects more competencies (see Hufen et al. 2008, 56).	
Malta		Decision *The Police v. Joseph Lebrun* in Hufen et al. (2008, 58)
Poland	Luchterhandt et al. (2007, 98) and Hufen et al. (2008, 68)	Art. 190 III Constitution; no longer than 12–18 months
Portugal	In case of omission Art. 283 II Constitution	Hufen et al. (2008, 73)
Romania	In case of *a priori* review according to Art. 18 III Act on Const. Court; see also Luchterhandt et al. (2007, 116)	Art. 31 III Act on Const. Court
Slovakia		Art. 125 III S. 2 Constitution sets a 6-month deadline; see also Luchterhandt et al. (2007, 163)
Slovenia	Luchterhandt et al. (2007, 183)	Art. 161 I S. 2–3 Constitution, no longer than 12 months; see also Luchterhandt et al. (2007, 182)
Spain	Hufen et al. (2008, 87), with examples	Hufen et al. (2008, 87)

Table A.2 Judicial directives and deadlines among supreme courts in the EU

Country	*Directive*	*Deadline*
Cyprus	Decisions regarding the constitutionality of a law apply only in the specific case brought to the court (see Luchterhandt et al. 2007, 287–288)	
Estonia	Hufen et al. (2008, 22)	Hufen et al. (2008, 23)
Ireland	Government often reacts before court proclaims decisions to prevent legal uncertainty (Hufen et al. 2008, 40)	Not used yet but also not legally ruled out for the future (Hufen et al. 2008, 40)
Netherlands	Art. 120 Constitution does not allow for any form of judicial review: "The constitutionality of Acts of Parliament and treaties shall not be reviewed by the courts."; see also Hufen et al. (2008, 59)	

References

Hufen, F., Nörr Stiefenhofer Lutz. (Eds.). (2008). *Beschränkung von Urteilswirkungen im Falle der Feststellung der Verfassungswidrigkeit von Rechtsnormen. Teil 2: Länderberichte*. Berlin: Bundesministerium der Finanzen.

Luchterhandt, O., Starck, C., Weber, A. (Eds.). (2007). *Verfassungsgerichtsbarkeit in Mittel- und Osteuropa. Teilband I: Berichte*. Baden-Baden: Nomos.

Ludewig, P. (2012). *Die zeitliche Beschränkung der Wirkung von Urteilen des EuGH im Vorabentscheidungsverfahren*. Berlin: Ducker und Humbolt.

Stone, A. (1992). *The Birth of Judicial Politics in France: The Constitutional Council in Comparative Perspective*. Oxford: Oxford University Press.

Appendix B: The Judicial-Policy-Dialogue Game

Step 1: Optimal policies by G in the final move.

Step 1.1 x_{g2}^{*1} **given** $U_G(ll, jd)$

$$
\begin{aligned}
U_G(ll, jd) &= -x_{g2}^2 - \alpha(x_{g2} - x_d)^2 \\
U_G(ll, jd) &= -x_{g2}^2 - \alpha x_{g2}^2 + 2\alpha x_{g2}x_d - \alpha x_d^2 \\
\frac{\partial U}{\partial x_{g2}} &= -2x_{g2} - 2\alpha x_{g2} + 2\alpha x_d \\
\frac{\partial U}{\partial x_{g2}} &= -2(x_{g2} + \alpha x_{g2} - \alpha x_d) \\
0 &= x_{g2} + \alpha x_{g2} - \alpha x_d \\
0 &= x_{g2}(1 + \alpha) - \alpha x_d \quad | + \alpha x_d \; | : (1 + \alpha) \\
x_{g2}^{*1} &= \frac{\alpha x_d}{\alpha + 1}
\end{aligned}
\tag{B.1}
$$

Step 1.2 x_{g2}^{*2} **given** $U_G(ll, j)$

$$
\begin{aligned}
U_G(ll, j) &= -x_{g2}^2 - \alpha(x_{g2} - 1)^2 \\
U_G(ll, j) &= -x_{g2}^2 - \alpha x_{g2}^2 + 2\alpha x_{g2} - \alpha \\
\frac{\partial U}{\partial x_{g2}} &= -2x_{g2} - 2\alpha x_{g2} + 2\alpha \\
\frac{\partial U}{\partial x_{g2}} &= -2(x_{g2} + \alpha x_{g2} - \alpha)
\end{aligned}
$$

B. G. Engst, *The Two Faces of Judicial Power*,
https://doi.org/10.1007/978-3-030-46016-7

$$0 = x_{g2} + \alpha x_{g2} - \alpha$$
$$0 = x_{g2}(1+\alpha) - \alpha \quad | + \alpha | : (1+\alpha)$$
$$x_{g2}^{*2} = \frac{\alpha}{\alpha+1} \tag{B.2}$$

Step 2: G's strategy in the final move...

Step 2.1: ...if C justifies with a directive

$$U_G(ll, jd) \geq U_G(l\neg l, jd) \Rightarrow -x_{g2}^2 - \alpha(x_{g2} - x_d)^2 \geq -1 - \alpha(1 - x_d)^2$$

$$\text{I. With } x_{g2}^{*1} \text{ (B.1): } -\left(\frac{\alpha x_d}{\alpha+1}\right)^2 - \alpha\left(\frac{\alpha x_d}{\alpha+1} - x_d\right)^2 \geq -1 - \alpha(1-x_d)^2$$

$$\text{II. Simplify } -\alpha\left(\frac{\alpha x_d}{\alpha+1} - x_d\right)^2 \text{ with common denominator}$$

$$-\alpha\left(\frac{\alpha x_d}{\alpha+1} - x_d\right)^2 \Rightarrow -\alpha\left(\frac{\alpha x_d - \alpha x_d - x_d}{a+1}\right)^2 \Rightarrow -\alpha\left(\frac{-x_d}{a+1}\right)^2 \Rightarrow \frac{-\alpha x_d^2}{(\alpha+1)^2}$$

$$\text{Substitute in I. \& simplify left part in I. } -\left(\frac{\alpha x_d}{\alpha+1}\right)^2 - \frac{-\alpha x_d^2}{(\alpha+1)^2}$$

$$\frac{-\alpha^2 x_d^2}{(\alpha+1)^2} - \frac{-\alpha x_d^2}{(\alpha+1)^2} \Rightarrow \frac{-\alpha^2 x_d^2 - \alpha x_d^2}{(\alpha+1)^2} \Rightarrow \frac{-\alpha x_d^2(\alpha+1)}{(\alpha+1)^2} \Rightarrow \frac{-\alpha x_d^2}{\alpha+1}$$

III. Binomial expansion in right part of I.:

$$-1 - \alpha(1-x_d)^2 = -1 - \alpha + 2\alpha x_d - \alpha x_d^2$$

$$\text{II. \& III. Back in I.: } \frac{-\alpha x_d^2}{\alpha+1} \geq -1 - \alpha + 2\alpha x_d - \alpha x_d^2 \quad | +1 | +\alpha | -2\alpha x_d | + \alpha x_d^2$$

$$\text{IV. Simplify left part in } \frac{-\alpha x_d^2}{\alpha+1} + 1 + \alpha - 2\alpha x_d + \alpha x_d^2 \geq 0$$

$$\text{Common denominator } -\frac{\alpha x_d^2}{\alpha+1} + \frac{\alpha+1}{\alpha+1} + \frac{\alpha^2+\alpha}{\alpha+1} - \frac{2\alpha^2 x_d - 2\alpha x_d}{\alpha+1} + \frac{\alpha^2 x_d^2 + \alpha x_d^2}{\alpha+1} \Rightarrow$$

$$\frac{2\alpha + 1 + \alpha^2 - 2\alpha^2 x_d - 2\alpha x_d + \alpha^2 x_d^2}{\alpha+1}$$

$$\text{Factorize } 2\alpha x_d \text{ in numerator } 2\alpha + 1 + \alpha^2 + 2\alpha x_d(-\alpha - 1) + (\alpha x_d)^2$$

$$\text{Simplifies to binomial formula } (-\alpha - 1)^2 + 2\alpha x_d(-\alpha - 1) + (\alpha x_d)^2$$

$$\text{Simplifies to binomial formula } (\alpha x_d - \alpha - 1)^2 \text{ with denominator } \frac{(\alpha x_d - \alpha - 1)^2}{\alpha+1}$$

$$\text{V. Hence, } U_G(ll, jd) \geq U_G(l\neg l, jd) \Rightarrow \frac{(\alpha x_d - \alpha - 1)^2}{\alpha+1} \geq 0$$

$$\text{VI.: V. True if denominator} \neq 0 \text{ hence, } \alpha + 1 = 0 \quad | -1 \Rightarrow \alpha = -1 \text{ hence, } \alpha \neq -1$$

This is always true as $\alpha > 0$ according to the modeling choices.

V. is true if nominator is positive, which is always true as it is squared.

Hence, according to VI. $U_G(ll, jd) \geq U_G(l\neg l, jd)$ always true.

G always l when $U_G(ll, jd) \cup U_G(l\neg l, jd)$

Step 2.2: ...if C justifies without a directive

$$U_G(ll, j) \geq U_G(l\neg l, j) \Rightarrow -x_{g2}^2 - \alpha(x_{g2} - 1)^2 \geq -1$$

$$\text{I. With } x_{g2}^{*2} \text{ (B.2)}: \ -\left(\frac{\alpha}{\alpha+1}\right)^2 - \alpha\left(\frac{\alpha}{\alpha+1} - 1\right)^2 \geq -1$$

$$\text{II. Simplify } -\left(\frac{\alpha}{\alpha+1}\right)^2 - \alpha\left(\frac{\alpha}{\alpha+1} - 1\right)^2 \text{ with common denominator}$$

$$-\left(\frac{\alpha}{\alpha+1}\right)^2 - \alpha\left(\frac{\alpha - \alpha - 1}{\alpha+1}\right)^2 \Rightarrow -\left(\frac{\alpha}{\alpha+1}\right)^2 - \alpha\left(\frac{-1}{\alpha+1}\right)^2$$

$$\text{Simplify further } \frac{-\alpha^2}{(\alpha+1)^2} - \frac{\alpha}{(\alpha+1)^2} \Rightarrow \frac{-\alpha(\alpha+1)}{(\alpha+1)^2} \Rightarrow \frac{-\alpha}{\alpha+1}$$

$$\text{III. Substitute in I.: } \frac{-\alpha}{\alpha+1} \geq -1$$

IV.: III. True if denominator $\neq 0$ hence, $\alpha + 1 = 0 \ | -1 \Rightarrow \alpha = -1$ hence, $\alpha \neq -1$

This is always true as $\alpha > 0$ according to the modeling choices.

$$\text{III. With } \alpha > 0 \text{ always } \frac{-\alpha}{\alpha+1} > -1 \text{ as } \frac{-\alpha}{\alpha+1} \rightarrow -1$$

Hence, according to IV. $U_G(ll, j) \geq U_G(l\neg l, j)$ always true.

G always l when $U_G(ll, j) \cup U_G(l\neg l, j)$

In sum, according to the final move of the JPD game the government's strategy (s_G) is (*Lemma 1*)

$$G^*(s_G) = \text{always } l \text{ with } \begin{cases} \frac{\alpha x_d}{\alpha+1} & \text{following } jd \\ \frac{\alpha}{\alpha+1} & \text{following } j \end{cases}$$

Step 3: C's strategy in the second move...

Step 3.1: Optimal directive by knowing G will legislate

$$U_C(jd, ll) = -(x_{g2} - C)^2 - \gamma(x_{g2} - x_d)^2$$

$$U_C(jd, ll) = -x_{g2}^2 + 2x_{g2}C - C^2 - \gamma x_{g2}^2 + 2\gamma x_{g2}x_d - \gamma x_d^2$$

$$\frac{\partial U}{\partial x_d} = 2\gamma x_{g2} - 2\gamma x_d$$

$$\frac{\partial U}{\partial x_d} = 2\gamma(x_{g2} - x_d)$$

$$0 = x_{g2} - x_d \quad | + x_d \mid \text{with } x_{g2} = x^{*1}_{g2} \text{ (B.1) following a directive}$$

$$x^*_d = x^{*1}_{g2} \tag{B.3}$$

The optimal directive to not become evaded is equal to G's final optimal policy.

Step 3.2 ... if C justifies with or without a directive

$$U_C(jd, ll) \geq U_C(j, ll) \Rightarrow$$

$$-(x_{g2} - C)^2 - \gamma(x_d - x_{g2})^2 \geq -(x_{g2} - C)^2 - \gamma(1 - x_{g2})^2$$

$$\text{I. With } x^{*1}_{g2} \text{ (B.1)},\ x^{*2}_{g2} \text{ (B.2)},\ x^*_d \text{ (B.3)}:$$

$$-(x^{*1}_{g2} - C)^2 - \gamma(x^{*1}_{g2} - x^{*1}_{g2})^2 \geq -(x^{*2}_{g2} - C)^2 - \gamma(1 - x^{*2}_{g2})^2$$

$$\text{Simplifies to: } -(x^{*1}_{g2} - C)^2 \geq -(x^{*2}_{g2} - C)^2 - \gamma(1 - x^{*2}_{g2})^2$$

$$\text{Binomial expansion \& rearrange:}$$

$$-(x^{*1}_{g2})^2 + 2x^{*1}_{g2}C - C^2 \geq -(x^{*2}_{g2})^2 + 2x^{*2}_{g2}C - C^2 - \gamma + 2\gamma x^{*2}_{g2} - \gamma(x^{*2}_{g2})^2$$

$$| + (x^{*2}_{g2})^2 \mid - 2x^{*2}_{g2}C \mid + C^2 \mid + \gamma \mid - 2\gamma x^{*2}_{g2} \mid + \gamma(x^{*2}_{g2})^2$$

$$\text{II. Factorize } x^{*1}_{g2} \text{ (B.1)} \,\&\, x^{*2}_{g2} \text{ (B.2)}:$$

$$x^{*1}_{g2}(-x^{*1}_{g2} + 2C) + x^{*2}_{g2}(x^{*2}_{g2} + \gamma x^{*2}_{g2} - 2C - 2\gamma) + \gamma \geq 0$$

$$\text{Plug in (B.1) \& (B.2):}$$

$$\frac{\alpha x_d}{\alpha+1}\left(-\frac{\alpha x_d}{\alpha+1} + 2C\right) + \frac{\alpha}{\alpha+1}\left(\frac{\alpha}{\alpha+1} + \gamma\frac{\alpha}{\alpha+1} - 2C - 2\gamma\right) + \gamma \geq 0$$

$$\text{III.: II. True if denominators } \neq 0 \text{ hence, } \alpha + 1 = 0 \mid -1 \Rightarrow \alpha = -1 \text{ hence, } \alpha \neq -1$$

This is always true as $\alpha > 0$ according to the modeling choices.

$$\text{IV.: II. With } \alpha > 0 \cap \gamma > 0 \text{ and solved for } C$$

$$\text{IV.1:}^{\dagger}\ x_d > 1 \cap C \geq \frac{\alpha^2(x_d - 1) - \gamma}{2\alpha(\alpha+1)(x_d - 1)}$$

$$\text{IV.2:}^{\dagger}\ x_d < 1 \cap C \leq \frac{\alpha^2(x_d - 1) - \gamma}{2\alpha(\alpha+1)(x_d - 1)}$$

Hence, according to III. and IV.

$$C^*(s_C) = \begin{cases} jd \text{ if} \begin{cases} x_d > 1 \cap C \geq \frac{\alpha^2(x_d-1)-\gamma}{2\alpha(\alpha+1)(x_d-1)} \\ x_d < 1 \cap C \leq \frac{\alpha^2(x_d-1)-\gamma}{2\alpha(\alpha+1)(x_d-1)} \end{cases} \\ j \text{ otherwise} \end{cases}$$

Steps marked † were calculated using Wolfram Alpha Pro (Wolfram Alpha LLC. 2017. Wolfram—Alpha. http://www.wolframalpha.com, accessed October 30, 2017.) and verified computing a simulation in R—Version 3.5.1.

Step: 3.3 ... if C justifies with a directive or does not justify

$$U_C(jd, ll) > U_C(\neg j, l) \Rightarrow -(x_{g2} - C)^2 - \gamma(x_d - x_{g2})^2 \geq -(x_{g1} - C)^2$$

I. With x_{g2}^{*1} (B.1), x_d^* (B.3), x_{g1}^* (= 0; see B.4 below):

$$-(x_{g2}^{*1} - C)^2 - \gamma(x_{g2}^{*1} - x_{g2}^{*1})^2 \geq -(x_{g1}^* - C)^2$$

Simplifies to: $-(x_{g2}^{*1} - C)^2 \geq -C^2$

Binomial expansion & rearrange: $-(x_{g2}^{*1})^2 + 2x_{g2}^{*1}C - C^2 \geq -C^2 \mid +C^2$

II. Factorize x_{g2}^{*1} (B.1): $x_{g2}^{*1}(-x_{g2}^{*1} + 2C) \geq 0$

Plug in (B.1): $\frac{\alpha x_d}{\alpha+1}\left(-\frac{\alpha x_d}{\alpha+1} + 2C\right) \geq 0$

III.: II. True if denominators $\neq 0$ hence, $\alpha + 1 = 0 \mid -1 \Rightarrow \alpha = -1$ hence, $\alpha \neq -1$

This is always true as $\alpha > 0$ according to the modeling choices.

IV.: II. With $\alpha > 0$ and solved for C

IV.1:† $x_d > 0 \cap C \geq \frac{\alpha x_d}{2\alpha+2}$

IV.2:† $x_d < 0 \cap C \leq \frac{\alpha x_d}{2\alpha+2}$

Hence, according to III. and IV.

$$C^*(s_C) = \begin{cases} jd \text{ if} \begin{cases} x_d > 0 \cap C \geq \frac{\alpha x_d}{2\alpha+2} \\ x_d < 0 \cap C \leq \frac{\alpha x_d}{2\alpha+2} \end{cases} \\ \neg j \text{ otherwise} \end{cases}$$

Step 3.4 ... if C justifies without a directive or does not justify

$$U_C(j, ll) > U_C(\neg j, l) \Rightarrow -(x_{g2} - C)^2 - \gamma(1 - x_{g2})^2 \geq -(x_{g1} - C)^2$$

I. With x_{g2}^{*2} (B.2) & x_{g1}^* (= 0; see B.4 below):

$$-(x_{g2}^{*2} - C)^2 - \gamma(1 - x_{g2}^{*2})^2 \geq -(x_{g1}^* - C)^2$$

Simplifies to: $-(x_{g2}^{*2} - C)^2 - \gamma(1 - x_{g2}^{*2})^2 \geq -C^2$

Binomial expansion & rearrange:

$$-(x_{g2}^{*2})^2 + 2x_{g2}^{*2}C - C^2 - \gamma + 2\gamma x_{g2}^{*2} - \gamma(x_{g2}^{*2})^2 \geq -C^2 \mid +C^2$$

II. Factorize x_{g2}^{*2} (B.2): $x_{g2}^{*2}(-x_{g2}^{*2} - \gamma x_{g2}^{*2} + 2C + 2\gamma) - \gamma \geq 0$

Plug in (B.2): $\frac{\alpha}{\alpha+1}\left(-\frac{\alpha}{\alpha+1}-\gamma\frac{\alpha}{\alpha+1}+2C+2\gamma\right)-\gamma\geq 0$

III.: II. True if denominators $\neq 0$ hence, $\alpha+1=0\ |-1\Rightarrow\alpha$
$= -1$ hence, $\alpha\neq -1$

This is always true as $\alpha>0$ according to the modeling choices.

IV.:† II. With $\alpha>0\cap\gamma>0$ and solved for $C\Rightarrow C\geq\frac{\alpha^2+\gamma}{2\alpha^2+2\alpha}$

Hence, according to III. and IV.

$$C^*(s_C)=\begin{cases} j \text{ if } C\geq\frac{\alpha^2+\gamma}{2\alpha^2+2\alpha}\\ \neg j \text{ otherwise}\end{cases}$$

In sum, according to the second move of the JPD game
the court's strategy (s_C) is *(Lemma 2)*

$$C^*(s_C)=\begin{cases} jd \text{ if } \begin{cases} x_d>x_{sq}\cap C\geq\frac{\alpha^2(x_d-1)-\gamma}{2\alpha(\alpha+1)(x_d-1)}\cap C\geq\frac{\alpha x_d}{2\alpha+2}\\ G<x_d<x_{sq}\cap C\leq\frac{\alpha^2(x_d-1)-\gamma}{2\alpha(\alpha+1)(x_d-1)}\cap C\geq\frac{\alpha x_d}{2\alpha+2}\\ x_d<G\cap C\leq\frac{\alpha^2(x_d-1)-\gamma}{2\alpha(\alpha+1)(x_d-1)}\cap C\leq\frac{\alpha x_d}{2\alpha+2}\end{cases}\\ j \text{ if } C\geq\frac{\alpha^2+\gamma}{2\alpha^2+2\alpha}\\ \neg j \text{ otherwise}\end{cases}$$

Step 4: G's strategy in the initial move...

Step 4.1: ... if C does not justify a referral

If C chooses not to justify a referral, G will want to present its optimal policy x^*_{g1} that can be obtained from optimization.

$$U_G(l,\neg j)=-x^2_{g1}$$
$$\frac{\partial U}{\partial x_{g1}}=-2x_{g1}$$
$$0=-2x_{g1}\ |:(-2)$$
$$x^*_{g1}=0 \tag{B.4}$$

This is rational as G is aware that the initial policy x_{g1} will become law if C does not justify a referral. Therefore, presenting the ideal policy x^*_{g1} at the own ideal point $G=0$ is the rational choice.

Step 4.2: ... if C justifies a referral presenting a directive

$$U_G(ll, jd) \geq U_G(\neg l, \emptyset) \Rightarrow -x_{g2}^2 - \alpha(x_{g2} - x_d)^2 \geq -1$$

I. With x_{g2}^{*1} (B.1) & x_d^* (B.3): $(-x_{g2}^{*1})^2 - \alpha(x_{g2}^{*1} - x_{g2}^{*1})^2 \geq -1$

Simplify & rearrange: $-(x_{g2}^{*1})^2 \geq -1 \mid : (-1) \Rightarrow (x_{g2}^{*1})^2 \leq 1$

Hence, due to quadratic form true if

$$x_{g2}^{*1} \in \mathbb{R}_{<0} \rightarrow x_{g2}^{*1} \geq -1$$

$$x_{g2}^{*1} \in \mathbb{R}_{>0} \rightarrow x_{g2}^{*1} \leq 1$$

II. According to I. G presents x_{g2}^{*1} as $-1 \leq x_{g2}^{*1} \leq 1$

This is rational as 1 is equal to the position of the status quo ($x_{sq} = 1$). G will only legislate in the initial move if the ideal policy pursued at the final move is as least as close to the own ideal point as the original status quo.

III. Plug in (B.1) in II.: $-1 \leq \frac{\alpha x_d}{\alpha + 1} \leq 1$

The denominators needs to be $\neq 0$ hence, $\alpha + 1 = 0 \mid -1 \Rightarrow \alpha = -1$

Hence, $\alpha \neq -1$. This is always true as $\alpha > 0$ according to the modeling choices.

IV. If $\alpha > 0$ solve for

$$x_d \text{ with } \frac{\alpha x_d}{\alpha + 1} \leq 1 \mid \cdot (\alpha + 1) \mid : \alpha \Rightarrow x_d \leq \frac{\alpha + 1}{\alpha}$$

$$x_d \text{ with } \frac{\alpha x_d}{\alpha + 1} \geq -1 \mid \cdot (\alpha + 1) \mid : \alpha \Rightarrow x_d \geq -\frac{\alpha + 1}{\alpha}$$

Hence, according to III. and IV. $U_G(ll, jd) \geq U_G(\neg l, \emptyset)$ is true only if

$$-\frac{\alpha + 1}{\alpha} \leq x_d \leq \frac{\alpha + 1}{\alpha}$$

Step 4.3: ... if C justifies a referral not presenting a directive

$$U_G(ll, j) \geq U_G(\neg l, \emptyset) \Rightarrow -x_{g2}^2 - \alpha(x_{g2} - 1)^2 \geq -1$$

I. Plug in x_{g2}^{*2} (B.2): $-\left(\frac{\alpha}{\alpha + 1}\right)^2 - \alpha\left(\frac{\alpha}{\alpha + 1} - 1\right)^2 \geq -1$

Simplify left part (with common denominator):

$$-\frac{\alpha^2}{(\alpha + 1)^2} - \alpha\left(\frac{\alpha - \alpha - 1}{\alpha + 1}\right)^2 \Rightarrow \frac{-\alpha^2}{(\alpha + 1)^2} - \frac{\alpha}{(\alpha + 1)^2}$$

factor out α in the numerator $\frac{-\alpha(\alpha + 1)}{(\alpha + 1)^2} \Rightarrow \frac{-\alpha}{\alpha + 1} \geq -1 \mid : (-1) \Rightarrow \frac{\alpha}{\alpha + 1} \leq 1$

II. The denominators needs to be $\neq 0$ hence, $\alpha + 1 = 0 \mid -1 \Rightarrow \alpha = -1$

Hence, $\alpha \neq -1$. This is always true as $\alpha > 0$ according to the modeling choices.

III. If $\alpha > 0$ then $\frac{\alpha}{\alpha+1} \leq 1$ always true, as $\frac{\alpha}{\alpha+1} \rightarrow 1$

Hence, according to II. and III. $U_G(ll, j) \geq U_G(\neg l, \emptyset)$ is always true.

G will always legislate in the first move when faced with $U_G(ll, j) \cup U_G(\neg l, \emptyset)$

In sum, according to the initial move of the JPD game

the government's strategy (s_G) is *(Lemma 3)*

$$G^*(s_G) \begin{cases} \neg l & \text{if } x_d > \frac{\alpha+1}{\alpha} \cup x_d < -\frac{\alpha+1}{\alpha} \\ l & \text{otherwise with } \; x^*_{g1} = G \end{cases}$$

Appendix C: Judicial Power in Germany and the EU

C.1 Hierarchical Cluster Analysis

Figure C.1 shows the dendrogram of a hierarchical cluster analysis using the unweighted pair-group method (option `average` in R). In this method, the dissimilarity between two groups is taken to be the average of all dissimilarities between the members of the groups (Kaufman and Rousseeuw 2005, 47). The dendrogram allows for an explorative analysis of the data showing three clusters which confirm the discussion from the main analysis. The preconditions to exercise judicial power in Germany cluster with the preconditions in Austria, Belgium, the Czech Republic, Latvia, Poland, Portugal, Slovenia, and Spain. This group of nine countries is distinct from the remaining countries, which fall in two clusters. The constitutional courts of France and Romania have traditionally been weak (Hönnige 2007; Kneip 2008, 648; Engst 2017, 297) and are at the lowest end of Fig. 3.2 in the main analysis, together with Bulgaria. The remaining countries form a cluster, having a midrange strength of the preconditions to exercise judicial power. The analysis was repeated using Ward's clustering method, which showed the same clusters (option `ward.D2` in R; see Murtagh and Legendre 2014). Overall, the assessment confirms that the preconditions of judicial power that exist in Germany are representative of half of the countries with constitutional courts in the EU.

B. G. Engst, *The Two Faces of Judicial Power*,
https://doi.org/10.1007/978-3-030-46016-7

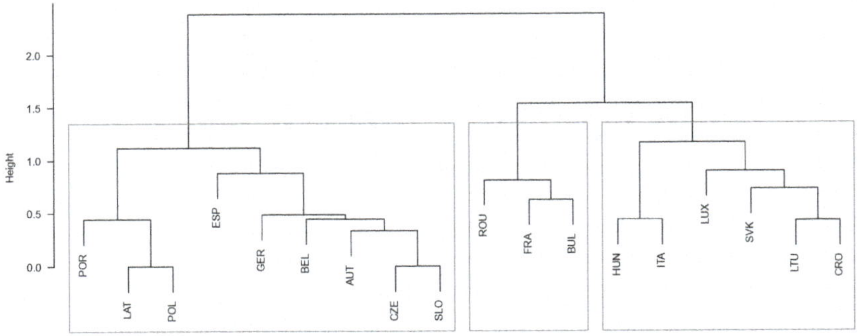

Fig. C.1 Dendrogram of average linkage cluster analysis of the indices on the two faces of judicial power

C.2 Robustness of the Indices on the Two Faces of Judicial Power

In Fig. C.2, the indices from Fig. 3.2 are computed based on two different weights. Instead of weighting the indices by the rule of law as measured by Freedom House (2017), the left panel of Fig. C.2 uses the rule of law as measured by the World Bank (2016) and the right panel of the figure weights the original indices by judicial independence as measured by Linzer and Staton (2015). I compute the weight, averaging the rule of law measured by the World Bank (2016) over the years 2012–2016 and afterwards I rescale the estimates (originally in the range from −2.5 to 2.5) to range between 0 and 1. Linzer and Staton's (2015) measure of judicial independence ranges between 0 and 1, but I average over the most recent five years that they report (2008–2012). They do not report an estimate for Slovakia. The correlation between the Freedom House (2017) measure and the measure by the World Bank (2016) is positive and very high, at 0.799. The correlation between the Freedom House (2017) measure and the measure by Linzer and Staton (2015) is positive and high, at 0.563.

Overall, the two panels confirm the previous analysis. The countries are located slightly differently in the left panel of Fig. C.2 compared with Fig. 3.2. Nevertheless, the changes are negligible since the respective cluster analysis (with the same specifications as chosen above) closely matches the results from the analysis in Fig. C.1 for the cluster which includes Germany (GER). The only exception is Portugal (POR), which no longer clusters

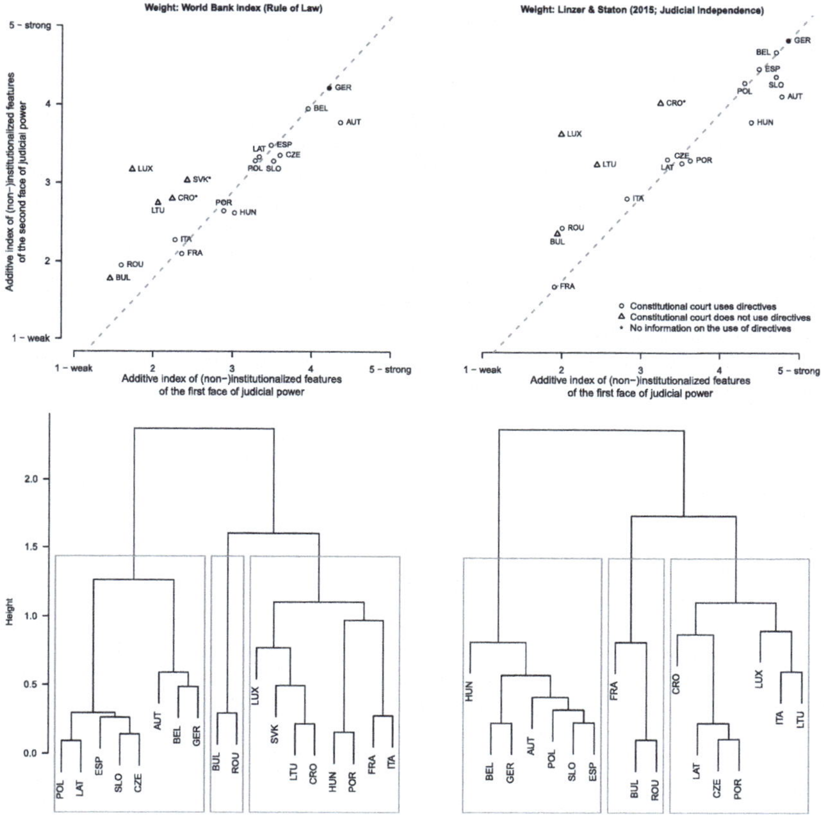

Fig. C.2 Robustness of differently weighted indices on the two faces of judicial power

with Germany, but overall the left panel in Fig. C.2—using the rule of law measured by the World Bank (2016)—shows similar patterns compared to the patterns in the main analysis.

The right panel of Fig. C.2 shows some variation compared to the original analysis. First, Hungary (HUN) clusters with Germany. Hungary had a very strong constitutional court in the past (Engst 2017), but in 2012 major constitutional reforms affected the power of the judiciary (see Grabenwarter et al. 2013). The scores estimated by Linzer and Staton (2015) range until 2012. Hence, later developments are not part of their scores. Second, the Czech Republic (CZE), Latvia (LAT) and Portugal do not cluster with Germany, while in the main analysis they do. Latvia and Portugal are also not very close to Germany in the original Fig. 3.2. A possible explanation is that the latent judicial independence scores from the IRT model run by Linzer and Staton (2015) address a different dimension than I seek to address. Their measure comprises multiple indicators to capture two commonly used dimensions: the judiciaries' *de facto independence* and the *de jure independence*. In Chapter 3, I argue that these concepts are court-centered, focusing on factors that constrain the judges, whereby I wish to place the judiciary in the separation of powers *and* account for a country's legal environment at large. This is why I regard the measure of the countries' rule of law as more appropriate for my purpose (see World Bank 2016; Freedom House 2017). The differences between these measures may explain the variation between the right panel in Figs. C.2 and 3.2, although the visual inspection speaks in favor of the robustness of the main finding.

References

Engst, B.G. (2017). Die vierte Gesetzeslesung. Verfassungsgerichte des deutsch-österreichischen Modells als Vetospieler. In V. Frick, O. W. Lembcke, and R. Lhotta (Eds.) *Politik und Recht. Umrisse eines politkwissenschaftlichen Forschungsfeldes* (pp. 281–301). Baden-Baden: Nomos.

Freedom House. (2017). *Freedom in the World*. https://freedomhouse.org (accessed February 21, 2018).

Grabenwarter, C., Hoffmann-Riem, W., Suchocka, H., Tuori, K., Velares, J. (2013). Opinion on the Fourth Amendment of the Fundamental Law of Hungary. *Venice Commission [European Commission for Democracy Through Law], 2013*(720), 1–32.

Hönnige, C. (2007). *Verfassungsgericht, Regierung und Opposition. Die vergleichende Analyse eines Spannungsdreiecks*. Wiesbaden: VS Verlag für Sozialwissenschaften.

Kaufman, L., Rousseeuw, P.J. (2005). *Finding Groups in Data: An Introduction to Cluster Analysis*. Hoboken: Wiley.

Kneip, S. (2008). Verfassungsgerichtsbarkeit im Vergleich. In O. W. Gabriel, and S. Kropp (Eds.) *Die EU-Staaten im Vergleich: Strukturen, Prozesse, Politikinhalte* (pp. 631–655). Wiesbaden: VS Verlag für Sozialwissenschaften.

Linzer, D.A., Staton, J.K. (2015). A Global Measure of Judicial Independence, 1948–2012. *Journal of Law and Courts*, *3*(2), 223–256.

Murtagh, F., Legendre, P. (2014). Ward's Hierarchical Agglomerative Clustering Method: Which Algorithms Implement Ward's Criterion? *Journal of Classification*, *31*(3), 274–295.

World Bank. (2016). *Worldwide Governance Indicators: Rule of Law Estimate, 2012–2016*. http://info.worldbank.org/governance/wgi/#home (accessed February 27, 2018).

Appendix D: The First Face of Judicial Power

D.1 Validation of the Government's Topic of Highest Interest

The following topics are identified:

- *Government operations* (CAP category 20), 12th legislative period; Christian Democrats and Liberal Party in government
- *Domestic macro-economic issues* (CAP category 1), 13th legislative period; Christian Democrats and Liberal Party in government
- *Labor and employment* (CAP category 5), 14th legislative period; Social Democrats and Green Party in government
- *Civil rights, minority issues and civil liberties* (CAP category 2), 15th legislative period; Social Democrats and Green Party in government
- *Labor and employment* (CAP category 5), 16th legislative period; Christian Democrats and Social Democrats in government.

Government operations and *domestic macro-economic issues* are the two topics with the highest frequency of words used when the Christian Democrats governed with the Liberal Party. Helmut Kohl was head of the government and some argue that he had no self-defined visions (see Wewer 1998, 15–16, for further references). However, the topic *government operations* is largely composed of words that address the intra-administrative organization of the state. Germany's reunification affected the organization of the

B. G. Engst, *The Two Faces of Judicial Power*,
https://doi.org/10.1007/978-3-030-46016-7

state and the fact that Kohl is seen as the "Chancellor of the Reunification" (Wewer 1998, 16–18) supports using the topic in the analyses for the 12th legislative period. The topic *macro-economic issues* is composed of words that characterize tax policies and investments to reduce poverty as well as unemployment. Indeed, common projects of the 13th legislative period were directed to safeguard Germany as a center of finance, industry, trade, and commerce. Moreover, the compulsory care insurance (*Pflegeversicherung*) was introduced, the legislature passed the austerity package to boost economic growth and employment, and finally a major tax reform as well as the reform of the pension system were initiated (von Homeyer 1998, 375–377). Therefore, *macro-economic issues* appropriately reflect on the 13th legislative period.

The topics identified as most important to the coalition of the Social Democrats and the Green Party were *labor and employment* as well as *civil rights, minority issues and civil liberties.* Immediately after taking office, the government initiated the Alliance for Employment (*Bündnis für Arbeit*) and waived laws by the former government that had weakened the position of employees (Blancke and Schmid 2003, 218). Chancellor Schröder and the British Prime Minister Blair of the Labor Party even published a working paper together, outlining a novel approach to labor market politics and the provision of welfare (Blancke and Schmid 2003, 218–219). The government reduced its direct efforts to reform the labor market during the middle of the legislative period but founded the "Hartz Commission" shortly before the election in 2002 (Blancke and Schmid 2003, 220). The commission drafted a major reform of the labor market, which was introduced over the course of the 15th legislative period (Schmid 2007). The fact that *civil rights, minority issues and civil liberties* are among the major topics of the 15th legislative period maybe explained with spillover effects across issue areas. It is plausible to assume that the labor market reform affected child and family affairs, which are by definition part of the policy area on civil liberties (see CAP coding 2–11, Bevan 2017). Moreover, the government addressed a number of minority issues. The rights of the LGBT community were strengthened while immigration rights became more restrictive in response to increasing terror attacks, especially the ones in the United States on September 11th (Egle and Zohlnhöfer 2007, 512–513). Therefore, the topics identified for the coalition between the Social Democrats and the Green Party are compelling.

It seems surprising that the topic identified for the grand coalition during the 16th legislative period is also *labor and employment*. However, in

Table D.1 Control variables to assess the first face of judicial power

Variable	*Description*	*Range*	*Median*	*Mean*
Impact on society	Indicates whether a topic addressed in a decision is of more than average importance to the society (1) or not (0)	0 – 1	0	0.23
Referral of law	Indicates whether a decision included the referral of (at least one) law	0 – 1	1	0.59
Senate	Indicates whether the First Senate (= 1) or the Second Senate (= 0) made a decision	0 – 1	1	0.57

some areas, like family affairs, the coalition continued reform efforts of the previous government (Gabriel et al. 2013, 176–177; Zohlnhöfer and Egle 2010, 579). Moreover, the Christian Democrats had originally supported the reform of the labor market in the second chamber (Zohlnhöfer and Egle 2010, 578). Therefore, the governing parties of the 16th legislative period shared an interest in labor market politics. The shared interest is supported by the idea that the grand coalition was a government of transition rather than one of novelty (Zohlnhöfer and Egle 2010, 579). Nevertheless, words that characterize the category of *labor and employment* are used almost as frequently as those that characterize *domestic macro-economic issues* in the 16th legislative period. Indeed, the grand coalition passed a large corporate tax reform and was able to establish a consolidated budget until the financial crisis of 2008 (Zohlnhöfer and Egle 2010, 578). Nevertheless, I assign the government *labor and employment* as a topic of interest to be consistent. The words that define the category are the ones used most frequently by the government. However, the measure should be treated with caution for the 16th legislative period.

D.2 Assessment of the Variables

Table D.1 summarizes the descriptions as well as measures of central tendency and dispersion for the control variables. In addition, Table D.2 summarizes the correlation matrix to assess the association between all variables. The age of an act and the referral of a law correlate moderately higher (0.436). This is unsurprising, although I accept this. There are also other types of referrals, which is why I keep the variable measuring the age of an act. Moreover, I account for the correlation at least to the extent that I

Table D.2 Correlation matrix of variables to assess the first face of judicial power

	Cohesiveness	*Days election*	*Gov.supp.*	*Age of act*	*Brief*	*Gov.topic*
Cohesiveness	1	0.129	−0.109	−0.029	0.002	0.098
Days election		1	0.153	0.011	−0.052	0.083
Gov.support			1	0.018	0.018	−0.037
Age of act				1	0.22	−0.028
Brief					1	0.107
Gov.topic						1

	Imp. (courts)	*Imp. (scholars)*	*Hearing*	*Doctrine*	*Imp. (society)*	*Sanction law*	*Senate*
Cohesiveness	0.063	−0.045	−0.01	0	0.01	−0.01	−0.027
Days election	0.048	0.04	−0.032	0.038	0.001	0.056	0.048
Gov.support	−0.01	−0.018	0.079	0.076	0.051	0.012	−0.042
Age of act	0.084	0.048	−0.096	−0.015	−0.153	0.436	0.141
Brief	0.063	0.154	0.16	0	−0.057	0.312	0.063
Gov.topic	0.02	0.007	0.067	−0.073	−0.098	0.033	0.036
Imp. (courts)	1	0.561	−0.085	−0.038	0.261	0.064	0.094
Imp. (scholars)		1	0.014	0.024	0.399	0.148	0.097
Hearing			1	0.171	0.116	0.069	−0.112
Doctrine				1	0.064	0.1	−0.166
Imp. (society)					1	−0.048	−0.052
Sanction law						1	0.028
Senate							1

Note: The outcome of the estimation was saved using the `xtable` package (Dahl 2016) in *R*

assess the robustness of the main analyses in the subsample which includes referrals based on at least on law only. Nevertheless, there is a higher correlation between the impact of a decision on courts and the impact on legal scholars (0.561). The correlation suggests that topics important to courts are also the ones discussed among scholars. Both measures address the same underlying dimension and I use only the impact on courts for the main analysis.

D.3 Empirical Assessment of the First Face of Judicial Power

Table D.3 summarizes multinomial logistic regressions estimated to conduct the subsample analysis in Sects. 4.4.2 and 4.4.3. The "w/o vague D"

Table D.3 Multinomial logistic regressions in subsamples to assess the first face of judicial power

	Dependent variable: judicial choice			
	Not J. vs. D. [w/o vague D]	*J. vs D. [w/o vague D]*	*Not J. vs. D. [only law]*	*J. vs D. [only law]*
Gov. cohesiveness	−3.300	−4.488	−2.274	−2.420
	(3.142)	(3.277)	(3.040)	(3.508)
Days to election	−0.433**	−0.246	−0.459**	−0.169
	(0.199)	(0.209)	(0.195)	(0.231)
Gov. support	−3.532***	−1.273	−2.827**	0.036
	(1.195)	(1.236)	(1.272)	(1.387)
Age of act	−0.491***	−0.354**	−0.237*	−0.297*
	(0.148)	(0.156)	(0.139)	(0.153)
Brief filed (= 1)	−0.403	−0.723**	−0.382	−0.301
	(0.300)	(0.316)	(0.297)	(0.347)
Gov. topic (= 1)	−0.850**	−0.536	−0.731*	−0.570
	(0.401)	(0.410)	(0.429)	(0.478)
Impact on courts (= 1)	−0.730**	−0.621*	−0.860***	−0.665*
	(0.312)	(0.333)	(0.321)	(0.384)
Oral hearing (= 1)	−0.813**	−0.051	−0.927***	−0.028
	(0.333)	(0.341)	(0.336)	(0.368)
Manifest doctrine (= 1)	−0.746***	−0.887***	−1.099***	−1.095***
	(0.286)	(0.306)	(0.293)	(0.347)
Impact on society (= 1)	0.297	0.090	0.018	−0.064
	(0.353)	(0.375)	(0.357)	(0.415)
Senate (= 1)	−1.045***	−0.445	−0.638**	−0.627*
	(0.301)	(0.321)	(0.294)	(0.340)
Referral of law (= 1)	−0.393	−1.399***		
	(0.363)	(0.367)		
Constant	14.468***	12.113***	10.595***	6.749*
	(3.565)	(3.708)	(3.430)	(3.940)
N	549		341	
logLik	−476.6348		−317.6894	
AIC	1005.27		683.3788	
PCP	0.59		0.56	
McFadden pseudo R^2	0.13		0.10	

Note: *p<0.10; **p<0.05; ***p<0.01. Not J. = Not justify; J. = Justify; D. = Justify with directive (which is the reference category)

model is based on decisions excluding vague directives. The "only law" model is based on decisions with referrals that include at least one law.

Figure D.1 summarizes simulated predicted probabilities and the first differences for the judicial choices using the Models 1, 2, and 3 in Table 4.2 which do not include any control variables. The simulations generate similar findings to the main analyses confirming the general robustness of the results.

D.4 Concluding Analysis Varying Costs Simultaneously

Table D.4 summarizes the multinomial logit models used to compute the concluding analysis. The "[only law, w/o vague]" model is used to simulate the quantities of interest shown in the main analysis. The "[only law]" Model from Table D.3 and the "[only law, vague as justify]" Model from Table D.4 are used to compute the quantities of interest for the robustness assessments in Fig. D.2.

The upper panel in Fig. D.2 confirms the robustness of the major findings shown in Sect. 4.6. Slight differences compared with the main analysis occur regarding the decisions simulated when the government's and the court's costs are high (dark gray dots). However, these changes do not affect the overall conclusions.

The ternary plot in the lower panel of Fig. D.2 looks similar to the ternary plot in Sect. 4.6. However, the square-shaped first difference between "Justify vs. Directive" in the right plot illustrates that the likelihood of the choice to present a directive is not significantly different compared with the likelihood of the choice to only justify a decision when the government faces low and the court faces high costs. This is the only difference compared with the main analysis and leads to a final assessment of the results using a logistic regression.

D.5 Logistic Regression to Assess the First Face of Judicial Power

In order to assess the notion that treating justified decisions and directives as separate choices or one choice does not lead to different results, I compute a logistic regression. The subsample of decisions is the same as used for the analysis in Sect. 4.6. The binary outcome variable takes the value of one when the court chooses to justify a decision or presents a directive

Table D.4 Multinomial logistic regressions of the concluding analysis on the first face of judicial power

	Dependent variable: judicial choice			
	Not J. vs. D. [only law, w/o vague]	*J. vs D.* [only law, w/o vague]	*Not J. vs. D.* [only law, vague as justify]	*J. vs D.* [only law, vague as justify]
Gov. cohesiveness	−4.073	−4.324	−4.129	−4.344
	(3.589)	(4.026)	(3.570)	(3.746)
Days to election	−0.920***	−0.645**	−0.913***	−0.728**
	(0.279)	(0.303)	(0.275)	(0.286)
Gov. support	−3.517**	−0.657	−3.374**	−0.942
	(1.460)	(1.568)	(1.432)	(1.462)
Age of act	−0.410**	−0.454**	−0.407**	−0.469***
	(0.165)	(0.179)	(0.169)	(0.173)
Brief filed (= 1)	−0.247	−0.162	−0.299	−0.131
	(0.338)	(0.385)	(0.335)	(0.359)
Gov. topic (= 1)	−0.658	−0.536	−0.803*	−0.569
	(0.478)	(0.521)	(0.474)	(0.478)
Impact on courts (= 1)	−0.872**	−0.649	−0.810**	−0.354
	(0.361)	(0.419)	(0.352)	(0.372)
Oral hearing (= 1)	−0.653*	0.228	−0.598	0.446
	(0.395)	(0.420)	(0.387)	(0.383)
Manifest doctrine (= 1)	−0.786**	−0.770**	−0.771**	−0.284
	(0.331)	(0.378)	(0.327)	(0.345)

(continued)

Table D.4 (continued)

	Dependent variable: judicial choice			
	Not J. vs. D. [only law, w/o vague]	*J. vs D.* [only law, w/o vague]	*Not J. vs. D.* [only law, vague as justify]	*J. vs D.* [only law, vague as justify]
Impact on society (= 1)	−0.160	−0.191	−0.083	−0.263
	(0.394)	(0.448)	(0.397)	(0.421)
Senate (= 1)	−0.918***	−0.925**	−0.934***	−0.921**
	(0.349)	(0.389)	(0.345)	(0.362)
Constant	17.322***	13.550***	17.236***	14.324***
	(4.361)	(4.797)	(4.315)	(4.464)
N	313		341	
logLik	−279.069		−312.301	
AIC	606.138		672.6021	
PCP	0.59		0.55	
McFadden pseudo R^2	0.10		0.11	

Note: *$p<0.10$; **$p<0.05$; ***$p<0.01$. Not J. = Not justify; J. = Justify; D. = Justify with directive (which is the reference category)

Table D.5 Comparison of predicted probabilities between models combining choices

Choices	*Average probability in percent*				*Model*
	G high costs C low costs	*G high cost C high cost*	*G low cost C low cost*	*G low cost C high cost*	
J. + D.	27.9	38.6	63	75.8	Multinomial
J. + D. coded 1	29.6	41.2	64.5	75.0	Binary
Not J. + J.	90.9	81.8	68.1	49.6	Multinomial
Not J. + J. coded 1	90.7	81.6	67.9	49.2	Binary
Not J. + D.	81.2	79.6	68.9	74.6	Multinomial
Not J. + D. coded 1	81.8	81.8	69.4	69.5	Binary

Note: Not J. = Not Justify; J. = Justify; D. = Directive. Simulated using the `zeligverse` package (Gandrud 2017)

Table D.6 Comparison between the use of vague directives at low and high costs

	Gov. support		*Days to election*	
	Lower quartile (High costs)	*Upper quartile (Low costs)*	*Lower quartile (High costs)*	*Upper quartile (Low costs)*
All directives	29	34	30	29
Vague directives	12	6	12	4
Share of vague directives	41.4%	17.6%	40.0%	13.8%

and zero when the court does not justify decisions. As quantities of interest, I simulate the average predicted probability of the combined choices to only justify a decision or present a directive, varying the same variables as in the main analysis. The average predicted probability from the logit model should be nearly similar to the sum of the predicted probabilities for the choices to only justify a decision and to present a directive from the multinomial model. This is the case according to the first two rows of Table D.5. The other rows in Table D.5 show that predicted probabilities from logistic regressions where either the choice to present a directive or the choice to only justify a decision is coded as zero are also not different compared with the multinomial analyses. This is why combining each choice or treating them separately does not lead to different results. For the reasons mentioned throughout Chapters 2 and 4, I treat the choices separately.

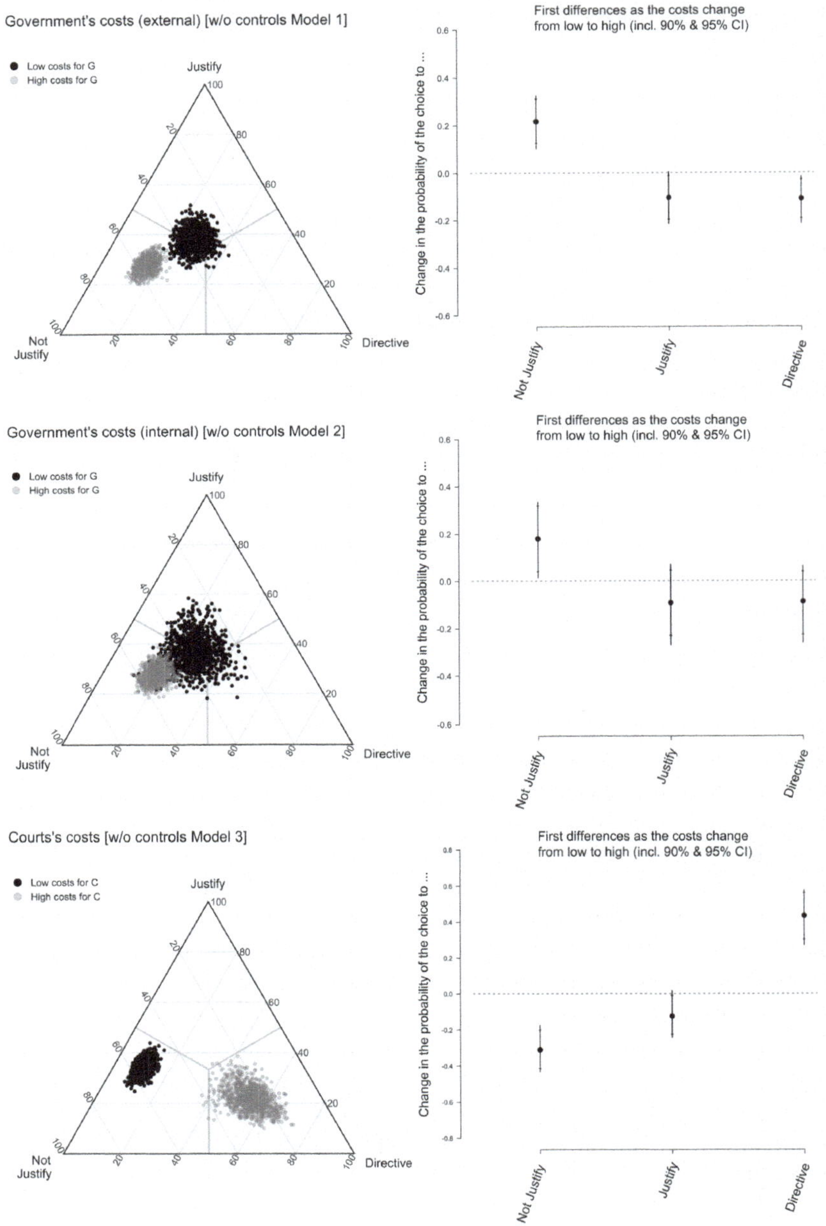

Fig. D.1 Robustness of judicial choices using models without control variables. Note: $N = 580$ Senate decisions by the GFCC; 1000 simulations from the respective Models in Table 4.2. Significant variables are varied according to the specifications in Table 4.3 while the other variables are held constant at their means

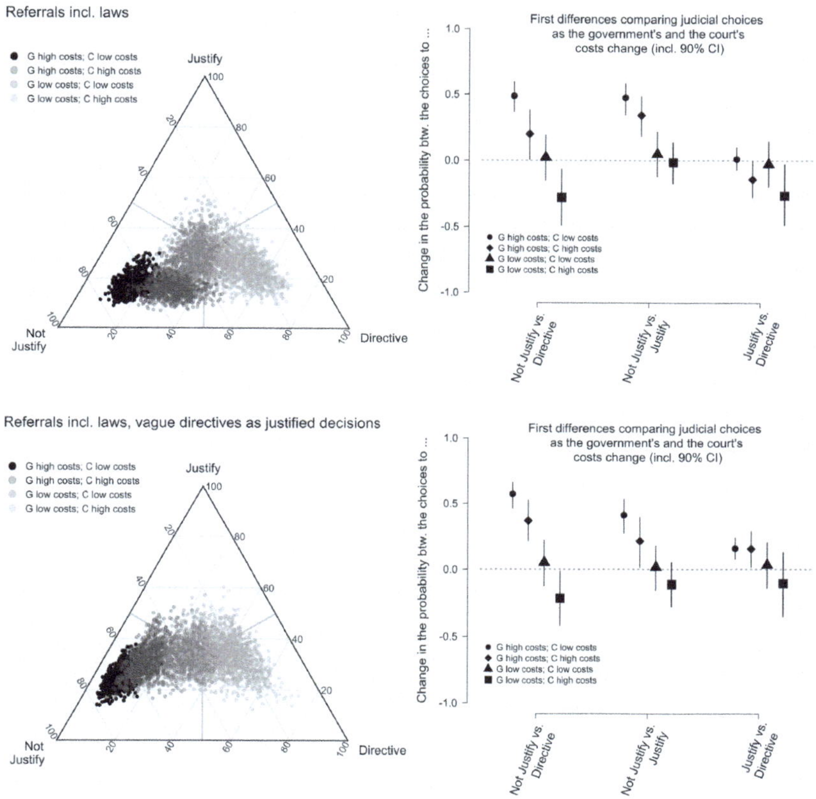

Fig. D.2 Robustness of the concluding analysis on the first face of judicial power. Note: $N = 341$ Senate decisions; 1000 simulations from the respective models in Tables D.3 and D.4. The variables that measure (1) the government's support, (2) the days to the next election, and (3) the impact on regular courts are varied according to Table 4.3. The other variables are held constant at their means

D.6 Opinion Clarity by Costs

Staton and Vanberg (2008, 513) argue that "[w]hen they [judges] expect resistance to their decisions, judges may use vague language in an attempt to mask noncompliance and to shield the court against the negative institutional consequences of open defiance." Resistance is particularly likely when the costs for the government to legislate are high. I assume for this brief descriptive assessment that the government's costs are high when the electoral support or the days until the next election are in the lower quartile. The government's costs of legislating are low when the electoral support or the days until the next election are in the upper quartile. Table D.6 shows that the share of vague directives is always larger at the lower quartile compared with the upper quartile. In other words, the court presents more vague directives when it anticipates resistances, which supports the considerations by Staton and Vanberg (2008).

References

Bevan, S. (2017). Gone Fishing: The Creation of the Comparative Agendas Project Master Codebook. *Comparative Agendas Project (CAP), 0.9.1*(Beta), August 26, 2017.

Blancke, S., Schmid, J. (2003). Bilanz der Bundesregierung Schröder in der Arbeitsmarktpolitik 1998–2002: Ansätze zu einer doppelten Wende. In C. Egle, T. Ostheim, and R. Zohlnhöfer (Eds.) *Das Rot-Grüne Projekt. Eine Billanz der Regierung Schröder 1998–2002* (pp. 215–238). Wiesbaden: Westdeutscher Verlag.

Dahl, D.B. (2016). xtable: Export Tables to LaTeX or HTML. *R Package* (Version 1.8-2).

Egle, C., Zohlnhöfer, R. (2007). Projekt oder Episode - was bleibt von Rot-Grün? In C. Egle, and R. Zohlnhöfer (Eds.) *Ende des rot-grünen Projekts. Eine Bilanz der Regierung Schröder 2002–2005* (pp. 511–535). Wiesbaden: VS Verlag für Sozialwissenschaften.

Gabriel, O.W., Bauknecht, J., Dageförde, M. (2013). Die Einstellungen der Bundesbürger zur Reform des Sozialstaates als Bestimmungsfaktor der Parteipräferenz. In B. Weßels, H. Schoen, and O. W. Gabriel (Eds.) *Wahlen und Wähler. Analysen aus Anlass der Bundestagswahl 2009* (pp. 174–205). Wiesbaden: Springer VS.

Gandrud, C. (2017). zeligverse: Easily Install and Load Stable Zelig Packages. *R package, V.0.1.1.*

Schmid, J. (2007). Arbeitsmarkt- und Beschäftigungspolitik - große Reform mit kleiner Wirkung? In C. Egle, and R. Zohlnhöfer (Eds.) *Ende des rot-grünen Projektes. Eine Bilanz der Regierung Schröder 2002–2005* (pp. 271–294). Wiesbaden: VS Verlag für Sozialwissenschaften.

Staton, J.K., Vanberg, G. (2008). The Value of Vagueness: Delegation, Defiance, and Judicial opinions. *American Journal of Political Science*, *52*(3), 504–519.

von Homeyer, I. (1998). Chronik der Ära Kohl 1982 bis 1998. In G. Wewer (Ed.) *Bilanz der Ära Kohl. Christlich-liberale Politik in Deutschland 1982–1998* (pp. 357–379). Wiesbaden: Springer Fachmedien Wiesbaden.

Wewer, G. (1998). Vom "Modell Deutschland" zur Standortdebatt. Zeitpunkt und Maßstäbe einer Bilanz der Ära Kohl. In G. Wewer (Ed.) *Bilanz der Ära Kohl. Christlich-liberale Politik in Deutschland 1982–1998* (pp. 7–58). Wiesbaden: Springer Fachmedien Wiesbaden.

Zohlnhöfer, R., Egle, C. (2010). Zwischen Reform und Blockade - die Bilanz der Großen Koalition 2005–2009. In C. Egle, and R. Zohlnhöfer (Eds.) *Die zweite Große Koalition. Eine Bilanz der Regierung Merkel 2005–2009* (pp. 578–596). Wiesbaden: VS Verlag für Sozialwissenschaften.

Appendix E: The Second Face of Judicial Power

E.1 Assessment of the Variables

Table E.1 shows only low correlations among all variables.

E.2 Logistic Regression to Assess the Second Face of Judicial Power

For initial insights, I compute a logistic regression. I coded an outcome variable taking the value 1 when a policy shift towards the court occurs between t and $t + 1$. This is the case in 98 out of the 277 proceedings. The logit model assumes that a policy shift occurs with a certain probability and does not occur with a certain inverse probability (see King 1989; Long 1997, Ch. 3). According to the results shown in Table E.2, a policy shift in direction of the court is significantly more likely when court decisions are cited in committee reports compared with when they are not cited.

E.3 Robustness Excluding the 16th Legislative Period

In Table E.3, the difference-in-differences estimation is replicated excluding the time of Germany's grand coalition from the analysis (16th legislative period). The findings confirm the robustness of the main analysis. The effect-size of the legal signal increases slightly. Bills exposed to legal signals

B. G. Engst, *The Two Faces of Judicial Power*,
https://doi.org/10.1007/978-3-030-46016-7

Table E.1 Correlation matrix of variables to assess the second face of judicial power

	Legal signal	*Consent bill*	*Opp. influence*	*Legal topic*
Legal signal	1	−0.049	−0.046	0.003
Consent bill		1	0.091	−0.092
Opp. influence			1	0.1
Legal topic				1

Table E.2 Logit models to explain policy shift in committees

Model	*Bivariate*			*With controls*		
DV	*Policy shift*			*Policy shift*		
Independent var.	*b*	*SE*		*b*	*SE*	
Legal Signal (= 1)	0.951	0.347	***	1.020	0.364	***
Consent Bill (= 1)				−0.201	0.269	
Opposition Influence				−4.577	2.668	*
Legal Topic (= 1)				1.159	0.405	***
12th Leg. Period				0.721	0.956	
13th Leg. Period				1.933	1.164	*
14th Leg. Period				1.995	1.306	
15th Leg. Period				2.427	1.564	
(Intercept)	−0.751	0.139	***	−0.559	0.303	*
BIC	363.676			387.2303		
Log Likelihood Final	−176.214			−168.3071		
Percent Correctly Predicted	56%			58%		

Note: $N = 277$; *$p<0.10$; **$p<0.05$; ***$p<0.01$. 16th legislative period as reference category for the 12th, 13th, 14th, and 15th legislative period

are on average significantly closer to the court than those not exposed to signals. However, the effect of a legal signal on policy shift over the course of a committee debate is small on average and insignificant.

E.4 Robustness with Stemmed Words Excluding Stop Words

In Appendix E.4, all findings are replicated using stemmed texts with the `SnowballC` package (Bouchet-Valat 2014) and excluding stop words with the `tm` package (Feinerer and Hornik 2018) in *R*. The findings confirm the robustness of the main analysis. Bills exposed to legal signals are on

Table E.3 Robustness of the difference-in-differences (w/o 16th LP)

Model	*Baseline*		*With controls*	
DV	*Policy shift*		*Policy shift*	
Independent var.	*b*	*SE*	*b*	*SE*
Legal Signal (= 1)	−0.352	0.125 ***	−0.326	0.125 ***
Time (after committee vote)	−0.003	0.064	−0.003	0.063
Legal Signal × Time	−0.028	0.177	−0.028	0.176
(Intercept)	1.228	0.045 ***	1.740	0.312 ***
R^2	0.04		0.06	
Adjusted R^2	0.03		0.04	

Note: N = 215 bills, 28 were exposed to a legal signal. *p<0.10; **p<0.05; ***p<0.01

average significantly closer to the court than those not exposed to signals. However, the average effect of a legal signal on policy shift over the course of a committee debate is only small and insignificant.

E.5 Robustness Using a Stricter Legal Signal

In Table E.6, the DiD analysis is replicated using a stricter version of a legal signal omitting vague references to the court's decisions only including clearly cited decisions identifiable via a number of reference or decision dates. The findings confirm the robustness of the main analysis.

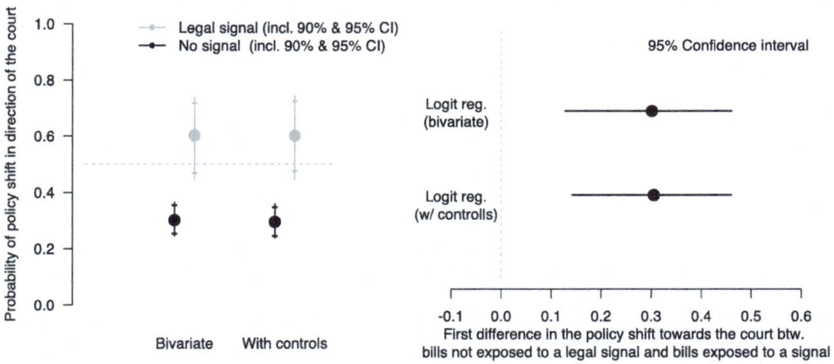

Fig. E.1 Robustness of predicted probabilities and first differences (stemmed texts w/o stop words). Note: N = 277 bills, of which 40 were negotiated under the influence of a legal signal

Table E.4 Robustness of the logit models (stemmed texts w/o stop words)

Model	*Bivariate*		*With controls*	
DV	*Policy shift*		*Policy shift*	
Independent var.	*b*	*SE*	*b*	*SE*
Legal Signal (= 1)	1.255	0.353 ***	1.284	0.364 ***
(Intercept)	−0.849	0.142 ***	−0.605	0.306 **
BIC	354.469		382.5447	
Log Likelihood Final	−171.6105		−165.9643	
Percent Correctly Predicted	57%		59%	

Note: $N = 277$; $^{*}p<0.10$; $^{**}p<0.05$; $^{***}p<0.01$

Bills exposed to legal signals are on average significantly closer to the court than those not exposed to signals. However, the effect of a legal signal on policy shift over the course of a committee debate is small on average and insignificant.

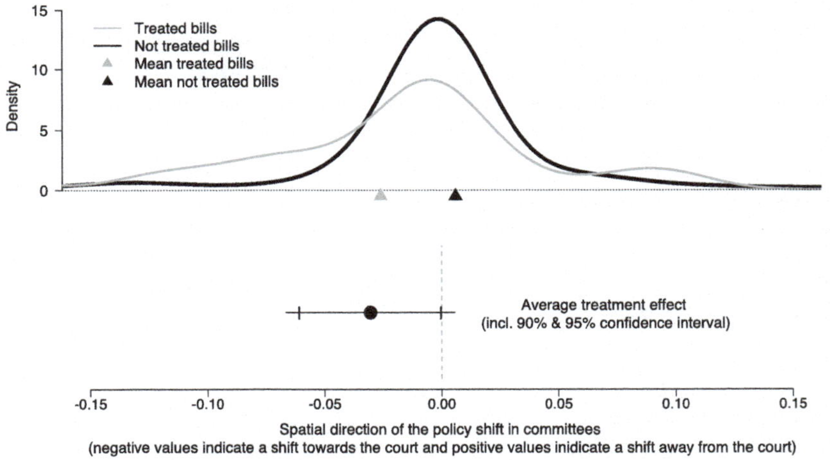

Fig. E.2 Robustness of the average treatment effect (stemmed texts w/o stop words). Note: $N = 277$ bills, of which 40 were negotiated under the influence of a legal signal

Table E.5 Robustness of the difference-in-differences (stemmed texts w/o stop words)

Model	*Baseline*		*With controls*	
DV	*Policy shift*		*Policy shift*	
Independent var.	*b*	*SE*	*b*	*SE*
Legal Signal (= 1)	−0.345	0.108 ***	−0.324	0.108 ***
Time (after committee vote)	0.006	0.058	0.006	0.058
Legal Signal × Time	−0.032	0.153	−0.032	0.152
(Intercept)	1.217	0.041 ***	1.144	0.070 ***
R^2	0.04		0.07	
Adjusted R^2	0.03		0.05	

Note: $N = 277$; *$p<0.10$; **$p<0.05$; ***$p<0.01$

Table E.6 Robustness of the difference-in-differences (stricter legal signal)

Model	*Baseline*		*With controls*	
DV	*Policy shift*		*Policy shift*	
Independent var.	*b*	*SE*	*b*	*SE*
Legal Signal (= 1)	−0.206	0.112 *	−0.202	0.111 *
Time (after committee vote)	0.001	0.055	0.001	0.055
Legal Signal × Time	−0.026	0.158	−0.026	0.157
(Intercept)	1.175	0.039 ***	1.141	0.067 ***
R^2	0.01		0.04	
Adjusted R^2	0.01		0.02	

Note: $N = 277$ bills, 34 were exposed to a legal signal. *$p<0.10$; **$p<0.05$; ***$p<0.01$

References

Bouchet-Valat, M. (2014). SnowballC: Snowball Stemmers Based on the C Libstemmer UTF-8 Library. *R Package*, *V.0.5.1*.

Feinerer, I., Hornik, K. (2018). tm: Text Mining Package. *R Package*, *V.0.7-5*.

King, G. (1989). *Unifying Political Methodology: The Likelihood Theory of Statistical Inference*. Cambridge: Cambridge University Press.

Long, J.S. (1997). *Regression Models for Categorial and Limited Dependent Variables*. Thousand Oaks: Sage.

Index

B. G. Engst, *The Two Faces of Judicial Power*,
https://doi.org/10.1007/978-3-030-46016-7

The manufacturer's authorised representative in the EU is Springer
Nature Customer Service Centre GmbH, Europaplatz 3, 69115 Heidelberg,
Germany. If you have any concerns regarding our products, please
contact ProductSafety@springernature.com

Printed and bound by CPI Group (UK) Ltd, Croydon, CR0 4YY
30/09/2026
02225644-0003